THE
OCCULT
IN THE
WESTERN WORLD

THE

OCCULT

IN THE

WESTERN WORLD

AN ANNOTATED BIBLIOGRAPHY

Cosette N. Kies

Library Professional Publications
1986

© 1986 by Cosette N. Kies. All rights reserved
First published in 1986 as a Library Professional
Publication, an imprint of The Shoe String Press, Inc.,
Hamden, Connecticut 06514

Printed in the United States of America

Library of Congress Cataloging-in-Publication Data

Kies, Cosette N., 1936–
    The occult in the western world.

    Includes index.
    1. Occult sciences—Bibliography   I. Title.
Z6876.K53   1986   [BF1411]   016.0019   86-7256
ISBN 0-208-02113-2

CONTENTS

PREFACE

The occult, defined as hidden secrets with attendant implications of arcane knowledge, is a field which has intrigued people throughout the centuries in many cultures. Every society, it seems, has had some element of the occult in its culture, some more predominantly than others. The word *occult* has a variety of meanings depending upon individual interpretation. To some the image of witches leaps to mind, while others consider the metaphysical nature of exotic religions. To some the word calls up visions of flying saucers, while others think of Ouija boards and ghostly voices. All these indeed are elements of the occult, in addition to many other subjects. Western occultism has a wide range of topics within its scope.

Although it may be fairly easy to agree on certain, distinct aspects of the occult, it is not so easy to delineate clearly the parameters of the occult field. These are gray and fuzzy. In recent decades especially, the boundaries have become even more blurred as popular interest in various subjects has waxed and waned. It would seem that there has never been a clear definition of what exactly is included in the occult. This ambiguity has been complicated further by the fact that some areas of the occult are claimed by other, more "respectable" and "legitimate" fields of learning as well. For example, aspects of magic and shamanism are clearly within the province of anthropology, while ancient myths and legends may be classified as history or literature. History is involved in most phases of the occult, as in theology. Curiously enough, most libraries catalog the majority of occult materials in the broader subject of psychology.

This confusion over definition, boundaries, and classification, not to mention a dubious scholarly reputation, has brought about a rather chaotic bibliographic state of affairs in the occult area. Since occult subjects have not clearly fallen within distinct subject fields, bibliographers charged with collection development in libraries have not always selected as widely and intelligently as they might have. Great public interest throughout the years has resulted in a high library theft rate of occult materials, causing further collection deficiencies.

Bibliographic control has been difficult for additional reasons. Reprints, sometimes with title changes, abound. Many smaller presses, private publishing operations, and vanity printers have turned out works in this area, a number of which have never appeared in trade bibliographies. Authors in the field have had a regrettable love of pseudonyms. The result of all this has been a bibliographic maelstrom for serious students, librarians, and scholars of the occult.

This book is intended to help these people and also casual readers who wish to read and do research in the occult area. It is meant to serve as a beginner's sourcebook, a start along the way. It is hoped that it will help individuals to select material appropriate to their various purposes.

The field of occult literature (nonfiction) is particularly rich at this time due to high public interest in the field over the past few decades. Publishers have been quick to provide titles in the various occult subject areas; the *Subject Catalog* of the Library of Congress bears witness to increased publishing activity in this area. During the five-year period 1960–1964 (pre-*Rosemary's Baby*), a total of 73 entries were cataloged for the library's collection in the general occult area. (This does not include those items dealing with specific occult areas such as witchcraft, demonology, folklore, astrology, etc.) Fifty-five percent of these books had American imprints. During the period from 1970 to 1974, there was a marked increase in the number of entries under "Occult Sciences" and its immediate subdivisions. In those years, 358 entries were listed, 32 percent of them with American imprints. The trend has continued to the present. In looking at acquisitions in the *Subject Catalog* for 1981 alone, one finds 79 entries, of which 32 were American imprints.

Another clue to the increased publishing activity and increased public interest in the occult can be observed in general bookstores. Specialty bookstores dealing with the occult have always existed in larger cities, but now general retail bookstores contain special occult sections, and they are growing in size.[1]

The emphasis in this book is on the occult as it is viewed today, although a number of classic, historic works are listed. Certain areas are covered in only a rather cursory way, and only as they pertain directly to specific occult areas. These include primitive religions, classical mythology, Eastern religions, legerdemain, Pentecostal religions and mystical branches of the accepted, major religions. In general, material included under the subject headings of "occult

---

1. D. J. R. Bruckner, "Occult Publishing," *New York Times Book Review*, 31 July 1983, 31.

sciences" and "superstition" in the *Library of Congress Subject Headings* (ninth edition) are covered.

Selection of the titles included was based on a number of criteria. The titles are in English, with the exception of a few items in series which are in major European languages. Monographs, generally at least a hundred pages in length, are listed. Although some historic classics are included, an effort was made to identify important modern works, as well as those which might be considered state-of-the-art. Other titles were selected as being representative of material published in certain fields. In some cases, rather weak items have been included because better works do not exist to cover a particular area. Emphasis has been placed on materials useful for reference, such as dictionaries, bibliographies, and encyclopedias. Only a few juvenile titles are provided, and only those whose contents are substantive. Fiction is not included. Finally, some items are listed because they are curiosity pieces or have achieved notoriety of some sort.

Each item has been assigned a unique number. Books in series are listed under a main number with added identifiers for individual titles. These series books are listed in the order given by their publishers rather than alphabetically. Entries are alphabetical (within sections) by author(s), editor, or compiler whenever possible. A full title follows with bibliographic information. The first bibliographic citation is that of the book examined by the author, and it matches the International Standard Book Number (ISBN) provided. When only one ISBN is given for a title appearing in both hardcover and paper, it is for the hard cover edition. Occasionally a Standard Book Number (SBN) is given, as is an infrequent International Standard Serial Number (ISSN). When a book has had a long, complicated publishing history, a note regarding its first publication is found in the annotation; series information is also given. A brief description of the work follows. Some occult terms, such as *UFOs* and *werewolves,* have been standardized for this book and variations are found only in titles. This applies also to the word which is correctly spelled foreword.

Appreciation is expressed by the author to the National Endowment for the Humanities for a Travel-to-Collections grant. Also, thanks are due to the staff members of libraries where the titles included in this work were examined: the Library of Congress, the New York Public Library, Columbia University Library, the American Association for Psychical Research Library, the University of Illinois Library, and Northern Illinois University Library. Particular appreciation is given to contributers to my own occult library: Joseph

Hewgley, Constance Kies, Mary Jane Lipshie, and JoAnn Mulvihill. Special thanks go to Nancy Harvey and Beth Nickels, who assisted in the preparation of the manuscript, and to my colleagues at Northern Illinois University for their interest and support for the project.

1
GENERAL WORKS ON THE OCCULT

Reality, n. The dream of a made philosopher. That which would
remain in the cupel if one should assay a phantom. The
nucleus of a vacuum.

Ambrose Bierce,
The Devil's Dictionary

For as long as there have been written records, there have been books
on the occult. Early attempts to uncover the mysteries of life which
described ideas, religious beliefs, and recipes for dealing with the
unknown are found on papyrus scrolls listed in ancient Egyptian
library records. As civilization advanced, more sophisticated systems
of recording knowledge evolved. As branches of knowledge were
clarified and defined, certain components of the area we now call the
occult became more distinct.

Definition of the occult has long been a matter of concern for
scholars. As society changes, so do the meanings of some words, and
the meaning of the word *occult* has changed throughout the ages.

An examination of occult literature, past and present, illustrates
how various authors have used the word in their exploration of
various aspects of speculation and information. This can be observed
by looking at the occult sections of bookstores, where materials the
book-buying public considers to be part of the field at any given time
are displayed.

Many definitions have been offered. According to Robert
Galbreath, the current concept of the occult includes anomalies of
human and natural history, psi phenomena, transpersonal experiences, occult sciences, arts or technologies, occult religions, and
metaphysical occultism.[1] Dictionary definitions tend to stress the

---

1. Robert Galbreath, "Occult and the Supernatural." from *Handbook of
American Culture* ed. by Thomas Inge. Westport, Conn.: Greenwood Press,
1980. 2 vols. 2: 213–4.

hidden and secret aspects of the word, along with implications of arcane knowledge systems employed to invoke and use mysterious powers.

In this book, the word *occult* is used in its widest sense to mean mysteries outside established religions. Most of the subjects listed under "Occult Sciences" and "Folklore" in the *Library of Congress Subject Headings* are covered, and a few additional terms have been added. The following areas of the occult are discussed: alchemy, amulets, animals (legends and stories), animism, astrology, auras, the Cabala, charms, clairvoyance, crystal gazing, demonology, the devil, divination, divining rods, dragons, dreams, druids and druidism, dryads, dwarfs, the elixir of life, the evil eye, extrasensory perception, fairies, flying saucers, fortune-telling, gematria, geographical myths, geomancy, ghosts, ghouls and ogres, giants, hauntings, incantations, initiations (in religion, folklore, etc.), legends, leopard men, levitation, magic, mana, manimals, mediums, monsters, myths, oracles, out-of-the-body experiences, palmistry, plant lore, psychical research, psychometry (occult sciences), reincarnation, satanism, santería, secret societies, second sight, sirens (mythology), spiritualism, sun worship, superstition, swan maidens, the tarot, theosophy, tree worship, vampires, voodooism, weather lore, werewolves, and witchcraft. A glossary of less common terms, along with other words used to describe occult materials, may be found on pages 191-199.

The literature of the occult has followed changing patterns through the centuries. In primitive times, and at the beginnings of ancient civilizations, religion, science, and philosophy blended in works which attempted to explain puzzling matters. With the introduction of Christianity to the Western world, efforts were made to eliminate from human consciousness and the written record those beliefs considered to be heretical. These beliefs included much of what is today called the occult. It might be overly simplistic to state that the ideas and systems of information which went underground in response to this suppression became the occult world. It is clear, however, that as a result of disapproval by Christian society, certain elements of unconventional belief became classified as occult, in part simply because they were not included in the official dogmas of society in the Western world. Even today, occult notions have an aura of being forbidden, which perhaps accounts, partially, for the continued fascination with them.

Until fairly recent times, societal disapproval of the occult manifested itself in extreme ways, including torture, legal punishment, and death. Centuries of persecution have added a touch of fear to the fascination with occult ideas. Best known of the persecutions were witchcraft trials and executions, which peaked in Europe in the sixteenth century. Literature of this period often focused on the evils of satanism and the identification of witches. A later century, sometimes called the "age of reason," discredited the notion that people actually could sell their souls to the devil in return for personal power.

Although occult beliefs and practices never seem to die out totally, certain periods of heightened interest can be identified. Following the late medieval and Renaissance concern with witchcraft and satanism, fascination with the occult focused on spiritualism and mysticism in the nineteenth century. Finally, renewed interest in the consideration of many occult systems and ideas has occurred during the past few decades and is presently very strong.

Writing and publishing in occult areas have attended these periods of high interest. Current interest in nearly all aspects of the occult and related areas such as mythology has resulted in a richer field of literature on the occult than ever before. Material covering all phases of the occult is available, although there is unevenness of coverage. It is important to apply guidelines for selection of materials in this field similar to those used in other, more familiar areas. As in any sort of selection, it is important to consider the author's qualifications, the reputation of the publishing house, and the treatment of contents. Such appraisal of occult materials will show that certain materials are valuable for research purposes, while others serve for casual readings or merely as curiosity items in a fascinating field. In this book, certain items are designated as "classic" works because of their historic value or because they have won outstanding critical evaluation through the years. Newer occult materials may be measured against these works, which have been noted for their excellence. For example, a French title not included in the main listing is Albert Louis Caillet's *Manuel bibliographique des sciences psychiques ou occultes* (Paris: Dorbon, 1912–13). Long held by scholars to be the finest example of a dictionary / encyclopedia in the field, reviewers often compare new works to it.

Material in this chapter covers books dealing with general aspects of the occult, items especially useful for quick reference work and / or beginning research in the area. The titles have been sorted into the following sections:

- Sourcebooks
- Bibliographies
- Library Catalogs
- One-Volume Dictionaries and Encyclopedias
- Multivolume Encyclopedias
- Series
- Atlases and Guides
- Histories, Overviews, and Classic Works
- Biographies

Sourcebooks

1. Drury, Nevill, and Tillet, Gregory. *The Occult Sourcebook.* London: Routledge & Kegan Paul, 1978. 236 pp. index. illus. bibliographies. ISBN 0-7100-8875-2.

> Illustrations by Elizabeth Trafford Smith. Short essays followed by bibliographic entries, some annotated. Contents: ESP, meditation and biofeedback, dreams, reincarnation, the origins of magic, supernatural and occult beings, ritual magic, ritual consciousness, magical equipment, the Golden Dawn, magical cosmology, the Quabalah, the tarot, the Tattvas, magical attack, sexual magic, Aliester Crowley: Lord of the New Aeon, hypnotism, auto-suggestion and relaxation, trance consciousness, out-of-the-body consciousness, drugs and mystical consciousness, shamanistic magic, ghosts and hauntings, spiritualism, possession, exorcism, faith healing, vampires, traditional witchcraft, modern witchcraft, traditional satanism, modern satanism, voodoo, Eastern mysticism, Eastern influence on the occult, theosophy, I Ching, astrology, numerology, palmistry, lost continents, inner-space rock music, occult art, who's who in the occult. British bias in the selection of titles for inclusion.

2. Hartmann, William C. *Who's Who in Occultism, New Thought, Psychism and Spiritualism (a Biography, Dictionary and Bibliography Combined in Distinctly Separate Sections).* Jamaica, N.Y.: Occult Press, 1927. 2d ed. 350 pp.

> First published in 1925 as *Hartmann's Who's Who in Occult, Psychic and Spiritual Realms.* Biographies broken down into sections, such as astrologers, psychic science, etc. Bibliographies are by subject with annotations. Also includes lists of libraries, publishers, periodicals (domestic, foreign, and discontinued) and a subject listing of magazine articles

dealing with occult subjects. Dated, but extremely useful for information about the period.

Bibliographies

3. Chicorel, Marietta, ed. *Chicorel Index to Parapsychology and Occult Books*. New York: Chicorel Library, 1978. 354 pp. ISBN 0-87729-202-2.

> Volume 24 in the Chicorel Index Series. An index to monographic material on various occult subjects. Thematic arrangement by broad and narrow subjects, such as demonology, alchemy, acupuncture, and the like. A number of titles are listed in more than one category. The titles, over 3,000 in all, reflect specific library holdings. The preface indicates that the publisher plans a new edition with more emphasis on Eastern religious aspects and influences relating to the occult.

4. Clarie, Thomas C. *Occult Bibliography: an Annotated List of Books Published in English, 1971 through 1975*. Metuchen, N.J.: Scarecrow Press, 1978. 454 pp. indexes. ISBN 0-8101-1152-9.

> A listing of nearly 2,000 titles, mostly annotated and arranged in alphabetical sequence by main entry. It does not claim to be all-inclusive (a bibliographer would be mad even to try!) and does pick up some reprints. Excludes works not reviewed in periodicals or "found" in any bookstore." Clarie awards stars for outstanding items, and includes a prioritized list of the ten best books for each year. Publishing trends are discussed for various occult subjects.

5. Clarie, Thomas C. *Occult / Paranormal Bibliography: an Annotated List of Books Published in English, 1976 through 1981*. Metuchen, N.J.: Scarecrow Press, 1984. 561 pp. indexes. ISBN 0-8108-1674-1.

> Similar in scope and arrangement to the previous item. Nearly 2,000 entries, mostly annotated, of books published during a six-year period. The prioritized list of the ten best books for each year is dropped. More attention is paid to reviewers' comments than in the previous work, although the number of reviews is less significant in the assignment of stars.

6. Eberhard, George M., comp. *Geo-Bibliography of Anomalies: Primary Access to Observations of UFO's, Ghosts, and Other Mysterious Phenomena*. Westport, Conn.: Greenwood Press, 1980. 1,115 pp. indexes. maps. ISBN 0-313-21337-2.

Covers Greenland, the U.S. (state by state) and Canada (province by province). Over 22,100 events of an unusual nature are arranged under place names, with citations to the newspaper(s) and / or periodical article(s) describing each event. A glossary defines the terms used. Indexes provide approaches by subjects, observers, ships, and Indian tribes.

7. Hyre, K. M., and Goodman, Eli. *Price Guide to the Occult and Related Subjects.* Los Angeles: Reference Guides, 1967. 380 pp.

A list of over 8,000 titles of out-of-print books from 39 used-book dealers' catalogs. Arranged alphabetically by author.

8. Melton, J. Gordon. *Magic, Witchcraft, and Paganism in America: a Bibliography Compiled from the Files of the Institute for the Study of American Religion.* New York: Garland, 1982. 231 pp. indexes. ISBN 0-8240-9377-1.

Garland Bibliographies on Sects and Cults series. Emphasis is on contemporary pagan and magical religious communities in America, but discusses historic European roots. Contains 1,500 items, some annotated.

9. Phillips, Leona Rasmussen, and Phillips, Jill M. *The Occult: Hauntings, Witchcraft, Dreams, and All Other Avenues of Paranormal Phenomena; an Annotated Bibliography.* New York: Gordon Press, 1976. 171 pp. ISBN 0-8490-0748-8.

This uneven work includes some long annotations in the *Cosmopolitan* girl style (lots of italics and exclamation marks). Only 45 titles are annotated. There is an essay on the occult in film, along with listings of occult fiction and nonfiction. No criteria for inclusion are provided.

10. Popenoe, Cris. *Books for Inner Development: the Yes! Guide.* Washington, D.C.: Yes! Bookshop, 1976, distributed by Random House. 383 pp. index. illus. ISBN 0-394-73294-4.

A bookstore catalog. Includes 8,000 items listed by subject. Does not include all occult areas; for example, astrology is excluded. Emphasis is on positive self-help books.

11. Popenoe, Cris. *Inner Development: the Yes! Bookshop Guide.* Washington, D.C.: Yes! Inc., 1979, distributed by Random House. 654 pp. index. illus. ISBN 0-394-73544-7.

A new edition of the catalog item 10), with 11,000 books organized into topics dealing with various inner-peace and mystic philosophies. Topics relating to nutrition have been dropped. Annotated. Updated by supplements.

Library Catalogs

12. *Alchemy and the Occult: a Catalogue of Books and Manuscripts from the Collection of Paul and Mary Mellon Given to Yale University Library.* New Haven, Conn.: Yale University Library, 1968–77. 4 vols. illus. ISBN 0-84573-118-1 (volumes 3–4).

Volumes one and two of this handsome set were compiled by Ian MacPhail. Volumes three and four were compiled by Laurence C. Witten II and Richard Pachella. Mary Mellon began this collection of rare books and manuscripts around 1940. Inspired by Jung, she dealt only with works of alchemy. After her death, her husband, Paul, continued her work, and broadened the scope of the collection to include other areas of the occult. The collection was presented to Yale in 1965. Consists of 160 books and 149 manuscripts. The catalog includes a number of facsimile pages.

One-Volume Dictionaries and Encyclopedias

13. Bowyer, Michael J. *Encyclopedia of Mystical Terminology.* South Brunswick, N.J.: A. S. Barnes, 1979. 135 pp. index. illus. ISBN 0-498-02262-5.

A single, alphabetical listing of terms used in religious cults, sects, societies, and languages. Broader in scope than most occult dictionaries, but it is not one of the better dictionaries in the field.

14. Cataldo, Gerald J., comp. *A Dictionary: Definitions and Comments from the Edgar Cayce Readings.* Virginia Beach, Va.: A.R.E. Press, 1973. 81 pp. ISBN 0-87604-064-4.

An official publication of the Edgar Cayce Foundation and Edgar Cayce's Association for Research and Enlightenment, Inc. A dictionary arrangement with appropriate passages from the works of the noted American spiritual healer and psychic.

15. Cavendish, Richard, ed. *The Encyclopedia of the Unexplained: Magic, Occultism and Parapsychology.* New York: McGraw-Hill, 1974; London: Routledge & Kegan Paul, 1974. 304 pp. index. illus. bibliography. ISBN 0-07-010295-3.

> J. B. Rhine served as a special consultant for articles on parapsychology. An American Library Association notable book of 1974. Emphasis is on events of the past two centuries. Indexes of persons and book titles.

16. Chambers, Howard V. *An Occult Dictionary for the Millions.* Los Angeles: Sherbourne Press, 1966. 160 pp.

> One alphabetical dictionary arrangement of definitions. "But the occult world is a large one, which frequently overlaps into both formal and informal religions, anthropology, astronomy, biology, medicine, religion, and sociology."—Foreword

17. Chaplin, James Patrick. *Dictionary of the Occult and Paranormal.* New York: Dell, 1976. 176 pp. illus. ISBN 440-01927-195.

> Reprint of a 1927 Dell publication, now out-of-print. Considered by some reviewers to be one of the best dictionaries published. Over 1,000 terms are defined; longer articles on magic topics, astrology, the devil, horoscopes, plant magic and the like are provided.

18. Drury, Nevill. *Dictionary of Mysticism and the Occult.* San Francisco: Harper & Row, 1985. 281 pp. ISBN 0-06-062094-3.

> Nearly 3,000 entries with cross-references. Covers ancient and modern occult and metaphysical terms. Dictionary arrangement with concise definitions.

19. Fodor, Nandor. *Encyclopedia of Psychic Science.* New Hyde Park, N.Y.: University Books, 1966; Secaucus, N.J.: Citadel Press, 1974. 416 pp. ISBN 0-8065-0429-5.

> Foreword to the University Books edition by Leslie Shepard, with a preface by Sir Oliver Lodge. Originally published by Arthurs Press in 1933. A classic in its own right, articles from this work have been reproduced in Shepard's *Encyclopedia of Occultism and Parapsychology* (see item 36). Especially good for biographical material.

20. Franklyn, Julian, ed. *A Dictionary of the Occult.* New York: Causeway Books, 1973; Detroit: Gale Research, 1981. 301 pp. ISBN 0-81034-085-2.

Originally published in England as *A Survey of the Occult* in 1935. Articles on occult practices, including material on subjects such as vampires and werewolves. Popular approach. Some longer articles with an index of "see" references to them from the over 1,000 entries.

21. Gettings, Fred. *Dictionary of Occult, Hermetic and Alchemical Sigils.* London: Routledge & Kegan Paul, 1981. 410 pp. index. bibliography. ISBN 0-7100-0095-2.

The term *sigils* refers to graphic symbols employed in describing certain occult practices. This specialized reference source is the only currently available work devoted exclusively to the meanings of these symbols.

22. Jack, Alex. *The New Age Dictionary.* Brookline, Mass.: Kantlaka Press, 1976. 244 pp. illus.

Contains the terminology of acupuncture, alchemy, Christian mysticism, gurus, Kabbalah, lost continents and tribes, mythology, natural foods, pyramid energy, radionics, sufism, UFOs, yoga, and others. Short entries for definitions. Quality paperback format.

23. King, Bruce [pseud. Zolar]. *The Encyclopedia of Ancient and Forbidden Knowledge.* Los Angeles: Nash 1970; New York: Popular Library, 1972; London: Abacus, 1973. 445 pp. illus. ISBN 0-285-62020-7.

Divided into two sections: ancient and forbidden knowledge (Cabalah, astral world, spiritualism, mind power), and the art of prophecy (astrology, numerology, tarot, crystal gazing, palmistry, phrenology). Includes a section on the occult meanings for the Hebrew alphabet.

24. Martin, Bernard W. *The Dictionary of the Occult.* London: Rider, 1979. 139 pp. ISBN 0-09-136880-4.

A brief-entry dictionary which attempts to make linkages between terms with "see" and "see also" references.

25. Poinsot, Maffeo Charles. *The Encyclopedia of Occult Sciences.* Detroit: Gale Research, 1972. 496 pp.

Reprint of a 1939 Tudor imprint. Useful from a historical perspective.

26. Riland, George. *The New Steinerbooks Dictionary of the Paranormal.* New York: Warner, 1982. 358 pp. ISBN 0-446-97010-7.

Nearly 2,800 entries. Most of the definitions are short; contains some longer articles. This is an updated version of a highly regarded work issued by the same publisher.

27. Spence, Lewis. *An Encyclopedia of Occultism: a Compendium of Information on the Occult Sciences, Occult Personalities, Psychic Science, Magic, Demonology, Spiritualism, Mysticism and Metaphysics.* New Hyde Park, N.Y.: University Books, 1960. 440 pp. index. illus. bibliography.

> Originally published by Routledge (London) in 1920, this classic work has been incorporated into Shepard's *Encyclopedia of Occultism and Parapsychology* (see item 36).

28. Underwood, Peter. *Dictionary of the Occult and Supernatural: an A to Z of Hauntings, Possession, Witchcraft, Demonology and Other Occult Phenomena.* London: Fontana, 1979. 389 pp. illus. bibliography. ISBN 0-00-634153-5.

> Illustrated by Marion Neville and originally published by Harrap (London) in 1978 as *Dictionary of the Supernatural*. Terms from the occult, the supernatural, and the psychical phenomena fields. Includes biographies.

29. Walker, Benjamin. *Man and the Beasts Within: the Encyclopedia of the Occult, the Esoteric and the Supernatural.* New York: Stein & Day, 1977. 343 pp. index. bibliography.

> Originally published by Routledge & Kegan Paul (London) in 1977 as *Encyclopedia of Esoteric Man*. Later issued by Paladin (London, 1979) as *Body Magic*. Covers the arcane side of human anatomy, physiology, and psychology. Fairly long articles, followed by bibliographies, describing 160 terms from anus and buttocks to vagina and xenophrenia.

30. Weaver, Graham. *A–Z of the Occult.* London: Everest, 1975. 175 pp. illus.

> This paperback covers about 200 terms. The author is a journalist, so terms are defined clearly in layman's language.

Multivolume Encyclopedias

31. Brookesmith, Peter, ed. *The Unexplained: Mysteries of Mind, Space and Time.* London: Marshall Cavendish, 1983. 8 vols. index in front of each volume. illus. maps. bibliographies. ISBN 0-86307-098-1 (set).

> A companion set to the publisher's *Man, Myth and Magic* (see following item). Evidently first issued in magazine format, since various topics

are discussed more than once, albeit differently, each time. Covers modern material, such as UFOs and the Loch Ness Monster (Nessie).

32. Cavendish, Richard, ed. *Man, Myth and Magic: an Illustrated Encyclopedia of the Supernatural.* New York, London: Marshall Cavendish, 1983. 2d ed. 12 vols. illus. bibliography. ISBN 0-86307-041-8 (set).

> Hailed by critics when the first edition appeared in 1970, this work has been improved greatly in its second edition under executive editor Yvonne Deutch. Previously scattered articles treating the same subject have been pulled together, and a much better grade of paper and binding have been used. The set covers the occult, parapsychology, anthropology, mythology, mysticism, spiritualism, and symbolism. There is an authoritative editorial board of experts from appropriate fields. Some pictures appear to have been chosen for sensational effect. Extensive bibliographies are not noticeably updated from the first edition.

33. Daniels, Cora Linn (Morrison), and Stevens, Charles McClellan. *Encyclopedia of Superstitions, Folklore & the Occult Sciences of the World: a Comprehensive Library of Human Belief and Practice in the Mysteries of Life.* Detroit: Gale Research, 1971; New York: Gordon Press, n.d. 3 vols. illus. ISBN 0-8102-3286-8.

> Facsimile reprint of the 1903 edition published by J. H. Yewdale & Sons Inc. (Chicago). Arranged alphabetically within a number of large chapters on subjects such as birth and child life, love and marriage, death, trades and occupations, etc. The emphasis is on superstitions, folklore, and customs. Specific bits of information are difficult to locate due to the lack of an index.

34. Hastings, James, ed. *Encyclopedia of Religion and Ethics.* New York: Scribner's, 1908–27; Edinburgh: T. & T. Clark, 1908–27. 13 vols.

> This standard work in the religious field includes long, signed articles on occult subjects. As such, it should not be overlooked by the conscientious scholar.

35. Phillips, Perrott, ed. *Out of This World: the Illustrated Library of the Bizarre and Extraordinary.* Milwaukee: Purnell Reference Books, 1979, dist. by Columbia House; England: Phoebus Pub. Co. / BPC Pub. Ltd., 1976–78. 24 vols. index. illus. ISBN 0-83939-975-8.

> Each volume of this set has articles on subjects within the categories of out-of-this world, mystery, bizarre, mythmakers, front page and peo-

ple. The subjects are similar to those frequently covered in American tabloids such as the *National Enquirer*. In addition to tales about Hollywood personalities and current events, reports are included on historical occult happenings. Compared to *The Unexplained* (item 31), this set is second best.

36. Shepard, Leslie A., ed. *Encyclopedia of Occultism and Parapsychology: a Compendium of Information on the Occult Sciences, Magic, Demonology, Superstitions, Spiritualism, Mysticism, Metaphysics, Physical Science, and Parapsychology*. Detroit: Gale Research, 1983–84. 3 vols. with update supplements. index. ISBN 0-8103-0196-2.

This new edition increases the original 1979–81 set from two to three volumes. The first edition incorporates articles from Fodor (item 19) and Spence (item 27). Articles in the second edition are updated and rewritten. Indexes animals and birds, demons, gems, geographic locations of phenomena, gods, periodicals, plants and flowers, societies and organizations, and paranormal phenomena.

Series

37. *The Occult*. James Webb, advisory editor. New York: Arno Press, 1976. 33 vols.

Reprints of classic occult works. Includes the following:

37.1. Adare, Viscount. *Experiences in Spiritualism with Mr. D. D. Home*. London, 1869. ISBN 0-405-07937-0.

37.2. Atwood, Mary Anne. *A Suggestive Inquiry into the Hermetic Mystery: with a Dissertation on the More Celebrated of the Alchemical Philosophers Being an Attempt towards the Recovery of the Ancient Experiment of Nature*. Belfast, 1920. rev. ed. ISBN 0-405-07938-9.

37.3 Benson, Robert Hugh. *The Necromancers*. London, 1909. ISBN 0-405-07939-7.

37.4. Blood, Benjamin Paul. *Pluriverse: an Essay in the Philosophy of Pluralism*. Boston, 1920. ISBN 0-405-07941-9.

37.5. Bonwick, James. *Irish Druids and Old Irish Religions*. London, 1894. ISBN 0-405-07042-7.

37.6. Britten, Emma Hardinge. *Nineteenth Century Miracles: or Spirits and Their Work in Every Country of the Earth. A Complete Historical Compendium of the Great Movement Known as "Modern Spiritualism."* New York, 1884. illus. ISBN 0-405-07943-5.

37.7. Cahagnet, Louis Alphonse. *The Celestial Telegraph: or, Secrets of the Life to Come Revealed through Magnetism. . . .* London, 1850. ISBN 0-405-07944-3.

37.8. Capron, E. W. *Modern Spiritualism: Its Facts and Fanaticisms, Its Consistencies and Contradictions.* Boston, 1855. ISBN 0-405-07945-1.

37.9. Davenport, Reuben Briggs. *The Death-Blow to Spiritualism: Being the True Story of the Fox Sisters, as Revealed by Authority of Margaret Fox Kane and Catherine Fox Jackson.* New York, 1888. ISBN 0-405-07949-4.

37.10. Dupotet de Sennevoy, Jean. *An Introduction to the Study of Animal Magnetism.* London, 1838. ISBN 0-405-0-7950-8.

37.11. Du Prel, Carl. *The Philosophy of Mysticism.* London, 1889. ISBN 0-405-07951-6.

37.12. *Five Years of Theosophy: Mystical, Philosophical, Theosophical, Historical and Scientific Essays, Selected from The Theosophist.* G.R.S. Mead, ed. London, 1894. 2d ed. ISBN 0-405-07966-4.

37.13. Hinton, Charles Howard. *The Fourth Dimension.* London, 1912. ISBN 0-405-07953-2.

37.14. Hinton, Charles Howard. *Scientific Romances. First and Second Series.* London, 1886 / 1922. ISBN 0-405-07954-4.

37.15. Hitchcock, Ethan Allen. *Remarks upon Alchemy and the Alchemists: Indicating a Method of Discovering the True Nature of Hermetic Philosophy; and Showing that the Search after the Philosopher's Stone Had Not for It's Object the Discovery of an Agent for the Transmutation of Metals. . . .* Boston, 1857. ISBN 0-405-07955-9.

37.16. Home, Mme. Daniel Dunglas. *D. D. Home: His Life and Mission.* London, 1888. ISBN 0-405-07956-7.

37.17. Jennings, Hargrave. *The Rosicrucians: Their Rites and Mysteries.* London, 1907. 4th ed. illus. ISBN 0-405-07957-5.

37.18. Kiesewetter, Karl. *Der Occultismus des Altertums.* Leipzig, 1895. ISBN 0-405-07958-3.

37.19. Kiesewetter, Karl. *Geschichte des Neueren Occultismus: Volume I and Volume II, Die Geheimwissenschaften*. Leipzig, 1891 / 1895. ISBN 0-405-07961-3.

37.20. Lacuria, Paul François Gaspard. *Les Harmonies de l'être exprimées par les nombres*. Paris, 1899. new ed. ISBN 0-405-07964-8.

37.21. London Dialectical Society. *Report on Spiritualism of the Committee of the London Dialectical Society: Together with the Evidence, Oral and Written, and a Selection from the Correspondence*. London, 1871. ISBN 0-405-07965-6.

37.22. *The Mediums and the Conjurors*. An Anthology with an Introduction by James Webb. ISBN 0-405-07967-2.

37.22.1. Maskelyn, John Nevil. *Modern Spiritualism: a Short Account of Its Rise and Progress, with Some Exposures of So-Called Spirit Media*. London, 1876.

37.22.2. Smith-Buck, George [pseud. Herr Dobler]. *Exposé of the Davenport Brothers*. Belfast, 1869.

37.22.3. Sexton, George. *Spirit-Mediums, and Conjurers: an Oration Delivered in the Cavendish Rooms, London, on Sunday Evening, June 15th, 1873*. London, 1873.

37.23. Moses, William Stainton. *Spirit Teachings through the Mediumship of William Stainton Moses*. London, 1924. ISBN 0-405-07968-0.

37.24. Myers, Frederic W. H. *The Subliminal Consciousness*. New York, 1976. ISBN 0-405-07952-4.

37.25. Nichols, T. L. *A Biography of the Brothers Davenport: with Some Account of the Physical and Psychical Phenomena Which Have Occurred in Their Presence, in America and Europe*. London, 1864. ISBN 0-405-07969-9.

37.26. Oliphant, Margaret. *Memoir of the Life of Laurence Oliphant and of Alice Oliphant, His Wife*. Edinburgh and London, 1892. new ed. ISBN 0-405-07970-2.

37.27. *A Quest Anthology*. New York, 1976. ISBN 0-405-07971-0.

37.28. Rivail, Hippolyte Leon Denizard [pseud. Allan Kardec]. *Spiritualist Philosophy: the Spirits' Book*. London, 1893. ISBN 0-405-07973-7.

37.29. Sinnett, Alfred Percival, ed. *Incidents in the Life of Madame Blavatsky: Compiled from Information Supplied by Her Relatives and Friends.* London, 1886. ISBN 0-405-07974-5.

37.30. *The Society for Psychical Research Report on the Theosophical Society.* New York, 1976. ISBN 0-405-07975-3.

37.31. Solovyoff (Solov'ev), Vsevolod Sergyeevich. *A Modern Priestess of Isis.* London, 1895. ISBN 0-405-07976-1.

37.32. Underhill, A. Leah. *The Missing Link in Modern Spiritualism.* New York, 1885. illus. ISBN 0-405-07977-X.

37.33. Zollner, Johann Carl Friedrich. *Transcendental Physics: an Account of Experimental Investigations from the Scientific Treatises of Johann Carl Friedrich Zollner.* Boston, 1888. illus. ISBN 0-405-07978-8.

38. Corliss, William R., comp. *Sourcebook Project* series. Glen Arm, Md.: Sourcebook Project, 1975–.

Articles originally appeared in science journals, e.g., *Nature, Science, Antiquity,* and more popular magazines, e.g., *Fate.* Those titles appearing with the word *Handbook* in them are longer and sometimes reprint material which has appeared already in a *Sourcebook.* Titles include the following:

38.1. *Ancient Man: a Handbook of Puzzling Artifacts.* 1978. ISBN 0-915554-03-8.

38.2. *Handbook of Unusual Natural Phenomena.* 1977.

38.3. *Incredible Life: a Handbook of Biological Mysteries.* 1981. ISBN 0-915554-07-0.

38.4. *Mysterious Universe: a Handbook of Astronomical Anomalies.* 1979. ISBN 0-915554-05-4.

38.5. *Strange Artifacts: a Sourcebook on Ancient Man.* 1976. ISBN 0-96007-122-9.

38.6. *Strange Life: a Sourcebook on the Mysteries of Organic Nature.* 1976. ISBN 0-96007-128-8.

38.7. *Strange Minds: a Sourcebook of Unusual Mental Phenomena.* 1976. ISBN 0-915554-003.

38.8. *Strange Planet: a Sourcebook of Unusual Geological Facts.* 1978. ISBN 0-96007-123-7.

38.9. *Strange Universe: a Sourcebook of Curious Astronomical Observations.* 1977. ISBN 0-915554-02-X.

38.10. *The Unexplained: a Sourcebook of Strange Phenomena.* 1976. ISBN 0-553-02812-X.

38.11. *Unknown Earth: a Handbook of Geological Enigmas.* 1980. ISBN 0-915554-06-2.

39. *The Supernatural.* Garden City, N.Y.: Doubleday, 1975–77; Danbury, Conn.: Danbury Press / Grolier, 1975–76. London: Aldus Books, 1975–76. 21 vols. index. illus. ISBN 0-7172-8105-1.

Originally published by Aldus, this supermarket-format encyclopedia set was first published by Doubleday as *A New Library of the Supernatural.* The final volume includes the index to the set, as well as an extremely useful biographical dictionary of occult personalities and authorities. There are no bibliographies or sources provided. Not scholarly, but very readable. Each volume covers a different subject and presents an overview of the title's topic. Occasionally, individual titles vary from their English to American editions; for example, the English *Mysterious Powers* is entitled *They Had Strange Powers* in its American edition.

39.1. Farson, Daniel. *Vampires, Zombies, and Monster Men.* ISBN 0-3851-1311-8.

39.2. Hall, Angus. *Monsters and Mythic Monsters.* ISBN 0-3851-1312-9.

39.3. Hall, Angus. *Signs of Things to Come.* ISBN 0-3851-1306-8.

39.4. Hall, Angus. *Strange Cults.* ISBN 0-3851-1324-2.

39.5. Holroyd, Stuart. *Dream World.* ISBN 0-3851-1325-0.

39.6. Holroyd, Stuart. *Magic, Words, and Numbers.* ISBN 0-3851-1313-7.

39.7. Holroyd, Stuart. *Minds Without Boundaries.* ISBN 0-3851-1320-X.

39.8. Holroyd, Stuart. *Psychic Voyages.* ISBN 0-3851-1322-6.

39.9. King Francis. *The Cosmic Influence.* ISBN 0-3851-1314-5.

39.10. King, Francis. *Wisdom from Afar.* ISBN 0-3851-1309-8.

39.11. Kingston, Jeremy. *Healing Without Medicine.* ISBN 0-3851-1319-6.

39.12. Kingston, Jeremy. *Witches and Witchcraft.*
ISBN 0-3851-1316-1.

39.13. Powell, Neil. *Alchemy, the Ancient Science.*
ISBN 0-3851-1323-4.

39.14. Smyth, Frank. *Ghosts and Poltergeists.*
ISBN 0-3851-1315-3.

39.15. Stemman, Roy. *Atlantis and the Lost Lands.*
ISBN 0-3851-1318-8.

39.16. Stemman, Roy, *Spirits and the Spirit World.*
ISBN 0-3851-1310-8.

39.17. Stemman, Roy. *Visitors from Outer Space.*
ISBN 0-3851-1317-X.

39.18. Wilson, Colin. *Enigmas and Mysteries.*
ISBN 0-3851-1327-8.

39.19. Wilson, Colin. *The Geller Phenomena.*

39.20. Wilson, Colin. *They Had Strange Powers.*
ISBN 0-3851-1308-8.

39.21. *Guide and Index.*

Atlases and Guides

40. Brandon, Jim. *Weird America: a Guide to Places of Mystery in the United States.* New York: Dutton, 1978. 244 pp. illus. maps.
ISBN 0-525-49491-9.

> A geographical guide to places in the U.S. where unusual happenings, ghost experiences, disappearances, and strange phenomena have been reported. Arranged by state. Stresses the sort of occurrences covered by Charles Fort (item 61).

41. Coleman Loren. *Mysterious America.* London: Faber & Faber, 1983. 176 pp. illus. bibliography. ISBN 0-571-12524-7.

> Arranged by phenomena subjects, such as alligators in sewers, sightings of wild kangaroos, and the like. Although the writing style is that of an investigative reporter, the references to other printed works increase its value for the serious scholar. Emphasis is on Fortean

mysteries. The lack of an index detracts from its value as a quick reference source.

42. Hitching, Francis. *The Mysterious World: an Atlas of the Unexplained*. New York: Holt, Rinehart & Winston, 1979; London: Pan, 1979. 256 pp. index. illus. maps. bibliographies. ISBN 0-03-044036-9.

> Originally published by Collins (London) as *The World Atlas of Mysteries* in 1978. Mysteries and unusual phenomena in a historic and geographic context. Includes items such as megalithic engineering, migration instinct, undeciphered writings, dragons, and UFO sightings.

43. Holzer, Hans. *The Directory of the Occult*. Chicago: Henry Regnery, 1974. 201 pp. ISBN 0-8092-8377-8.

> Arranged by state. Rates, as well as lists, various types of psychics and occult practitioners. Also includes groups and organizations, and a glossary of terms.

44. Pepper, Elizabeth, and Wilcock, John. *Magical and Mystical Sites: Europe and the British Isles*. New York: Harper & Row, 1977. 304 pp. index. illus. bibliography. ISBN 0-06-090656-1.

> An historical approach to occult happenings in various parts of Europe. Divided into three parts: the ancient world, the Continent, and Great Britain. No current events information is included other than the Loch Ness Monster.

45. St. Clair, David. *The Psychic World of California*. Garden City, N.Y.: Doubleday, 1972. 323 pp. index.

> Results of the author's personal travels and investigations. Divided into southern, central and northern California. Short history in the final chapter.

46. Steiger, Brad. *Psychic City: Chicago*. Garden City, N.Y.: Doubleday, 1976. 186 pp. illus. bibliography. ISBN 0-385-01362-0.

> An occult profile of what is reported to be a very psychic city. Journalistic approach includes interviews with such occult leaders as the editor and publisher of *Fate* magazine. The appendix, by J. Gordon Melton, is a directory to organizations, spiritualist churches, and leaders of the Chicago occult society.

47. Strachan, Françoise, ed. *The Aquarian Guide to Occult, Mystical, Religious, Magical London and Around*. London: Aquarian Press, 1970. 180 pp. illus.

A paperback directory to practitioners, associations, bookstores, schools, and groups of the occult in the London area. Fairly lengthy descriptions of services and their scope, as well as a bit of history. Addresses provided. A few rituals and spells conclude the book.

48. Wilcock, John. *A Guide to Occult Britain: the Quest for Magic in Pagan Britain.* London: Sidgwick & Jackson, 1976. 143 pp. index. illus. bibliography. ISBN 0-283-98237-3.

Five tours arranged to include various magical sites. Specific routes are suggested for London, the south of England, Devon and Cornwall, Wales, eastern and northern England, Scotland and northwestern England.

49. Wilcock, John. *An Occult Guide to South America.* New York: Book Division of Laurel Tape & Film, 1976, distributed by Stein & Day. 222 pp. illus. bibliography. ISBN 0-8128-2106-X.

One of the most useful features of this title is its bibliography, arranged by country. Otherwise, the book has been dismissed by some critics as superficial.

Histories, Overviews, and Classic Works

50. Adams, William Henry Davenport. *Curiosities of Superstition, and Sketches of Some Unrevealed Religions.* Detriot: Singing Tree, 1971. 328 pp.

Originally published by J. Masters (London) in 1882. Victorian writing style with little original material. Nothing on Latin America. Contents: Buddhism, Magianism, Jewish superstitions, Brahmanism, Hindu mythology, Chinese beliefs, Australia, savage races of Asia, Africa, and the Zulus, Zabianism and serpent worship, North American Indians, Eskimos, flagellants, Scotland, and second sights.

51. Agrippa von Nettesheim, Heinrich Cornelius. *Three Books of Occult Philosophy or Magic. Book One—Natural Magic Which Includes the Early Life of Agrippa, His Seventy-four Chapters on Natural Magic, New Notes, Illustrations, Index, and Other Origins and Selected Matter.* London: Aquarian Press, 1971; New York: Samuel Weiser, 1971. 283 pp. illus. ISBN 0-85030-083-5.

Edited in part by Willis F. Whitehead. Translation of book one of *De Occulta Philosophia*, first published in 1510. This translation and edition was published first by Hahn & Whitehead (Chicago) in 1897. The second and third books were not published. New foreword by Leslie Shepard. Many reprint editions of this work exist. Deals primarily with the use of magic to learn about nature and God.

52. Baring-Gould, Sabine. *Curious Myths of the Middle Ages.* Ann Arbor, Mich.: Humphreys, 1967; New Hyde Park, N.Y.: University Books, 1967. 660 pp. illus.

> Introduction by Leslie Shepard. Explores folklore and superstition during the Middle Ages.

53. Barrett, Francis. *The Magus, or Celestial Intelligences: Being a Complete System of Occult Philosophy: In Three Books Containing the Ancient and Modern Practice of the Cabalisitc Art, Natural and Celestial Magic, &; Showing the Wonderful Effects that May Be Performed by a Knowledge of the Celestial Influences, the Occult Properties of Metals, Herbs, and Stones, and the Application of Active to Passive Principles.* Secaucus, N.J.: Citadel Press, 1967; Leicester, Eng.: Vance Harvey, 1970. 198 pp. reprint. illus.

> First published by Lackington, Allen, & Co. (London) in 1801. The reprint edition by Citadel Press includes a fine, 10-page bibliographic note by Timothy d'Arch Smith regarding the history and biography of the book and author. This was an early attempt to pull together all the occult knowledge of the time. It portrays the Cabala as part of a whole occult / magical system. The original 1801 edition has hand-tinted aquatints of the demons of hell, as well as other handsome illustrations. Primary emphasis is on magic.

54. Bertrand, Michel, and Angelini, Jean [pseud. Jean-Michel Angebert]. *The Occult and the Third Reich: the Mystical Origins of Nazism and the Search for the Holy Grail.* New York: McGraw-Hill, 1975; New York: Macmillan, 1974. 306 pp. index. illus. bibliography. ISBN 0-02-502150-8.

> Translated by Lewis A.M. Sunberg from the original French, *Hitler et la tradition cathare.* Explores the roots of German mysticism and its particular glorification in the Nazi dream. Based on the premise that Hitlerism was merely one brief chapter in the continuing struggle between neopaganism and Christianity.

55. Bessy, Maurice. *Pictorial History of Magic and the Supernatural.* London: Spring Books, 1964. 317 pp. illus.

Originally published as *Histoire en 1000 images de la magie* by Editions du Pont Royal. Translated by Margaret Crosland and Alan Daventry. No index, bibliography, or footnotes. Coffee-table book format. Useful primarily as a picture source, but the lack of an index or table of contents limits even this use.

56. Buckland, Raymond. *The Anatomy of the Occult*. New York: Samuel Weiser, 1977. 151 pp. illus. bibliographies. ISBN 0-87728-304-4.

A general overview of the occult scene by a self-proclaimed witch.

57. Burland, Cottie Arthur. *The Magical Arts: a Short History*. London: Arthur Books, 1966; New York: Horizon, 1966. 196 pp. index. illus.

An international, once-over-lightly approach. Fine summary of subjects that is not judgmental in tone. Provides a good overview from a sane perspective.

58. Calkins, Carroll C. *Mysteries of the Unexplained*. Pleasantville, N.Y.: Readers' Digest Association, 1983, distributed by Random House. 320 pp. illus. bibliography. ISBN 0-89577-146-2.

Popular, reporter style; profusely illustrated. Contents include prophecies, anomalies, coincidences, spontaneous human combustion, inexplicable crimes and assaults, appearances and disappearances, monsters, spectral incursions, strange things from above, UFOs, atmospheric and astronomical oddities, cures and immunities, and signs and wonders.

59. Constant, Alphonse Louis [pseud. Eliphas Lèvi]. *The Great Secret: or, Occultism Unveiled*. New York: Samuel Weiser, 1969. 192 pp.

First published in Paris in 1898 as *Le grand arcane; ou, L'occultisme deviolé*. An influential occultist, Lèvi is often quoted. Deals mainly with the concept of evil.

60. Crow, William Bernard. *A History of Magic, Witchcraft and Occultism*. Hollywood, Calif.: Wilshire Book Co., 1972; London: Abacus, 1972. 320 pp. index. bibliographic footnotes. ISBN 0-349-10640-1.

First published by Aquarian Press (London), this book provides good detail, despite a confusing organization.

61. Fort, Charles. *The Complete Book of Charles Fort.* New York: Dover, 1975. 4 vols. in one. ISBN 0-486-230945.

> Reprint of Fort's *The Book of the Damned* (1919), *New Lands* (1923), *Lo!* (1931), and *Wild Talents* (1923). Fort was the first writer in this century really to capture the public interest with his dramatic accounts of unusual events ignored by science. The Fortean Society has been named in his honor.

62. Franklyn, Julian. *A Survey of the Occult.* London: Arthur Baker, 1935. 301 pp.

> Contributions by Dr. F. E. Budd, J. H. Mozley, S. G. Soal, and Alastair Baxter. An attempt to combine ancient occult beliefs with modern scientific advances. A series of longish articles with references to smaller topics makes this book almost encyclopedic in nature. Contents include the following: alchemy, astrology, black magic, Buddhist occultism, Chinese occultism, devil worship, English literature and the occult, fairies, ghosts, history of occult ideas, illusion and hallucination, Indian occultism, literature of occultism, Moslem occultism, occultism in ancient Greece and Rome, psychotherapy and psychic phenomena, spiritualism, the vampire, the werewolf, white magic, and witchcraft.

63. Galbreath, Robert, ed. *The Occult: Studies and Evaluations.* Bowling Green, Ohio: Bowling Green University Popular Press, 1972. 126 pp. bibliographies.

> Originally published as the Winter 1971 (vol. 5, no. 3) issue of *The Journal of Popular Culture.* Contains nine scholarly essays, including the excellent bibliographic survey by Galbreath mentioned in the introductory comments to this chapter.

64. Gibson, Walter Brown, and Gibson, Litzka R. *The Complete Illustrated Book of the Psychic Sciences.* Garden City, N.Y.: Doubleday, 1966. 403 pp. index. illus.

> Illustrations by Murray Keshner. Glossary included in the introduction. Includes the following: astrology, cartomancy, colorology, fortune-telling by dice, domino divination, dream interpretation, graphology, numerology, moleosophy, palmistry, phrenology, physiognomy, radiesthesia and other phenomena (dowsing, Ouija, crystal gazing), superstitions and omens, tasseography, telepathy, and yoga.

65. Godwin, John. *Occult America.* Garden City, N.Y.: Doubleday, 1972. 314 pp. index. illus.

Summary of occult happenings in America with an emphasis on contemporary developments. The author interviewed many occult practitioners to obtain information. Glossary provided. Subjects covered in the text include L. Ron Hubbard, Edgar Cayce, Eckankar, saucerians, etc.

66. Godwin, John. *This Baffling World.* Toronto: Bantam, 1971–73. 3 vols. illus.

Reprint of the 1968 publication by Hart (New York) in one volume. Pictorial research by Marion Geisinger. A basic survey on a wide range of subjects.

67. Gould, Rupert T. *Oddities: a Book of Unexplained Facts.* New York: Bell, 1965. 3d ed. 228 pp. index. illus. maps. ISBN 0-517-18012-X.

Introduction by Leslie Shepard. First published in 1928. Carefully documented accounts of mysteries, including the moving coffins of Barbados, the ships on ice seen by Sir John Franklin, Orffyreus' wheel (a powerless machine), the Auroras and other doubtful islands, Mersenne's number (a mathematical puzzle), Bottineau (wizard of Mauritius), and the planet Vulcan. Gould is the author of other works on unexplained phenomena, including *Enigmas*, published in 1929.

68. Grant, James. *The Mysteries of All Nations: Rise and Progress of Superstition, Laws Against and Trials of Witches, Ancient and Modern Delusions, Together with Strange Customs, Fables and Tales Relating to Mythology—Days and Weeks—Miracles—Poets and Superstition—Monarchs, Priests, and Philosophers—Druids—Demonology—Magic and Astrology—Divination—Signs, Omens, and Meanings—Amulets and Charms—Trials by Ordeal—Curses and Evil Wishes—Dreams and Visions—Superstition in the Nineteenth Century.* Detroit: Gale Research, 1971. 640 pp.

First published by Reid & Sons (Leith, England) in 1880. Many tales and legends, primarily from the Near East, ancient Egypt, Greece, and Rome, plus European customs. Lengthy notes in the table of contents serve as an index.

69. Grillot de Givry, Emile Angelo. *Witchcraft, Magic and Alchemy.* Boston: Houghton Mifflin, 1931, 1954. 395 pp. index. illus.

Translated by J. Courtney Leek. An illustrated version is published by Gale Research and Harrap. A number of other reprint editions by various publishers also exist.

70. Grim, Patrick. *Philosophy of Science and the Occult.* New York: State University of New York Press, 1982. 336 pp. index. illus. bibliography. ISBN 0-87395-572-2.

> SUNY Series in Philosophy. This collection of papers presents reasons for the separation of the sciences and the pseudosciences. Includes general history and considerations, astrology, parapsychology, study of UFOs, and the ancient astronaut hypothesis.

71. Hall, Manly P. *Collected Writings of Manly P. Hall.* Los Angeles: The Philosophical Research Society, n.d., 3 vols. illus.

> Originally published in various places and formats, primarily in periodicals and pamphlets. These are more ephemeral pieces; monographs are not included. Wide range of subjects.

72. Holiday, Frederick William. *The Dragon and the Disc: an Investigation into the Totally Fantastic.* New York: Norton, 1973; London: Futura, 1973; Sidgwick & Jackson, 1973. 247 pp. index. illus. maps. bibliography. ISBN 0-393-06336-4.

> An exploration of the long history and universality of occult beliefs. Definite British slant. Contents include dragons (also the Loch Ness Monster), mysterious discs, ley lines, etc. Strong Celtic flavor to the selections.

73. Hunt, Douglas. *Handbook on the Occult.* London: Arthur Baker, 1967. 219 pp.

> Based on *Exploring the Occult*, published in the Pan Piper series. Contents include spiritualism, hauntings, astral projection, dreams, reincarnation, hypnosis, telepathy (clairvoyance and precognition), healing and radiesthesia, yoga, Tibetan Buddhism, the Hierarchy, astrology, black magic, and human oddities.

74. Jacolliot, Louis. *Occult Science in India and among the Ancients, with an Account of Their Mystic Initiations and the History of Spiritualism.* New Hyde Park, N.Y.: University Books, 1970. 274 pp.

> Originally published in Paris (1884) as *Spiritisme dans le monde*. Translation by William L. Feit. Includes some information on the Cabala.

75. Kerr, Howard, and Crow, Charles L., eds. *The Occult in America: New Historical Perspectives.* Champaign: University of Illinois Press, 1983. 240 pp. index. illus. ISBN 0-2520-0983-5.

Bibliographical notes at the ends of chapters. Centers on religious thought in occult matters. Includes coverage of the dark age of American occultism, 1760–1848, women in occult America, and UFOs and the search for scientific legitimacy.

76. Leahey, Thomas Hardy, and Leahey, Grace Evans. *Psychology's Occult Doubles: Psychology and the Problem of Pseudoscience.* New York: Nelson-Hall, 1983. ISBN 0-88229-717-1.

Examines the problems "legitimate" science has had in dealing with various occult ideas and possible truths. An excellent, up-to-date survey.

77. Mitchell, John, and Richard, Robert J.M. *Phenomena: a Book of Wonders.* New York: Pantheon Books, 1977; London: Thames & Hudson, 1977. 128 pp. illus. bibliographical references. ISBN 0-394-41596-5.

A coffee-table book describing oddities of a Fortean nature. The authors stress that the concept of reality is probably much wider than the commonly accepted view.

78. O'Keefe, Danielle Lawrence. *Stolen Lightning: the Social Theory of Magic.* New York: Random House, 1982. 598 pp. index. ISBN 0-394-71634-5.

Available both in hardcover and paperback. A view of the occult, synthesizing the sociological, anthropological, and psychological perspectives. A series of postulates suggests certain characteristics of magic as it has pervaded civilization and various societies.

79. Readers' Digest. *Into the Unknown.* Pleasantville, N.Y.: The Readers' Digest Association, 1981. 352 pp. index. illus. bibliography. ISBN 0-89577-098-9.

Contains short, profusely illustrated articles on UFOs, clairvoyance, telepathy, animal ESP, mind-over-matter, reincarnation, ghosts and poltergeists, ancient unknowns, earth shrines, Atlantis, powers of the brain, psychic healing, witchcraft, monsters, divination, astrology, spiritualism, dreams, out-of-the-body experiences, and possession and exorcism.

80. Sanderson, Ivan Terence. *Investigating the Unexplained: a Compendium of Disquieting Mysteries of the Natural World.* Englewood Cliffs, N.J.: Prentice-Hall, 1972. 339 pp. index. illus. maps. bibliography. ISBN 0-13-502229-0.

The author is a noted naturalist whose theories are controversial but well worth considering. Appendixes list cases of spontaneous combustion and of falls of mysterious objects from the sky.

81. Schuré, Edouard. *From Sphinx to Christ: an Occult History*. San Francisco: Harper & Row, 1982. London: Garber Communications, 1981. 284 pp. ISBN 0-06067-124-6.

English edition published under the title *Evolution Divine*. First American edition appeared in 1970, published by Rudolf Steiner (Blauvelt, N.Y.).

82. Shadowitz, Albert, and Walsh, Peter. *The Dark Side of Knowledge: Exploring the Occult*. Reading, Mass.: Addison-Wesley, 1976. 305 pp. index. illus. bibliography. ISBN 0-201-07331-5.

Quality paperback written in a journalistic style. Includes information on magic, witchcraft, psychic phenomena, altered states, mysticism, UFOs, and astrology.

83. Shumaker, Wayne. *The Occult Sciences in the Renaissance: a Study in Intellectual Patterns*. Berkeley: University of California Press, 1972. 284 pp. index. illus. bibliography. ISBN 0-520-02021-9.

A scholarly treatment of astrology, white magic, witchcraft, alchemy, and Hermes Trismegistus.

84. Somerlott, Robert. *"Here Mr. Splitfoot": an Informal Exploration into Modern Occultism*. New York: Viking Press, 1971. 311 pp. index. illus. bibliography. ISBN 0-670-36876-8.

A chatty, readable account of the historic development of occultism in the world today. Includes pieces on Eusapia Paladino, Leonora Piper, the Fox sisters, Arthur Ford, Daniel Dunglas Home, John Dee, Edgar Cayce, and Peter Hurkos. Emphasis primarily on psychics, although prophecy and other occult notions are covered as well.

85. Stewart, Louis. *Life Forces: a Contemporary Guide to the Cult and Occult*. Kansas City: Andrews & McMeel, 1980. 567 pp. index. illus. bibliographies. ISBN 0-8362-7903-4.

An appendix at the end contains a directory of occult and related organizations. Divided into three main sections: spiritual sciences, the occult bible, and the dissenting viewpoint. Based on the premise that the occult is not so much a set of beliefs as a system of knowledge. Includes a number of modern developments, such as Rolfing and orgone boxes.

86. Thomas, Keith Vivian. *Religions and the Decline of Magic: Studies in Popular Beliefs in Sixteenth- and Seventeenth-Century England.* New York: Scribner's, 1971, 1973; Harmondsworth, Eng.: Penguin, 1973. 853 pp. index. bibliography. ISBN 0-68410-602-7.

> Originally published by Weidenfeld & Nicolson (London) in 1971. Anthropological, scholarly study of the decline of belief in the supernatural among the lower classes of England during the English Renaissance. Considered to be very influential on the works of other scholars.

87. Thorndike, Lynn. *A History of Magic and Experimental Sciences.* New York: Macmillan and Columbia University Press, 1923–58. 8 vols. indexes.

> A well-documented history with chapters devoted to general historical periods (centuries), as well as personalities, the development of the discipline, and various practices. Considered a landmark work in the field.

88. Waite, Arthur Edward [pseud. Grant Orient]. *Complete Manual of Occult Divination.* New Hyde Park, N.Y.: University Books, 1972. 2 vols. ISBN 0-8216-0063-X.

> A reprint of a title first published in England under Waite's pseudonym in the 1890s. Waite was an earnest and prolific writer on occult matters. He succeeded Aleister Crowley as head of the Golden Dawn.

89. Waite, Arthur Edward. *The Occult Sciences: a Compendium of Transcendental Doctrine and Experiment, Embracing an Account of Magical Practices; of Secret Societies in Connection with Magic: of the Professors of Magical Arts; and of Modern Spiritualism, Mesmerism, and Theosophy.* New Hyde Park, N.Y.: University Books, 1962. New York: Dutton, 1923. 292 pp. ISBN 0-8216-0214-4.

> First printed in 1891 by Trubner (London) and reprinted in 1923. Includes information on the principles of black and white magic, talismans, divining rods, Cabala, Rosicrucians, Freemasons, mesmerism, spiritualism, and theosophy.

90. Watson, Lyall. *Supernature: the Natural Guide to the Supernatural.* Garden City, N.Y.: Anchor / Doubleday, 1973; London: Hodder & Stoughton, 1973; Coronet, 1974. 344 pp. index. bibliography. ISBN 0-385-00744-2.

> Discusses man's relationship to the natural world in a supernatural way. The author states; "All the best science has soft edges . . ." (p. x).

91. Wheatley, Dennis. *The Devil and All His Works*. London: Hutchinson, 1971; New York: American Heritage Press, 1971. 302 pp. index. illus. maps.

> Coffee-table book format with fine pictures (sources provided). Part I includes invisible influences (mesmerism, hypnotism, faith healing, telepathy and premonitions). Part II covers predestination (astrology, numerology, cheirognomy, cartomancy, clairvoyance, psychometry, clairaudience, oracles, necromancy, haruspicy, and other means of divination). Part III deals with beliefs in early ages. Part IV describes beliefs in the past 2,500 years. Part V discusses witches and warlocks. There is a final section on the "way," since Wheatley apparently believed in the "right-hand path," espoused in his occult novels.

92. *The World Almanac Book of the Strange*. New York: Signet / New American Library, 1977. 482 pp. illus. ISBN 0-451-07784-9.

> A compendium by the editors of *The World Almanac*. An excellent survey of mysterious things, archaeological ruins, occult happenings, and the like. A brisk, skeptical tone prevails. A sequel, *The Second Book of the Strange*, is not as well done as this first volume.

93. Yates, Frances Amelia. *The Occult Philosophy in the Elizabethan Age*. London: Routledge & Kegan Paul, 1979. 217 pp. index. illus. bibliographic references. ISBN 0-7100-0320-X.

> The importance of Jewish mysticism and the Cabala, often overlooked in studying the Renaissance, is the theme of this book. It includes a section on the influence of occult philosophy on English writers such as Spenser, Marlowe, Chapman, and Shakespeare.

Biographies

94. Ebon, Martin. *They Knew the Unknown*. New York: World, 1971; New American Library, 1972. index. bibliography.

> Includes information on the role of the occult in the lives of Kant, Schopenhauer, Shelley, Lincoln, Hugo, the Brownings, Mark Twain, William James, Strindberg, A. R. Wallace, Arthur Conan Doyle, Edison, William McDougall, Freud, Jung, Yeats, Alexis Carol, Maeterlinck, MacKenzie King, Thomas Mann, Gilbert Murray, Alduous Huxley, Upton Sinclair, and C. J. Ducasse.

95. Haining, Peter, ed. *The Magicians: the Occult in Fact and Fiction*. New York: Taplinger, 1972. 219 pp. illus. ISBN 0-8008-5045-9.

Published by P. Owen (London) in 1972 as *The Magicians: Occult Stories*. Introduction by Colin Wilson. Includes chapters on Huysman, Lèvi, Blavatsky, Crowley, Yeats, Machen, Fortune, Doyle, Rohmer, Spence, Blackwood, and Gardner.

96. Hamon, Count Louis [pseud. Cheiro]. *Mysteries and Romances of the World's Greatest Occultists.* London: Herbert Jenkins, 1935. 315 pp.

Part I deals with historical figures—Cagliostro, Doctor Dee, Edward Kelley, Elias Ashmole, Pierre Le Clerc, Van Galgebrok, and Paulo Phinn. Part II discusses twentieth-century occult celebrities—Princess Zisky, Herr Zunklehorn, Mme. Gutjen Send, Eusapia Paladino, Mme. Blavatsky, Mrs. Annie Besant, William Q. Judge, Mrs. Katherine Tingley, Krishnamurti, Sir Oliver Lodge, Camille Flammarion. Also covers occult experiences of famous people.

97. McIntosh, Christopher. *Eliphas Lèvi and the French Occult Revival.* London: Rider, 1972, 1975. 238 pp. index. illus. bibliography. ISBN 0-09-112270-8.

An account of the revival of occult interest in nineteenth-century France. Emphasis is on the life and times of Lèvi (whose birth name was Constant), considered a leader in the movement.

98. Wilson, Colin, with Christmas Humphreys and others. *Dark Dimensions: a Celebration of the Occult.* New York: Everest House, 1978. 236 pp.

Nine biographies: Blavatsky, Rasputin, Crowley, Nikola Tesla, "Hellfire" Dashwood, Mesmer, Nostradamus, Uri Geller, and Gurdjieff.

2
TRADITIONAL WITCHCRAFT
AND SATANISM

WITCH, n. (1) An ugly and repulsive old woman, in a wicked
    league with the devil. (2) A beautiful and attractive young
    woman, in wickedness a league beyond the devil.
                                            Ambrose Bierce,
                                       The Devil's Dictionary

For many people, the term *occult* is synonymous with witchcraft. In
that context, witchcraft is usually thought of in its traditional sense—
as a heresy prosecuted first by the Catholic Church and later by
Protestant sects. Witchcraft came into popular attention in the late
Middle Ages in Europe, peaked in Germany in the sixteenth century,
lingered on in the rest of the Continent and Great Britain for another
century or so, and flared up in America only during the seventeenth
century, in New England.

The literature dealing with traditional witchcraft and satanism
therefore tends to be historical and religious in nature. Often scholarly, it deals with those concepts of why and how persecutions came
about at certain times and in certain places. Recently, the psychological and sociological aspects of witchcraft have been examined as well.

For those interested in bibliographic essays dealing with witchcraft as a scholarly activity, three articles are recommended:

1. George Lincoln Burr, "The Literature of Witchcraft," *Papers
of the American Historical Association*, 4 (1890): 37–66.

2. H. C. Midelfort, "Recent Witch Hunting Research, or
Where Do We Go from Here?" *Papers of the Bibliographical Society of
America*, 62 (1968): 373–420.

3. Donald Nugent, "Witchcraft Studies, 1959–1971: a Bibliographical Survey," *Journal of Popular History*, 5 (1971): 710–25.

A dominant theme throughout these scholarly works is the
question, Did the accused actually believe and practice witchcraft? As
with any historical speculation, there appear to be as yet no definitive
answers.

For the purpose of describing what is included in this chapter, some definitions follow. Witchcraft involves the practice of certain arcane spells learned from demonic sources. Satanism is the worship of Satan as a superior, or preferred, god. Demonology is the examination of evil spirits from various cultures, most often those described as tempters and torturers in the Judeo-Christian tradition.

Material in this chapter is organized as follows:

- General Reference Works
- Histories and Overviews
- Works Arranged by Country:
  Great Britain, France,
  Italy, America

General Reference Works

99. Anglo, Sydney, ed. *The Damned Art: Essays in the Literature of Witchcraft*. London: Routledge & Kegan Paul, 1977. 258 pp. index. bibliographic references. ISBN 0-7100-8589-3.

> A useful volume concerning the literature of witchcraft, primarily fifteenth and sixteenth century documents from Germany, Italy, France, England, Scotland, and New England. Includes material on Johann Weyer, Jean Bodin, Reginald Scott, Georges Gifford, King James I, Pierre de Lancre, Cotton Mather, John Bell, Heinrich Kramer, and Jacob Sprenger.

100. Collin de Plancy, Jacques Albin Simon. *A Dictionary of Witchcraft*. New York: Philosphical Library, 1965. 125 pp.

> Edited and translated by Wade Baskin. The Philosophical Library has published a number of short-entry dictionaries on different occult subjects, most of which have been criticized for their brevity and superficiality.

101. Cornell University Libraries. *Witchcraft: Catalogue of the Witchcraft Collection of Cornell University Library*. Millwood, N.Y.: KTO Press, 1977. 644 pp. index. ISBN 0-527-19705-X.

> Edited by Martha J. Crow and indexed by Jane Marsh Dickmann, this important work includes a 50-page introduction by Rossell Hope Robbins. It consists of 12,000 catalog-card entries for nearly 3,000 books and manuscripts in the Cornell Witchcraft Collection, probably the best collection in the country on witchcraft. The subject approach in the index makes this a particularly useful source.

102. Del Cervo, Diane M., ed. *Witchcraft in Europe and America: Guide to the Microfilm Collection.* Woodbridge, Conn.: Research Publication, 1983. 104 microfilm reels.

> A total of 1,099 books dealing with witchcraft have been preserved on microfilm. Additional subject areas include demonology, theology, canon law, civil law, narratives, history, literature, and science / medicine. Major European languages are represented, in addition to English and Latin. Covers material from the thirteenth century to the end of the nineteenth century. Most items are from the Cornell Witchcraft Collection and the Henry Charles Lea Collection at the University of Pennsylvania.

103. Ericson, Eric. *The World, the Flesh, the Devil: a Biographical Dictionary of Witches.* New York: Mayflower Books, 1981; England: New English Library, Ltd., n.d. 285 pp. illus. ISBN 0-8317-9512-3.

> Fairly short but informative biographies of individuals known to be, or accused of being, witches. International in scope, the work focuses on English witches of past centuries.

104. Lehner, Ernest, and Lehner, Johanna. *Devils, Demons, Death, and Damnation.* New York: Dover, 1971. 174 pp. illus. ISBN 0-486-22751-0.

> A picture source from Dover's clip art-book series. A limited number of these illustrations may be used in any one publication without violating copyright laws. Most of the material concerns the devil, demons, and the apparently overwhelming fascination with death. The majority are reproductions of old woodcuts and etchings.

105. Newall, Venetia. *The Encyclopedia of Witchcraft and Magic.* New York: A & W Visual Library, 1974; Dial Press, 1974; London: Hamlyn, 1974. 191 pp. index. illus. bibliography. ISBN 0-600-33077-X.

> Introduction by Richard M. Dorson. Brief articles, 142 in all, with ample, accurate illustrations. Coffee-table book format. A quick, good introduction to terms and important names in the field.

106. Robbins, Rossell Hope. *Encyclopedia of Witchcraft and Demonology.* New York: Crown, 1959; London: Peter Nevill, 1959. 571 pp. illus. bibliography.

> An excellent work which treats witchcraft in its traditional sense. Entries and articles reflect solid scholarship.

107. Valiente, Doreen. *An ABC of Witchcraft Past and Present.* London: Robert Hale, 1973; New York: St. Martin's. 1973. 377 pp. indexes. illus. ISBN 0-7091-3164-X.

> The compiler of this work is a self-proclaimed witch. Indexes are arranged by subjects, places, and people. Includes areas outside the subject of witchcraft, such as vampires, scrying (divination); and phallic worship.

108. Wilson, Colin. *Witches.* New York: A & W Publishers, 1982. 160 pp. index. illus. ISBN 0-88365-575-6.

> A coffee-table book profusely illustrated by Una Woodruff. Consists of short descriptions of famous witches in history, mostly English.

Histories and Overviews

109. Ashton, John. *The Devil in Britain and America.* San Bernardino, Calif.: Borgo Press, 1980; Hollywood, Calif.; Newcastle, 1972, 1980; Detroit: Gale Research, 1974; New York: Gordon Press, 1976. 363 pp. illus. bibliography. ISBN 0-87777-008-9.

> Reprint of an 1896 edition published by Ward and Downey (London). Study of seventeenth and eighteenth century witchcraft. Includes testimonies of some of the condemned.

110. Barojar, Julio Caro. *The World of Witches.* Chicago: University of Chicago Press, 1964. 313 pp. index. illus. bibliography.

> The Nature of Human Society series. Translated by O. N. V. Glendinning from the original, *Las Brujas y su mundo* (Madrid: Revista Occidente, 1961). A frequently cited, scholarly work on the classical background of witchcraft, the rise of witchcraft, the crisis of witchcraft in the Basque country, the decline of witchcraft, and modern witchcraft. Subscribes cautiously to the Murray (see items 151 and 152) theory that witchcraft may well be part of a long-lived cult. Considered an important work in the field.

111. Carus, Paul. *History of the Devil and the Ideas of Evil, from the Earliest Times.* LaSalle, Ill.: Open Court, 1974; New York: Land's End Press, 1969; Bell, 1974. 496 pp. illus. ISBN 0-87548-3070.

> First published in 1900. A historical study of the appeal of evil in the Western world. Scholarly.

112. Cavendish, Richard. *The Black Arts.* New York: Putnam, 1967; Capricorn Books, 1968. 373 pp. illus. bibliography.

> Putnam published a later version (1975) under the title *The Powers of Evil.* Considered a good basic overview.

113. Cohn, Norman. *Europe's Inner Demons: an Enquiry Inspired by the Great Witchhunt.* New York: Basic Books, 1975; New American Library, 1977. 304 pp. index. illus. bibliography. ISBN 0-465-02131-X.

> Columbus Centre Series on Medieval Witchcraft. Cohn suggests that the witchcraft trials began later than originally thought.

114. Ebon, Martin. *The Devil's Bride: Exorcism, Past and Present.* New York: Harper & Row, 1974; New American Library, 1975; London: Cassell, 1975. 245 pp. bibliography. ISBN 0-06-062114-1.

> Published by Cassell (England) under the title *Exorcism, Past and Present,* in 1975. Describes actual case studies, mostly historic, in which demons were exorcised. The author views his subject from a psychological perspective and concludes that exorcism may have therapeutic value in and of itself. It is clear that he does not believe in the existence of demons.

115. Guazzo, Francesco Maria. *Compendium Maleficarum.* London: Muller, 1970; New York: Barnes & Noble, 1970. 206 pp. illus. bibliography.

> Reprint of a 1929 edition. Edited with notes by Montague Summers. Translated by E. E. Ashwin. An important, historical work on witchcraft, first published in the seventeenth century in Italy. (see item 131).

116. Harrison, Michael. *The Roots of Witchcraft.* Secaucus, N.J.: Citadel Press, 1972; London: Muller, 1973; Tandem, 1975. 278 pp. index. illus. bibliography. ISBN 0-584-10232-1.

> Traces the theme of the fertility cult from its rise in pre-Christian Europe to present-day witchcraft. Strong Celtic theme.

117. Hughes, Pennethorne. *Witchcraft.* London: Penguin, 1965; Baltimore: Penguin, 1965. 236 pp. illus. bibliography. A Pelican Book.

> General overview of the subject with a definite British focus. Includes modern witchcraft in the final chapter.

118. Institoris, Henricus. *The Malleus Maleficarum of Heninrich Kramer and Jacob Sprenger.* New York: Dover, 1971; London: Rodker, 1928; Arrow Books, 1971. 277 pp. ISBN 0-486-22802-9.

Translated with notes and bibliography by Montague Summers. Originally published in 1485. Roughly translated as "The Witches' Hammer," this treatise was written by two Dominican friars who traveled about Germany investigating witchcraft claims and witches. Considered the authority for identifying witches, what constitutes witchcraft, and how to bring proceedings against witches.

119. Jong, Erica. *Witch.* New York: Abrams, 1981. 176 pp. illus. ISBN 0-8109-1765-3.

A coffee-table book with illustrations by Joseph A. Smith of ethereal appearing witches throughout history, practicing their spells and undergoing torture. The book glorifies the feminist aspects of witchcraft.

120. Kieckhefer, Richard. *European Witch Trials; Their Foundations in Popular and Learned Culture, 1300–1500.* London: Routledge & Kegan Paul, 1976; Berkeley: University of California Press, 1976. 181 pp. index. illus. bibliography. ISBN 0-7100-8314-9.

A careful and scholarly investigation of witchcraft records from the late medieval period. The author makes the point that the lower classes were concerned with magic and sorcery, while more learned individuals looked for deliberate cases of devil worship.

121. Kittredge, George Lyman. *Witchcraft in Old and New England.* Cambridge, Mass.: Harvard University Press, 1929; New York: Russell & Russell, 1929. 641 pp. index. bibliography.

A noted scholar in the field, Kittredge includes references to modern-day practices. Emphasis is on the historic background of witchcraft. Strong folklore theme throughout.

122. Lea, Henry Charles. *Materials toward a Study of Witchcraft.* New York: Thomas Yoseleff, 1957; London: W. H. Allen, 1958. 3 vols.

Originally published in 1939, this is an important sourcebook for case studies and persecution accounts. No bibliography. Most of the material was taken from Lea's own collection of witchcraft, now in the library of the University of Pennsylvania.

123. *A Manual of Exorcism: Very Useful for Priests and Ministers of the Church.* New York: Hispanic Society of America, 1975, distributed by Interbook. 141 pp. ISBN 0-913456-46-2.

Translated from the Spanish by Eunice Beyersdorff. Includes an appendix with actual prayers to use during an exorcism. Reproduction of a historic text which covers the reasons for exorcism and the general procedures to follow.

124. Maple, Eric. *The Dark World of Witches*. New York: A. S. Barnes, 1964; London: Pan, 1962. 209 pp. illus. bibliography.

Includes references to modern-day witchcraft, but the emphasis is on the traditional European style of the craft. Readable, standard work.

125. Marwick, Max G., ed. *Witchcraft and Sorcery; Selected Readings*. Magnolia, Mass.: Peter Smith, 1971; Harmondsworth, Eng.: Penguin, 1970. 416 pp. bibliographies.

The Penguin Modern Sociology Readings series. An anthology of articles on witchcraft from around the world, mostly of primitive societies, prior to the current century.

126. Master, Robert E. L. *Eros and Evil: the Sexual Psychopathology of Witchcraft*. Baltimore: Penguin, 1962. 322 pp. bibliography.

An important work on the sex psychology and pathology of the ancient craft. Explores the fascination with deviant sexual practices that pervade the accounts of witchcraft persecutions and trials.

127. Oesterreich, Traugott Konstantin. *Possession, Demoniacal and Otherwise, among Primitive Races, in Antiquity, the Middle Ages, and Modern Times*. New York: R. R. Smith, 1930. 400 pp.

Translated by D. Ibberson. A study of the nature of possession with various historical viewpoints regarding it.

128. Parrinder, Geoffrey. *Witchcraft: European & African*. London: Faber & Faber, 1958, 1963. index. bibliography. ISBN 571-06416-7.

An exploration of witchcraft from both its European and its African roots. Contents include witches' meetings, black masses, confessions, witchcraft trials (in both Britain and New England), witchcraft in the Near East, modern African witchcraft, and modern witchcraft.

129. Philpott, Kent. *Manual of Demonology and the Occult*. Grand Rapids, Mich.: Zondervan, 1973. 191 pp. bibliography.

Description of the various demoniacal aspects by a contemporary minister. Includes glossary.

130. Ravensdale, Tom, and Morgan, James. *The Psychology of Witchcraft: an Account of Witchcraft, Black Magic and the Occult.* New York: Arco, 1974; Edinburgh: J. Bartholomew, 1974. 200 pp. index. illus. ISBN 0-668-03501-3.

> Forword by Sir Alec Kirkbride. A successful attempt to combine the history and development of witchcraft and satanism on the international scale.

131. Remi, Nicolas, and Guazzo, Francesco Maria. *Demonolatry.* London: Muller, 1970; Secaucus, N.J.: University Books, 1974. 2 vols. ISBN 0-8216-0215-2.

> Reprint of a title first published in translation by J. Rodker (London) in three books. Translated by E. A. Ashwin and edited by Montague Summers. Preface by Leslie Shephard. Volume one is a reprint of the book *Demonolatry*, a translation of Remi's sixteenth century work, *Daemonlatreiae Libri Tres.* Volume two is a translation of Guazzo's *Compendium Maleficarum* (see item 115).

132. Rhodes, Henry Taylor Fowkes. *The Satanic Mass: a Sociological and Criminological Study.* London: Arrow Books, 1973; Rider, 1954; Secaucus, N.J.: Citadel Press, 1974. 254 pp. index. bibliography. ISBN 0-09-906960-1.

> Originally published by Rider (London) in 1954. An essential study, considered the definitive work on historic satanic masses.

133. Rose, Elliott. *A Razor for a Goat: a Discussion of Certain Problems in the History of Witchcraft and Diabolism.* Toronto: University of Toronto Press, 1962. 257 pp. bibliography.

> Primarily a historical study; one chapter is devoted to modern-day witchcraft. Often cited by scholars in the field.

134. Russell, Jeffrey Burton. *The Devil: Perceptions of Evil from Antiquity to Primitive Christianity.* Ithaca, N.Y.: Cornell University Press, 1977. 276 pp. index. illus. bibliography. ISBN 0-8014-0938-1.

> The first volume in what is to be a four-volume history of concepts of the devil. This title covers the period from early times to shortly after the end of the New Testament. The principal theme is evil and how it is personified in the idea of the devil. Very scholarly. The author has written other books on this subject: *Witchcraft in the Middle Ages; A History of Witchcraft, Sorcerers, Heretics, and Pagans; Satan: the Early Christian Tradition;* and *Lucifer: the Devil in the Middle Ages.*

135. Scott, Sir Walter. *Demonology and Witchcraft: Letters Addressed to J. G. Lockhart, Esq.* London: Routledge, 1887; Secaucus, N.J.: Citadel Press, 1970; New York: Bell, 1970. 320 pp.

> A frequently reprinted work, first published in the nineteenth century. Full of pious Victorianisms and Scott's own opinions on witchcraft evils.

136. Strachan, Françoise. *Casting Out Devils.* London: Aquarian Press, 1972; New York: Samuel Weiser, 1972. 127 pp. bibliography. ISBN 0-85030-085-1.

> A religious discussion of evil and its nature. International in scope. Not on exorcism, per se, although the title implies this.

137. Summers, Montague. *The Geography of Witchcraft.* London: Routledge & Kegan Paul, 1978; Evanston, Ill.: University Books, 1958. 623 pp. index. illus. ISBN 0-7100-7617-7.

> First published in 1927 by Kegan Paul. A companion to item 138. Much emphasis on location, particularly on New England. A true believer in evil, Summers dramatizes the punishment of those who were thought to have sinned.

138. Summers, Montague. *History of Witchcraft and Demonology.* New York: University Books, 1956. 353 pp. illus. bibliography.

> First published by Knopf (New York) in 1926. This and the previous title are well-known works by a somewhat controversial author. Summers claimed to be a priest and wore vestments, but no record of his ordination has been found to date. A sincere believer in evil, witchcraft, and devil worship, he advocated their avoidance.

139. Trevor-Roper, Hugh Redwald. *Crisis of the Seventeenth Century: Religion, the Reformation and Social Change.* New York: Harper & Row, 1967. 486 pp. illus. bibliographic footnotes.

> Published by Melbourn (London) as *Religion, the Reformation and Social Change.*

140. Ward, Arthur Sarsfield [pseud. Sax Rohmer]. *The Romance of Sorcery.* New York: Paperback, 1970; Venus Freeway, 1973; Causeway Books, 1973; Dutton, n.d.. 214 pp.

> A sprightly account of famous (and infamous) witches and magicians with an emphasis on well-known personalities. The author wrote the

popular Dr. Fu Manchu novels. Includes accounts of sorcery, witches, and black magic.

141. Wedeck, Harry Ezekial. *A Treasury of Witchcraft: a Sourcebook of the Magic Arts.* New York: Philosophical Library, 1961; New York: Citadel Press, 1966. 271 pp. illus. bibliography.

> A historic view of witchcraft. Emphasis is on the magical spells incorporated by witches into their rites and practices.

142. White, Andrew Dickson. *History of the Warfare of Science with Theology in Christendom.* New York: Dover, 1960; Appleton, 1932. 2 vols.

> First published in 1896. Much of the text deals with witchcraft history. The author was president of Cornell and founder of its famous witchcraft collection.

143. Williams, Charles. *Witchcraft.* New York: Meridian Books, 1959. 316 pp.

> First published in 1941. A history portraying witchcraft as part of a total philosophic system.

144. Williams, Selma R., and Williams, Pamela J. *Riding the Night Mare: Women and Witchcraft.* New York: Atheneum, 1978. 228 pp. index. illus. bibliography. ISBN 0-689-30633-4.

> A feminist approach to the history of witchcraft. Makes the argument that women were accused of witchcraft throughout the ages in order to keep them subservient.

145. Woods, William Howard, comp. *Casebook of Witchcraft: Reports, Depositions, Confessions, Trials, and Executions for Witchcraft during a Period of Three Hundred Years.* New York: Putnam, 1974. 216 pp. ISBN 0-399-11403-3.

> A dispassionate, scholarly treatment of the European witch trials.

146. Zacharias, Gerhard. *The Satanic Cult.* London: Allen & Unwin, 1980. 181 pp. illus. ISBN 0-04-133008-0.

> Translated by Christine Trollope from the original, *Satanskult und schwarze Messe* (Munich: Limes Verlag, 1970). An historic overview of satanic worship.

See also item 39.12.

Works Arranged by Country: Great Britain

147. Adams, William Henry Davenport. *Witch, Warlock, and Magician: Historical Sketches of Magic and Witchcraft in England and Scotland.* Detroit: Gale Research, 1973. 428 pp. bibliography.

> First published by J. W. Bouton (New York) in 1889. An account of witchcraft in England and Scotland, with emphasis on the seventeenth century.

148. Ewen, Cecil Henry L'Estrange. *Witch Hunting and Witch Trials: the Indictments for Witchcraft from the Records of 1373 Assizes Held for the Home Circuit A.D. 1559–1736.* New York: Dial Press, 1929; MacVeagh, 1929; London: Kegan Paul, Trench, Trubner, 1929. 345 pp. illus.

> An often-cited overview and analysis of the trials.

149. Ewen, Cecil Henry L'Estrange. *Witchcraft and Demonianism: a Concise Account Derived from Sworn Depositions and Confessions Obtained in the Courts of England and Wales.* New York: Barnes & Noble, 1970. 495 pp. illus. bibliography.

> Reprint of a book first published by Heath Cranton (London) in 1933, taken from trial and official records of the period.

150. Hole, Christina. *Some Episodes in the History of English Witchcraft.* New York: Scribner's, 1947; Collier, 1947; London: B. T. Batsford, 1945; Totowa, N.J.: Rowan & Littlefield, 1977. 167 pp. illus. bibliography.

> Illustrated by Mervyne Peake. An often-cited, well-regarded overview.

151. Murray, Margaret Alice. *The God of the Witches.* London: Faber & Faber, 1931; New York: Doubleday, 1960; London: Oxford University Press, 1970. 222 pp. index. illus. bibliographic references.

> The second of Murray's anthropological works which suggests that witchcraft as a pagan belief has survived underground in England and has been practiced throughout history. Its roots, according to her theory, are in the Dianic fertility cult.

152. Murray, Margaret Alice. *The Witch-Cult in Western Europe: a Study in Anthropology.* London: Oxford University Press, 1921. 303 pp. index. bibliographic footnotes.

A study of pagan fertility cults in Great Britain. Murray's work inspired Gerald Gardner, who probably was most responsible for the twentieth century revival of witchcraft in Great Britain and America.

153. Rosen, Barbara. *Witchcraft*. New York: Taplinger, 1969; London: Edward Arnold, 1969. 407 pp. illus. bibliography.

> The Stratford-Upon-Avon Library series. A reprinting of 25 pamphlets from Elizabethan and Jacobean England with modernized spelling. Some passages omitted. Glossary included.

France

154. Huxley, Aldous Leonard. *The Devils of Loudun*. New York: Harper & Row, 1952; Harmondsworth, Eng.: Penguin, 1971; London: Chatto & Windus, 1952; 374 pp. illus. bibliography. ISBN 0-06-080-226-X.

> Used as the basis for the film *The Devils*. The account of a well-known case in witchcraft history of a convent of nuns who became convinced that they were bewitched.

155. Lewis, Dominic. *The Soul of Marshal Gilles de Raiz*. London: Eyre & Spottiswoode, 1952. 209 pp. maps. bibliography.

> An account of the notorious French marshal who devoted himself to a life of debauchery and satanism in seventeenth century France.

156. Michelet, Jules. *Satanism and Witchcraft: a Study in Medieval Superstition*. Secaucus, N.J.: Citadel Press, 1939. 322 pp. bibliography.

> A number of reprintings with various dates are available. Translated by A. R. Allinson from *La Sorcière*. Concentrates on witchcraft in medieval and Renaissance France. Considered by some to be a very important work.

Italy

157. Leland, Charles Godfrey. *Aradia: the Gospel of the Witches*. London: Daniel, 1974; New York: Samuel Weiser, 1974. 133 pp. ISBN 0-85207-124-8.

Introduction by Stewart Farrar. A facsimile of a work originally published by D. Nutt (London) in 1899. A classic which includes many Italian witchcraft legends, as well as nineteenth century practices.

United States

158. Beard, George Miller. *The Psychology of the Salem Witchcraft Excitement of 1692: and Its Practical Application to Our Own Time.* Stratford, Conn.: J. E. Edwards, 1971. 112 pp.

First published by Putnam (New York) in 1882. An account of the witchcraft trials compared to those of Cadet Whittaker and Charles Guiteau.

159. Booth, Sally Smith. *The Witches of Early America.* New York: Hastings House, 1975. 238 pp. index. bibliography.

Focuses primarily on witchcraft in New England. A sociological and psychological approach.

160. Boyer, Paul, and Nissenbaum, Stephen. *Salem Possessed: the Social Origins of Witchcraft.* Cambridge, Mass.: Harvard University Press, 1974. 231 pp. index. illus. maps. bibliography. ISBN 0-674-78525-8.

Concentrates on daily life as it may have existed in Salem and describes the social and economic changes which brought on tensions. Points out the various factions within the community and how jealousies between them may have produced the witchcraft accusations. Also suggests that class consciousness may have played a role.

161. Demos, John Putnam. *Entertaining Satan: Witchcraft and the Culture of Early New England.* New York: Oxford University Press, 1982. 543 pp. ISBN 0-19503-131-8.

Using a psychological approach, the author suggests that the Salem witchcraft accusations were prompted by subconscious pre-oedipal rage against mothers.

162. Hansen, Chadwick. *Witchcraft at Salem.* New York: New American Library, 1969. 318 pp. index. illus. bibliography.

The author advances the theory that witchcraft actually was practiced in Salem.

163. Jackson, Shirley. *The Witchcraft of Salem Village.* New York: Popular Library, 1976; Random House, 1956. 176 pp. illus. ISBN 0-445-031-62-X.

> Landmark Books series. Illustrations by Lili Rethi. A well-written and lucid account by a Gothic writer of what may have happened in Salem. Part of a juvenile series.

164. Mather, Increase, and Mather, Cotton. *The Wonders of the Invisible World: Being an Account of the Tryals of Several Witches by Cotton Mather, D.D. . . . A Farther Account of the Tryals by Increase Mather, D.D.* London: John Russel Smith, 1862. 291 pp.

> A historic title by the noted colonial figures, the Mathers, father and son.

165. Nevins, Winfield S. *Witchcraft in Salem Village in 1692, Together with a Review of the Opinions of Modern Writers and Psychologists in Regard to the Outbreak of the Evil in America.* New York: Burt Franklin, 1971. 273 pp. illus. bibliography. ISBN 0-8337-4300-7.

> Reprint of a work originally published in 1916 by Franklin.

166. Starkey, Marion Lena. *The Devil in Massachusetts: a Modern Enquiry into the Salem Witch Trials.* New York: Alfred A. Knopf, 1949; Garden City, N.Y.: Doubleday, 1961. 310 pp. bibliography.

> An often-cited work. It has been suggested in historical circles that never have so few people (the original colonists of Massachusetts) been studied by so many scholars.

3
MODERN WITCHCRAFT AND SATANISM

Satan, n. One of the Creator's lamentable mistakes, repented in
sashcloth and axes. Being instated as an archangel, Satan
made himself multifariously objectionable and was finally
expelled from Heaven. Halfway in his descent he paused,
bent his head in thought a moment and at last went back.
"There is one favor that I should like to ask," said he.
"Name it."
"Man, I understand, is about to be created. He will
need laws."
"What, wretch! you his appointed adversary,
charged from the dawn of eternity with hatred of his
soul—you ask for the right to make his laws?"
"Pardon; what I have to ask is that he be permitted
to make them himself."
It was so ordered.

Ambrose Bierce,
The Devil's Dictionary

Widespread publicity of present-day events involving witchcraft and
satanism clearly indicate their practice today. Lurid accounts of ritualistic satanic ceremonies and photographs of nude witches performing
their rites are evidence of witchcraft and satanism in the modern age.

As with traditional witchcraft and satanism, there are two
mainstreams of these practices to be considered in modern times.
One is "white" witchcraft, usually based on Celtic, Dianic, and / or
other pagan fertility beliefs. The other is "black" witchcraft, or satanism, which involves devil worship, satanic practices, and, sometimes perverted sexuality and murder. It is the "black" rites which
most often receive media attention. One can only hope that this
publicity does not serve merely to inspire their imitation by others.

The literature of modern witchcraft and satanism could be said
to have begun with Margaret Murray (see items 151 and 152) and
furthered by Gerald Gardner, with embellishments. It is easy to see
how Gardner's fascination with the sexual aspects of the rites may
have been picked up and twisted by others into present-day sa-

tanism. Followers of the ideas of "wicca," sometimes called "the old religion," turned to the way of modern witchcraft. Modern day witches do not perform favorable spells only, but their spells of revenge seem mild compared to the rites practiced by satanists.

Modern witches and satanists do not practice in secret. Their writings are easily found, purchased, and read. Whether or not their spells work is a matter of opinion.

A bibliographic essay on the subject by Carol Mitchell, "The 20th Century Witch in England and the United States: an Annotated Bibliography," is found in the *Bulletin of Bibliography* (vol. 39, no. 2, pp. 69–83). It should be noted at this point that most of the currently available literature on modern witchcraft and satanism is in the Western tradition. Witchcraft as practiced in primitive societies will be examined in a later chapter.

Listings in this chapter are divided into three subsections:

- General Overviews
- Favorable (Advocacy) Approaches
- Anti-Witchcraft Works

General Overviews

167. Fritscher, John. *Popular Witchcraft*. Secaucus, N.J.: Citadel Press, 1973; Bowling Green, Ohio: Bowling Green University Popular Press, 1972. 192 pp. illus. bibliographic notes. ISBN 0-8065-0380-7.

> Bowling Green edition published with the title *Popular Witchcraft Straight from the Witch's Mouth*. A good account of American sorcery. Contents include harping bazaar, the medium as medium, the selling of the Age of Aquarius, sex and witchcraft, and straight from the witch's mouth. The final section contains interviews with practicing witches, not how-to-do-it recipes. Based on the premise that satanism pervades much of today's pop culture.

168. Haining, Peter. *The Anatomy of Witchcraft*. London: Souvenir Press, 1972; Ontario: J. M. Dent, 1972; New York: Taplinger, 1972. 212 pp. illus. bibliography. ISBN 0-8008-0201-2.

> Frontiers of the Unknown series. Appendixes include some rituals. Contemporary practices are explored in Britain, America, and California; the ancient craft is covered in Europe, behind the Iron Curtain, and through voodoo.

169. Hershman, Florence. *Witchcraft Today.* New York: Modern Promotions, n.d. 155 pp.

> A sensationalized, dramatic account of witchcraft and satanism in daily life in the U.S. during the 1970s. Based on interviews and personal experiences.

170. Holzer, Hans. W. *The Witchcraft Report.* New York: Ace Books, 1973. 222 pp.

> Covers regional witchcraft in the U.S. Includes a potpourri of initiation rites and spells along with a list of occult shops. The author is research director for the New York Committee for the Investigation of Paranormal Occurrences.

171. Seabrook, William Buehler. *Witchcraft: Its Power in the World Today.* New York: Harcourt, Brace, 1940. 387 pp. illus.

> An anecdotal account of the revival of witchcraft in the twentieth century.

172. Sebald, Hans. *Witchcraft: the Heritage of a Heresy.* Oxford: Elsevier, 1978. 262 pp. index. illus. map. bibliography. ISBN 0-444-99058-5.

> A scholarly work on modern-day witchcraft in a district of Switzerland. Divided into three parts: the setting of witchcraft, the working of witchcraft, and the meaning of witchcraft.

173. Smith, Susy. *Today's Witches.* Englewood Cliffs, N.J.: Prentice-Hall, 1970; New York: Award Books, 1971. 180 pp. bibliography. ISBN 0-13-924555-3.

> A full-fledged believer in the occult when she wrote this book, Smith, in a clear and journalistic style, nevertheless provides a straightforward account of contemporary witchcraft in the U.S., Canada, Mexico, Haiti, and Great Britain.

Favorable (Advocacy) Approaches

174. Adler, Margot. *Drawing Down the Moon: Witches, Druids, Goddess-Worshippers, and Other Pagans in America Today.* New York: Beacon Press, 1979. 455 pp. ISBN 0-670-28342-8.

> An investigation of pre-Christian groups in the U.S. today, sympathetically examined by a witch, granddaughter of Alfred Adler. Appendixes

cover rituals, publications, organizations, and other sources of information.

175. Bidart, Gay-Darlene. *The Naked Witch.* New York: Pinnacle, 1975. 212 pp. ISBN 0-523-00529-6.

The use of witchcraft for a fabulous personal and sex life.

176. Buckland, Raymond. *Ancient and Modern Witchcraft.* New York: HC Publications, 1970. 153 pp. bibliography.

A testimonial to the positive values to be found in witchcraft as a way of life.

177. Buckland, Raymond. *Witchcraft from the Inside.* St. Paul: Llewellyn, 1975. 2d rev. ed. 144 pp. illus. bibliography. ISBN 0-87542-049-4.

A Llewellyn Occult Manual. First edition published in 1971. Buckland is a trained anthropologist and self-proclaimed witch in the Gardnerian tradition. He is also the founder and director of the Museum of Witchcraft and Magick. The book espouses wicca.

178. Crowther, Arnold, and Crowther, Patricia. *The Secrets of Ancient Witchcraft with the Witches' Tarot.* Secaucus, N.J.: University Books, 1974. 218 pp. illus. bibliography. ISBN 0-8216-0221-7.

Introduction by Leo Martello. An examination of the symbolism of witchcraft in tarot card art. In the Gardnerian tradition. Enthusiastically pro-nature.

179. Farren, David. *Living with Magic.* New York: Simon & Schuster, 1974. 319 pp. index. bibliography. ISBN 0-671-21805-0.

This, along with its sequel, *The Return of Magic,* provide insights from an ex-Jesuit married to a witch. Farren does a good job of relating current American witchcraft practices to the past. Well-documented.

180. Frost, Gavin, and Frost, Yvonne. *A Witch's Grimoire of Ancient Omens, Portents, Talismans, Amulets, and Charms.* West Nyack, N.Y.: Parker, 1979. 225 pp. illus. ISBN 0-13-961557-1.

Two leaders of the church of wicca provide simple, easy-to-follow directions for getting what you want in life. Includes material adapted from powwow doctors. Very pro–witchcraft.

181. Gardner, Gerald Brosseau. *The Meaning of Witchcraft*. London: Aquarian Press, 1959; New York: Samuel Weiser, 1971; Magickal Childe, 1984. illus, bibliography.

> This and the following title incorporate Gardner's whole philosophy of witchcraft. Very influential in the current witchcraft revival in Great Britain and the U.S.

182. Gardner, Gerald Brosseau. *Witchcraft Today*. New York: Citadel Press, 1955, 1970; Magickal Childe, 1984. 158 pp. illus. ISBN 0-939708-03-5.

> Introduction by Margaret Murray. First published in 1954. A strong and persuasive argument in favor of following ancient pagan ways rather than the Christian beliefs of conventional society.

183. Holzer, Hans. *Heather: Confessions of a Witch*. New York: Mason & Lipscomb, 1975; Pocket Books, 1975. 226 pp.

> A witch's life, principles, and practices, as told to a prolific occult author.

184. Huebner, Louise. *Never Strike a Happy Medium*. Los Angeles: Nash, 1970. 334 pp. illus. ISBN 0-8402-1161-9.

> The cheerful account of what it is like to be a witch.

185. Huebner, Louise. *Witchcraft for All*. Los Angeles: Nash, 1969; London: Alan Wingate, 1970; Tandem, 1971; New York: Bantam, 1973. ISBN 0-426-05995-6.

> A modern witch's spellbook. Huebner is the official witch of Los Angeles. The Tandem edition was published as *Power through Witchcraft*.

186. Johns, June. *King of the Witches: the World of Alex Sanders*. New York: Coward McCann, 1969. 154 pp. illus.

> Alex Sanders, England's Anton LaVey, is the subject of this admiring biography. Includes rites and personal spells.

187. Lady Sheba [pseud.]. *The Grimoire of Lady Sheba*. St. Paul: Llewellyn, 1974. 2d rev. ed. 227 pp. illus.

> The secrets of a modern witch, first published in 1972 by Llewellyn. Part II contains the text of *The Book of Shadows*, the ancient "bible" of witchcraft.

188. LaVey, Anton Szandor. *The Compleat Witch: or, What to Do When Virtue Fails.* New York: Dodd, Mead, 1971; Lancer Books, 1972. 274 pp. illus. bibliography. ISBN 0-3960-6266-0.

> Sexual guide by the most notorious modern satanist and founder of the Church of Satan in San Francisco. LaVey believes that sexual energy produces great occult power.

189. LaVey, Anton Szandor. *The Satanic Bible.* New York: Avon, 1969; New Hyde Park, N.Y.: University Books, 1969. 272 pp. illus. ISBN 0-380-01539-0.

> Introduction by Burton H. Wolfe. Outlines LaVey's principles. ". . . Anton LaVey brought Satan out of the closet and the Church of Satan is the fountainhead of contemporary satanism" (Introduction).

190. LaVey, Anton Szandor. *The Satanic Rituals.* New York: Avon, 1972; Secaucus, N.J.: University Books, 1972. 220 pp. ISBN 0-380-01392-4.

> A collection of satanic ceremonies. Set up like a play script to enable various celebrants to speak their lines correctly.

191. Leek, Sybil. *The Best of Sybil Leek.* New York: Popular Library, 1974. 253 pp. bibliography.

> A gathering of some of Leek's more popular and influential writings. Leek was an English witch who promoted her ideas in the U.S. popular media.

192. Leek, Sybil. *The Complete Art of Witchcraft.* New York: World, 1971; London: Frewin, 1975; New York: New American Library, n.d.. 205 pp. illus.

> Includes theoretical and philosophical bases for the practice of witch-craft, as well as actual rituals and spells. A strong argument is made for living harmoniously with nature through witchcraft.

193. Leek, Sybil. *Diary of a Witch.* Englewood Cliffs, N.J.: Prentice-Hall, 1968; New York: New American Library, 1969; London: Frewin, 1975. 187 pp. bibliographic references.

> An account of a famous witch's life, with emphasis on her early, formative years. "Witches have always been good at getting bad press" (chapter 1).

194. Martello, Leo Louis. *Black Magic, Satanism and Voodoo*. New York: HC Publications, 1972. 192 pp. bibliography.

> Focuses on devil worship. The author is media-oriented, as well as a self-proclaimed witch and homosexual.

195. Martella, Leo Louis. *Weird Ways of Witchcraft*. New York: HC Publications, 1969. 224 pp. illus. bibliography.

> An Allograph Book. A survey of witchcraft today, with some history of powwow.

196. Morrison, Sarah Lyddon. *The Modern Witch's Spellbook: Everything You Need to Know to Cast Spells, Work Charms and Love Magic, and Achieve What You Want in Life through Occult Powers*. Secaucus, N.J.: Citadel Press, 1971; New York: David McKay, 1971. 246 pp. index. illus. bibliography.

> A witch's grimoire with emphasis on love spells. Based on her own original experiments rather than historic recipes. Very personal, with the author's opinions interspersed throughout.

197. Paine, Lauran. *Witchcraft and the Mysteries*. New York: Taplinger, 1975; London: Robert Hale, 1975. 192 pp. index. illus. bibliography. ISBN 0-8008-8377-2.

> A good survey by a witch of historic practices which could be used today. Includes her philosophy and material on Satan.

198. Sevarg, Luba. *The Do-It-Yourself Witchcraft Guide*. New York: Award Books, 1971. 153 pp. illus.

> A serious outline of how to apply various witchcraft principles to daily life.

199. Valiente, Doreen. *Where Witchcraft Lives*. London: Aquarian Press, 1962. 112 pp. bibliography.

> An overview of the universality of witchcraft as practiced today by a self-proclaimed Gardnerian witch.

200. Weinstein, Marion. *Positive Magic: Occult Self-Help*. Custer, Wash.: Phoenix, 1981. rev. ed. 293 pp. ISBN 0-919345-01-8.

> Good basic witchcraft (rather than magic, as the title implies) manual. Understandable directions on how to make witchcraft a lifestyle.

201. Wolfe, Burton H. *The Devil's Avenger: a Biography of Anton Szandor LaVey*. New York: Pyramid Books, 1974. 272 pp. illus.

An account of LaVey's flamboyant life and his elevation to the leadership of satanism in the U.S. today.

Anti-Witchcraft Works

202. Bainbridge, William Sims. *Satan's Power: a Deviant Psychotherapy Cult*. Berkeley: University of California Press, 1978. 312 pp. index. illus. bibliography. ISBN 0-5200-3546-1.

An account of actual cults in California. Includes the following: rumors of Satan, social implosion, God at Xtal, in search of the miraculous, paradise misplaced, power society, gods and their symbols, cure of souls, the separation, new beginning, and the triumph of Satan.

203. Cruz, Nicky. *Satan on the Loose*. Old Tappan, N.J.: F. H. Revell Co., 1973; New York: New American Library, 1974. 158 pp.

The author of *The Cross and the Switchblade* describes his childhood in Puerto Rico with occult parents. Upon his conversion to Christianity he became anti-occult. Includes advice on fighting the devil.

204. Ebon, Martin, ed. *The Satan Trap: Dangers of the Occult*. Garden City, N.Y.: Doubleday, 1976. 276 pp. ISBN 0-385-07941-9.

"Occult powers are not playthings. They open us to influences we do not know, and at times cannot control" (p. vii). Presents a variety of tales about getting sucked into satanic beliefs and practices. To illustrate, the title of one account is "The Death of a Teen-Age Witch." Needless to say, no one comes to a good end.

205. Ebon, Martin, ed. *Witchcraft Today*. New York: Signet, 1971. 144 pp.

A good survey of the work of modern witches, such as Sybil Leek, and satanists, such as Anton LaVey. Some material on Canada.

206. Lindsey, Hal. *Satan Is Alive and Well on Planet Earth*. New York: Bantam, 1974; Grand Rapids, Mich.: Zondervan, 1972. 238 pp. bibliographic notes. ISBN 0-553-24406-X.

With C. C. Carlson. The author of *The Late Great Planet Earth* takes on the terrors of satanism. "Consider what is said about this clever character, Satan. Anyone who has dominated history as he has cannot be ignored, especially in these days" (Introduction).

207. Logan, Daniel. *America Bewitched: the Rise of Black Magic and Spiritualism.* New York: William Morrow, 1973. 187 pp. index. bibliography. ISBN 0-688-00221-8.

A psychic reviews the fascination with evil in America and warns of its consequences. Many anecdotes.

208. Shepard, Leslie A. *How to Protect Yourself against Black Magic & Witchcraft.* Secaucus, N.J.: Citadel Press, 1978. 162 pp. index. bibliography. ISBN 0-8065-0646-6.

Contents include the new menace of black magic and witchcraft, how magic works, medical and psychological aspects, basic self-protection, active defense and countermeasures, exorcism, the power of healthy religion, and a special listing of recordings and index of names.

209. Smith, Michelle, and Pazder, Lawrence. *Michelle Remembers.* New York: Congdon & Lattès, Inc., 1980; London: Michael Joseph, 1981; Sphere, 1981. distributed by St. Martin's. illus. ISBN 0-312-92531-X.

A graphic account of a woman's psychoanalysis in which she recalls the horrors of being a satanic victim during her childhood in Vancouver, British Columbia.

4
MAGIC AND THE HERMETIC ARTS

Magic, n. An art of converting superstition into coin. There are
other arts serving the same high purpose, but the discreet
lexicographer does not name them.

Ambrose Bierce,
The Devil's Dictionary

Magic is separate from witchcraft because of its non-reliance on
inverted Christian beliefs. In other words, sorcerers use magic to
achieve power but do not consider this magic to be provided by the
devil and his minions. It is not viewed as a gift from evil sources but
rather as a combination of abilities and scientific principles based on
mystical knowledge. It is true that one of the best-known sorcerers of
legend, Faust, sold his soul to the devil, but his action can be ascribed
to ambition beset by lack of achievement. Although sorcerers often
were suspected of dealing in devil worship, it cannot be shown that
such was actually the case.

The connection between magic (sometimes called magick) and
legerdemain is plain to see. The stage magician of today, however,
achieves results through the use of illusion rather than the hermetic
arts. The proper magician, magus, or sorcerer achieves results
through the use of spells and mysterious powers. Some magicians
who have claimed such powers throughout the ages have been mere
charlatans. It is no wonder that legitimate magicians, such as
Houdini, have devoted much effort to the unmasking of unprincipled
cheats who claimed supernatural abilities in order to gull the public.

An interesting piece on seventeenth-century magical spells is
that by Katherin E. Briggs, "Some Seventeenth-Century Books of
Magic," published in *Folk-Lore, the Transactions of the Folk-Lore Society,*
64 (December 1953), pages 446–62.

In contemporary times, much of the wiccan (white witchcraft)
repertoire of spells can be regarded as magical in nature, harking back
to ancient times and religions, such as druidism. Also, spells practiced for the sake of evil can be considered part of the hermetic arts.
Personal power seems to be a common aim in the practice of magic
today. In this chapter, materials are listed that treat magic in its

usually accepted sense, that of using mysterious rites and spells to obtain certain results. Prophecy and some divination systems will be covered in later chapters. The monographs in this chapter are divided into the following groups:

- General Works
- Amulets and the Evil Eye
- Herbs, Cures, and Spells
- Gypsy Lore
- Alchemy
- Jewish Mysticism and the Cabala
- Numerology
- I Ching

General Works

210. Bardon, Franz. *Frabat the Magician*. Wuppertal, West Germany: Ruggeberg, 1982, distributed by Llewellyn. 206 pp.

A thinly disguised autobiography of a modern magician describing the development of his beliefs. Considered to be the final book of the author's trilogy on magic, left unfinished at the time of his death.

211. Baskin, Wade. *The Sorcerer's Handbook*. New York: Philosophical Library, 1974; London: Owen, 1974. 635 pp. illus. ISBN 0-8022-2112-2.

A useful, one-volume encyclopedia with over 2,000 entries. Including biographies, occult terms, and numerological meanings. Actual practices and spells are given also.

212. Blum, Ralph. *The Book of Runes: a Handbook for the Use of an Ancient Oracle: the Viking Runes*. New York: St. Martin's, 1982. 126 pp. illus. bibliography. ISBN 0-312-09002-1.

A guide to using runic characters for a better understanding of direction in one's life. A package edition with rune stones is available. Originally used by the ancient Viking and North Sea cultures.

213. Bonewits, Philip Emmons Isaac. *Real Magic: an Introductory Treatise on the Basic Principles of Yellow Magic*. Berkeley, Calif.: Creative Arts, 1979. rev. ed. 282 pp. illus. bibliography. ISBN 0-916870-19-7.

First published by Coward-McCann (New York) in 1971. Includes a glossary. The author defines yellow magic as that which combines the human mind with the nervous system. Provides a great deal of introductory material on the occult in general.

214. Butler, Eliza Marian. *The Myth of the Magus.* Cambridge, Eng.: Cambridge University Press, 1979; Westport, Conn.: Hyperion Press, 1979. 282 pp. index. illus. bibliography ISBN 0-521-29554-8.

First published by Cambridge in 1949. A history of the magus, including information on famous magicians such as Simon Magus, Merlin, Faust, Dee, and Kelley. Also includes a section on pre-Christian rites and ceremonies. Suggests that European magic followed two mainstreams of thought and practice: Solomonic and Faustian.

215. Butler, Eliza Marian. *Ritual Magic.* Cambridge, Eng.: Cambridge University Press, 1979. 328 pp. index. illus. bibliography. ISBN 0-521-22563-9.

Originally published by Cambridge in 1949. The main focus of this title is on magic and sorcery, although witchcraft also is present. Includes rituals of conjuration used by European magicians.

216. Carroll, David, and Saxe, Barry. *Natural Magic: the Magical State of Being.* New York: Arbor House, 1977, distributed by Dutton. 340 pp. index. illus. bibliography. ISBN 0-87795-152-7.

A study of the theory of white magic. Contents: case for magic; what is magic?; Freud versus Faust: the psychology of magic; the ether; occult phenomena and the higher worlds; the energies of magic; the magical state of being; the unity of magical medicines, omens; rain-making; why magic fails today; and the end of the world, the final paradox.

217. Cavendish, Richard. *A History of Magic.* New York: Taplinger, 1977; London: Weidenfeld & Nicolson, 1977; Sphere, 1978. 180 pp. index. illus. bibliography. ISBN 0-8008-3886-6.

Reviewers seem a bit disappointed with this title, probably because of the author's distinguished reputation as a scholar in the field. Contents include ancient Rome and the East, Christianity and the Middle Ages, the Renaissance and witch mania, and the modern revival.

218. Conway, David. *Magic: an Occult Primer.* New York: Dutton, 1972; St. Albans, Eng.: Mayflower, 1974; London: Cape, 1974. 334 pp. illus. bibliography. ISBN 0–525–15010–2.

A survey of magic as a science and how it fits into natural law. Egyptian and Cabala rituals are included, as well as material on talismans and other magical techniques.

219. Crowley, Aleister. *The Confessions of Aleister Crowley*. New York: Bantam, 1971; Hill & Wang, 1970; Mystic Arts, 1970. 1,059 pp. index. illus. SBN 553-05820-195.

The abridged autobiography of the "wickedest man who ever lived." Originally in six volumes. This version was edited by John Wymonds and Kenneth Grant and contains their notes. Crowley's notorious life led to his involvement with a number of secret, magical societies in Europe at the turn of the century. His confessions provide a fascinating, sympathetic view of his ideas.

220. Crowley, Aleister. *Magick in Theory and Practice*. New York: Samuel Weiser, 1974; London: Routledge & Kegan Paul, 1973. 511 pp. ISBN 0-87728-254-4.

Originally published by Lecran Press (Paris) in 1911. Probably the best of Crowley's usually confusing books about magical theory and practice. This version is edited by John Symonds and Kenneth Grant. Needless to say, the emphasis is on magic for purposes of evil and personal power.

221. Denning, Melita, and Phillips, Osborne. *The Magical Philosophy*. St. Paul: Llewellyn, 1974–75. 5 vols. illus.

A series of instructional books based on the practices of the magical society of Aurom Solis.

221.1. *The Robe and the Ring*. ISBN 0-85742-176-8.

221.2. *The Apparel of High Magic*. ISBN 0-85742-177-6.

221.3. *The Sword and the Serpent*. ISBN 0-87542-178-4.

221.4. *The Triumph of Light*. ISBN 0-87542-179-2.

221.5. *Mysteria Magica*. ISBN 0-87542-180-6.

222. Gonzàlez-Wippler, Migene. *The Complete Book of Spells, Ceremonies and Magic*. New York: Crown, 1978; London: Barrie & Jenkins, 1978. 1,376 pp. index. illus. bibliography. ISBN 0-517-52885-1.

Divided into two parts: history, evolution, and general techniques of magic; and actual rituals and spells. International in scope.

223. Hohman, Johann Georg. *The Long Lost Friend: a Collection of Mysterious & Invaluable Arts & Remedies, for Man as Well as Animals.* Harrisburg, Pa.: Thomas F. Scheffer, Printer, 1856. 72 pp.

First published in 1818 in Reading, Pennsylvania, as *Der lange verborgene Freund, oder; getreuer und christlicher Unterricht für jedermann, enthaltend: Wunderbare und probmässige Mittel und Kunste, sowohl für die Menschen als das Vieh.. . .* The basic spellbook for use in "powwow," part of the Pennsylvania Dutch system of popular witchcraft. Based on the teachings of Hohman, a nineteenth-century mystic who combined folklore remedies with Christianity into a system of spells.

224. *The Illustrated Library of Sacred Imagination.* New York: Crossroad, 1976 (?), dist. by Macmillan as the Illustrated Library of Religion and Mythology. 10 vols. illus. bibliographies. ISBN 0-8245-0621-9.

A series of beautiful illustrated books on various mysteries throughout the world and throughout history.

224.1. Matthews, John. *The Grail: Quest for the Eternal.* ISBN 0-8245-0035-0.

224.2 Lanny, Lucia. *Egyptian Mysteries: New Light on Ancient Spiritual Knowledge.* ISBN 0-8245-0055-5.

224.3. Payne, Peter. *Martial Arts: the Spiritual Dimension.* ISBN 0-8245-0034-2.

224.4. Sharkey, John. *Celtic Mysteries: the Ancient Religion.* ISBN 0-8245-0059-8.

224.5. Michell, John F. *The Earth Spirit: Its Ways, Shrines and Mysteries.* ISBN 0-8245-0057-1.

224.6 Zolla, Elemire. *The Androgyne: Reconciliation of Male and Female.* ISBN 0-8245-0065-2.

224.7. Halifax, Joan. *Shaman: the Wounded Healer.* ISBN 0-8245-0066-0.

224.8 Lawlor, Robert. *Sacred Geometry: Philosophy and Practice.* ISBN 0-8245-0062-8.

224.9. Bancroft, Anne. *Zen: Direct Pointing to Reality.* ISBN 0-8245-0068-7.

224.10. Coxhead, David, and Hiller, Susan. *Dreams: Visions of the Night.* ISBN 0-8245-0064-4.

225. King, Francis. *The Magical World of Aleister Crowley.* New York: Coward, McCann & Geoghegan, 1978. 210 pp. index. illus. bibliography. ISBN 0-698-10884-1.

> Originally published in 1977 by Weidenfeld & Nicolson (London). An objective view of the notorious Crowley's life. Recognition is given to the development of his rituals.

226. King, Francis. *Ritual Magic in England: 1887 to the Present Day.* London: New English Library, 1972; Spearman, 1970. illus. bibliography. ISBN 0-450-01346-4.

> Published in the U.S. (New York: Macmillan, 1971) as *The Rites of Modern Occult Magic.*

227. King, Francis, and Skinner, Stephen. *Techniques of High Magic.* New York: Destiny, 1976; London: C. W. Daniel, 1976. 228 pp. ISBN 0-89281-030-0.

> Basic concepts of magic presented in a practical way for the novice magician. Includes Western magic, I Ching, tarot, and alchemy.

228. Knight, Gareth. *History of White Magic.* New York: Samuel Weiser, 1978; London: Mowbray, 1978. 236 pp. index. illus. ISBN 0-264-66446-9 (Mowbray edition).

> Historical approach to ancient mystery religions, the Renaissance and alchemy, the Rosicrucians and Freemasons, and the nineteenth century and contemporary revivals.

229. Mafteah Shelomo. *The Key of Solomon the King.* New York: Samuel Weiser, 1974; London: Kegan Paul, Trench, Trubner, 1909; Routledge & Kegan Paul, 1972. 126 pp. illus. ISBN 0-87728-211-0.

> Originally published by G. Redway (London) in 1888. Translated by S. Liddell MacGregor Mathers. Foreword by Richard Cavendish. A translation of supposedly ancient documents which Mathers claimed were the secrets of King Solomon. Includes discussion of black and white magic, in addition to rituals and spells.

230. Metzner, Ralph. *Maps of Consciousness: I Ching, Tantra, Tarot, Alchemy, Astrology, Actualism.* New York: Collier, 1971, 1974; Macmillan, 1971; London: Macmillan Collier, 1971, 1974. 161 pp. illus. bibliographic references. ISBN 0-02-077400-1.

> A good introduction to a number of magical systems. The entries are short and lucidly written with documentation.

231. *The Necronium.* London: Corgi, 1980; New York: Barnes Graphics, 1978; St. Helier, Eng.: Spearman, 1978. 184 pp. illus. bibliography. ISBN 0-552-98093-5.

> A mysterious book which may well be a hoax written by a contemporary British author (rumored to be Colin Wilson). Nevertheless, there are those who claim it works as a grimoire. Some say it is an ancient Arab work, and that it was endorsed by the horror writer H. P. Lovecraft. Others claim Lovecraft invented the tome as literary license.

232. Norvell. *Amazing Secrets of the Mystic East.* West Nyack, N.Y.: Parker, 1980. 227 pp. ISBN 0-13-023754-X.

> Magical secrets and spells based on Eastern mysticism. Includes material on white magic, mantras, pyramid power, Chinese beliefs, yoga, yin-yang, I Ching, and others. Presented in an easy-to-read style.

233. Redgrove, Herbert Stanley. *Magic and Mysticism: Studies in Bygone Belief.* New Hyde Park, N.Y.: University Books, 1971. 205 pp. illus. bibliographical references.

> Originally published as *Bygone Beliefs*. A basic overview of historical mysticism.

234. Regardie, Israel. *A Garden of Pomegranates.* St. Paul: Llewellyn, 1970, 1971; London: Thorsons, 1970. 160 pp. illus.

> Background and discussion of the hermetic arts.

235. Seligmann, Kurt. *Magic, Supernaturalism, and Religion.* New York: Pantheon Books, 1973; London: Allen Lane, 1971. 342 pp. index. illus. bibliography.

> Illustrated by the author. Alternate titles: *The Mirror of Magic* (first English edition in 1956) and *The History of Magic* (New York: Pantheon Books, 1948). Explores the relationship of magic to dream consciousness.

236. Smith, Richard Furnald. *Prelude to Science: an Exploration of Magic and Divination.* New York: Scribner's, 1975. 129 pp. index. illus. bibliography. ISBN 0-684-14370-4.

> Emphasis on astrology. The author also covers I Ching, Cabalah, magic, oracles, and tarot. "To safeguard the reader against this kind of reasoning [to discard magic and divination out of hand], I have tried to define the boundaries of science as closely as possible and have

acknowledged the presence of values on both sides of the boundaries" (Preface).

237. Waite, Arthur Edward. *The Book of Black Magic and of Pacts: Including the Rites and Mysteries of Gnostic Theurgy, Sorcery, and Infernal Necromancy.* London: George Redway, 1898; Chicago: De-Laurence, Scott, 1910. 296 pp. illus.

> A classic work by a noted author and historian of occult and magical matters. A later edition (1961) was published by Citadel Press (Secaucus, N.J.) as *The Book of Ceremonial Magic: a Complete Grimoire* (ISBN 0-8065-0208-8).

See also items 39.6, 39.9, 39.11., 78

Amulets and the Evil Eye

238. Albertus Magnus, Saint. *The Book of Secrets of Albertus Magnus: of the Virtues of Herbs, Stones and Certain Beasts; also a Book of the Marvels of the World.* London: Oxford University Press, 1973. 128 pp. ISBN 0-19-812502-X.

> Edited by Michael G. Best and Frank H. Brightman. The magical secrets of a fabled thirteenth century mystic and magus. Includes astrology, and herbal and amulet magic.

239. Budge, Sir Ernest Alfred Thompson Wallis. *Amulets and Talismans.* New York: Dover, 1978; Collier, 1970. New Hyde Park, N.Y.: University Books, 1961. 543 pp. index. illus. bibliographic notes in text. ISBN 0-486-23573-4.

> Originally published by Oxford University Press (London) in 1930. Covers amulets from Egypt, Ethiopia, Persia, Arabia, Israel, Phoenicia, Sumeria, Syria, and Babylonia; also religious groups (Coptic, Gnostic, Hebrew, Mandaean); and forms (rings, stones, swastikas, crosses, evil eyes); plus some material on divination, the hand of Fatimah, and other topics.

240. Elworthy, Frederick Thomas. *The Evil Eye: an Account of This Ancient and Widespread Superstition.* Secaucus, N.J.: Citadel Press, n.d. facsimile edition. 471 pp. index. illus. bibliographic references. ISBN 0-8065-0801-9.

> A reproduction of the original edition published in 1895 by John Murray (London). Includes materials on sympathetic magic, tree wor-

ship, totems, amulets, horns, horseshoes, gestures, crosses, and other related matters. Considered a classic on the subject.

241. Evans, Joan. *Magical Jewels of the Middle Ages and the Renaissance, Particularly in England.* Detroit: Gale Research, 1975; Oxford: Clarendon Press, 1922. 264 pp. index. bibliographic references. ISBN 0-486-23367-7.

> Originally published in 1922 by Clarendon (Oxford, England). An interesting and scholarly account of mysticism attached to gems during the medieval and Renaissance periods.

242. Gregor, Arthur S. *Amulets, Talismans and Fetishes.* New York: Scribner's, 1975. 120 pp. index. illus. bibliography. ISBN 0684-14460-3.

> Written for children, this excellent title is crammed with useful information. Drawings by Anne Burgess show various kinds of amulets and talismans. A dictionary of amulets is included. Information on the evil eye, string and knot magic, symbols, and gems is provided.

243. Kunz, George Frederick. *The Curious Lore of Precious Stones.* New York: Dover, 1971; London: Constable, 1971. 406 pp. illus. bibliography. ISBN 0-486-22227-6.

> Originally published in 1913 by J. P. Lippincott (Philadelphia), with the subtitle "Being a description of their sentiments and folklore, superstitions, symbolism, mysticism, use in medicine, protection, prevention, religion, and divination, crystal gazing, birthstones, lucky stones and talismans, astral, zodiacal, and planetary."

244. Maloney, Clarance, ed. *The Evil Eye.* New York: Columbia University Press, 1976. 335 pp. index. illus. bibliographies. ISBN 0-231-04006-7.

> Results of a symposium on the evil-eye belief held at the 1972 meeting of the American Anthropological Association. Fifteen papers explore the psychological, social, economic, and historic aspects of the evil-eye tradition in many different cultures. The first 12 chapters deal with specific evil-eye beliefs. The last three chapters synthesize and generalize the evil eye's meaning and associated behavior.

245. Villiers, Elizabeth. *The Book of Charms.* New York: Simon & Schuster, 1973. 144 pp. index. illus. ISBN 0-671-21775-5.

> Originally published as *The Mascot Book* by T. Werner Laurie Ltd. (London) in 1923. Contents include origins and mythology; signs,

sigils, and talismans; stones, jewels, and beads; days, numbers, and colours; animal kingdom and plants; metals and miscellaneous charms.

Herbs, Cures, and Spells

246. Buckland, Raymond. *Practical Candle Burning*. St. Paul: Llewellyn, 1970. 153 pp. ISBN 0-87542-048-6.

> A Llewellyn Occult Guide. Includes information on rites, formations of candles, and the significance of color and appropriate spells.

247. Budge, Sir Ernest Alfred Thompson Wallis. *The Divine Origin of the Craft of the Herbalist*. Ann Arbor, Mich.: Grand River Books, 1971. 96 pp. illus.

> Originally published by Culpepper House (London) for the Society of Herbalists in 1928. Scholarly work on early uses of herbs in healing and magic.

248. Clark, Linda A. *The Ancient Art of Color Therapy*. Old Greenwich, Conn.: Devin-Adair, 1975. 145 pp.

> Examines the psychological and physical effects of various colors and light on humans, animals, and plants. Case studies are included. Information on the effects of colors of food, light, water, and gems, as well as auras and color breathing.

249. Crow, William Bernard. *The Occult Properties of Herbs and Plants*. Wellingborough, Eng.: Aquarian Press, 1980. 2d ed. 96 pp. index. ISBN 0-85030-196-3.

> Paths in Inner Power series. First published in 1969. Covers the use of herbs in alchemy, astrology, healing, magic, and religion. Includes the druidical tree alphabet.

250. Haggard, Howard Wilcox. *Devils, Drugs, and Doctors: the Story of the Science of Healing from Medicine-Man to Doctor*. New York: Harper Bros., 1929. 405 pp. illus.

> Published in other editions: Blueribbon Bks. (New York), 1929, 193-(?), 194-(?); Heinemann (London), 1929; Halcyon (New York), 1929; Harper (New York and London), 1930, 1933, 1936; Eastman-Kodak (CBS Radio Series), 1931–32; Pocket Books (New York), 1946.

251. Hansen, Harold A. *The Witch's Garden*. Santa Cruz, Calif.: Unity Press, 1978. 128 pp. index. illus. bibliography. ISBN 0-913300-47-0.

> Translated by Muriel Crofts from *Heksens Urtegard*. Concentrates on hallucinatory and poisonous herbs, such as mandrake, henbane, nightshade, hemlock, thorn apple, and monkshood. The appendix gives information on the infamous spell in *Macbeth*.

252. Jacobs, Dorothy. *Cures and Curses*. New York: Taplinger, 1967. 144 pp.

> A practical, how-to-do-it book on casting simple spells.

253. Maple, Eric. *Magic, Medicine & Quackery*. South Brunswick, N.J.: A. S. Barnes, 1968. 192 pp. illus.

> A readable account of the history and development of legitimate medicine and its attendant, less "scientific" sister, alternative medicine.

254. Middleton, John, comp. *Magic, Witchcraft, and Curing*. Austin: University of Texas Press, 1976. 346 pp. index. map. bibliography. ISBN 0-292-75031-5.

> Texas Press Sourcebooks in Anthropology, no. 7. Originally published by the Natural History Press for the American Museum of Natural History (Garden City, N.Y.) in 1967. A scholarly work on the curing aspects of magic. International in scope and authorship. Focuses primarily on primitive societies.

Gypsy Lore

255. Bowness, Charles. *Romany Magic*. Wellingborough, Eng.: Aquarian Press, 1973. 96 pp. index. ISBN 0-85030-106-8.

> Facts and legends about the gypsies. Set up as a one-volume encyclopedia in which each topic (such as family lore, the evil eye, and Romany magic) is followed by a series of shorter entries providing details on the subject. A glossary of Romany terms is included.

256. Clebert, Jean-Paul. *The Gypsies*. London: Penguin, 1969. 282 pp.

> A sociological / anthropological look at gypsies and their folklore, magical beliefs, and practices, as well as their history and way of life.

257. Derlon, Pierre. *Secrets of the Gypsies.* New York: Ballantine Books, 1977. 230 pp. ISBN 0-345-15405-8.

> Translated by Joan Smyth from *Traditions occultes des gitans.* Describes the life and magical practices of the gypsies as learned by someone who was brought up in the Romany way.

258. Leland, Charles Godfrey. *Gypsy Sorcery and Fortune Telling.* New Hyde Park, N.Y.: University Books, 1962; New York: Dover, 1971; Magnolia, Mass.: Peter Smith, 1972. 271 pp. index. illus.

> Introduction to this reprint edition by Margery Silver. Originally published in 1891. The author views gypsies as "carriers" of witchcraft throughout the ages. Compares gypsy beliefs with other magical systems.

259. Martin, Kevin [pseud.]. *The Complete Gypsy Fortune Teller.* London: Arlington, 1973; St. Albans, Eng.: Mayflower, 1975. 315 pp. illus. bibliography.

> Originally published by Putnam (New York) in 1970. More emphasis on fortune-telling techniques than on magical beliefs.

260. Trigg, Elwood B. *Gypsy Demons and Divinities: the Magic and Religion of the Gypsies.* Secaucus, N.J.: Citadel Press, 1974. 238 pp.

> Preface by Edward Evans-Pritchard. An overview of gypsy lifestyle, containing many details regarding superstitions and folklore.

Alchemy

261. Albertus, Frater. *The Alchemist's Handbook: Manual for Practical Laboratory Alchemy.* New York: Samuel Weiser, 1974. 124 pp. illus. ISBN 0-87728-181-5.

> A contemporary alchemist provides how-to-do-it instructions.

262. Aquinas, Saint Thomas. *Aurora Consurgen: a Document Attributed to Thomas Aquinas on the Problem of Opposites in Alchemy.* New York: Bollinger, 1966. 555 pp.

> The disputed author, an Italian student of Albertus Magnus, probably did not dabble in magic as his legend sometimes presumes.

263. Burland, Cottie Arthur. *The Arts of the Alchemists.* New York: Macmillan, 1967, 1968; London: Weidenfeld & Nicolson, 1967. 224 pp. illus. bibliography.

> Good introduction to the subject. Includes historical development.

264. Butler, Eliza Marian. *The Fortunes of Faust.* Cambridge, Eng.: Cambridge University Press, 1952. 365 pp. illus. bibliography.

> The third volume in the author's trilogy on magic (see items 214 and 215).

265. Chkashige, Masumi. *Oriental Alchemy.* New York: Samuel Weiser, 1974. 110 pp.

> Originally published in 1936. Discussion of the little-known art of alchemy in China and Japan.

266. Doberer, Kurt Karl. *The Goldmakers: 10,000 Years of Alchemy.* Westport, Conn.: Greenwood Press, 1972. 301 pp. illus. bibliography. ISBN 0-8371-6355-2.

> Translated by E. W. Dickes. An anecdotal history of alchemy with some attention to the transmutation of metals.

267. Eliade, Mircea. *The Forge and the Crucible: the Origins and Structure of Alchemy.* Chicago: University of Chicago Press, 1978. 2d ed. 238 pp. index.

> Translated from the Franch (Paris: Flammarion, 1956) by Stephen Corrin. Originally published as *Forgerous et alchimistes.* An account of alchemy by the distinguished scholar from the University of Chicago.

268. French, Peter J. *John Dee: the World of an Elizabethan Magus.* London: Routledge & Kegan Paul, 1972. 254 pp. index. illus. bibliography. ISBN 0-7100-7158-2.

> An excellent biography of Elizabeth I's magician and alchemist, a fabled personality.

269. Holmyard, Eric John. *Alchemy.* London: Penguin, 1957; Baltimore: Penguin, 1968. 281 pp. index. illus.

> Contains a brief listing of "authorities" at the beginning of the book. Glossary included. An international, historical survey of alchemy.

270. Holzer, Hans. *Star of Destiny.* New York: Day Books, 1981.
192 pp. index. illus. bibliography. ISBN 0-8128-7041-7.

> Originally published by Stein & Day in 1974 as *The Alchemist.* A novelized account of Rudolf von Habsburg, Holy Roman emperor in the sixteenth century. Holzer claims to have based the book on an old manuscript he found in a tomb in Prague.

271. Jung. Carl Gustav. *Psychology and Alchemy.* Princeton, N.J.: Princeton University Press, 1968. 581 pp. illus. bibliography.

> Volume 12 of the Collected Works. Bollingen series, no. 20. Long interested in the occult, Jung particularly was intrigued by the symbolism to be found in alchemy and its application to psychology.

272. Kelley, Edward. *The Stone of the Philosophers.* New York: Samuel Weiser, 1970. 153 pp. illus.

> Translation, with notes, by A. E. Waite of *Tractatus duo Egregie.* First published in Hamburg in 1676. This Weiser edition is reprinted from an 1893 edition. Kelly is a noted name in alchemical history.

273. Klossowski de Rola, Stanislas. *Alchemy: the Secret Art.* New York: Bounty Books / Crown, 1973; Avon, 1973; London: Thames & Hudson, 1973. 128 pp. illus.

> Translated by Margaret Sansone Scouten from *Les confidences d'un voyant* (Paris: Editions Alsatis, 1969). The short text discusses the true nature of alchemy. Fine illustrations make this an outstanding work on the subject.

274. Palmer, Philip Mason, and More, Robert Pattison, eds. *The Sources of the Faust Tradition from Simon Magus to Lessing.* New York: Haskell House, 1965; Octagon Books, 1936, 1966. 300 pp. bibliographic footnotes.

> First published in 1936. An interesting study of the Faust legend throughout history.

275. Paracelsus. *The Hermetic and Alchemical Writings of Aureolus Philippus Tehophrastus Bombast, of Hohenheim, called Paracelsus the Great.* New Hyde Park, N.Y.: University Books, 1967; Berkeley, Calif.: Shambhala, 1976, distributed by Random House. 2 vols. index. illus. bibliography. ISBN 0-87773-082-2 (vol. 1).

> Reprint of an 1894 edition published in London by J. Elliot. Edited by Arthur Edward Waite. Volume one deals with the transmutation of

metals; volume two covers hermetic medicine and philosophy. Probably the best edition of Paracelsus' works presently available.

276. Pritchard, Alan. *Alchemy: a Bibliography of English-Language Writings.* London: Routledge & Kegan Paul, 1980. 439 pp. index. ISBN 0-7100-0472-9.

> A useful tool, key to the many writings available in this area of the occult.

277. Read, John. *Prelude to Chemistry: an Outline of Alchemy.* London: G. Bell, 1936, 1939; New York: Macmillan, 1937. 327 pp. illus. maps. bibliography.

> A good overview and introduction.

278. Redgrove, Herbert Stanley. *Alchemy: Ancient and Modern.* New York: Barnes & Noble, 1969, 1973; Wakefield, Eng.: E. P. Publishers, 1973. 2d ed. 141 pp. illus. bibliographic references. ISBN 0-06-495809-4.

> Originally published in 1922. Introduction by H. J. Sheppard. A clear rendering concerning the relationship of alchemy to science. Includes the idea that alchemy is, in many ways, more of a philosophical search than a chemical one.

279. Reyner, John Hereward. *Diary of a Modern Alchemist.* London: Spearman, 1974. 155 pp. index. illus. ISBN 0-85435-172-8.

> A follower of the philosophies of Gurdjieff and Sufism, the author believes the alchemists were searching for spiritual truth.

280. Sadoul, Jacques. *Alchemists and Gold.* New York: Putnam, 1972; London: Spearman, 1972. 284 pp. index. illus. ISBN 0-399-10990-0.

> Translated by Olga Sieveking from *Le trésor des alchimistes* (Paris: Editions Publications Primières, 1970). Part one covers the history of alchemy; part two, the lives of major alchemists; and part three, the materials and techniques used in making the philosopher's stone. Glossary included.

281. Silberer, Herbert. *The Hidden Symbolism of Alchemy & the Occult Arts.* New York: Dover, 1971; Magnolia, Mass.: Peter Smith, 1972. 451 pp. bibliography. ISBN 0-486-20972-5.

> Translated by Smith Ely Jelliffe from *Probleme der Mystik und ihrer Symbolik.* Originally published in English under the title *Problems of*

Mysticism and Its Symbolism in 1917. The main theme concerns the author's search for hidden symbolism among the works of famous occultists, alchemists, and Rosicrucians. A very mystical approach.

282. Waite, Arthur Edward, and Barrett, Francis. *Alchemists through the Ages: Lives of the Famous Alchemistical Philosophers from the Year 850 to the Close of the 18th Century, Together with a Study of the Principles and Practice of Alchemy, Including a Bibliography of Alchemical and Hermetic Philosophy.* Blauvelt, N.Y.: Rudolf Steiner, 1970. 315 pp. illus.

> Reprint of the 1888 edition published under the title *Lives of Alchemystical Philosophers* in London. First published as *The Lives of the Adepts in Alchemystical Philosophy.* This title has been ascribed to Francis Barrett, although it was published anonymously. Waite served as editor of the contemporary edition.

283. Yates, Frances Amelia. *Giordano Bruno and the Hermetic Tradition.* Chicago: University of Chicago Press, 1964; London: Routledge & Kegan Paul, 1964; New York: Vintage, 1969. 466 pp. bibliographic footnotes.

> A scholarly account of hermetic history.

See also items: 37.2, 37.15, 39.13.

Jewish Mysticism and the Cabala

284. Abraham ben Simeon of Worms. *The Book of Sacred Magic of Abra-Melin the Mage.* New York: Dover, 1975; Causeway Books, 1974, illus. ISBN 0-486-23211-5.

> Reprint of the second edition of the title published by J. M. Watkins (London) in 1900. Introduction to the Causeway edition by Michael Cord. A translation of the magical writings of a Jewish magician. Contains an autobiography, along with techniques and many diagrams.

285. Albertson, Edward. *Understanding the Kabbalah.* Los Angeles: Sherbourne Press, 1973. 135 pp. illus.

> For the Millions series. A short, easy-to-understand, beginner's book.

286. Butler, Walter Ernest. *Magic and the Qabalah.* London: Aquarian Press, 1964. 107 pp. illus.

An introductory piece discussing the magical elements found in the Cabala.

287. Constant, Alphonse Louis [pseud. Eliphas Lèvi]. *The Mysteries of the Qabalah: or the Occult Agreement of the Two Testaments: as Contained in the Prophecy of Ezekiel and the Apocalypse of St. John.* Wellingborough, Eng.: Thorsons, 1974; New York: Samuel Weiser, 1974. 285 pp. illus. IBSN 0-7225-0268-0.

> Studies in Hermetic Tradition, vol. 2. A work by the nineteenth century French occultist.

288. Cook, Roger. *The Tree of Life: Image for the Cosmos.* New York: Avon, 1974; London: Thames & Hudson, 1974. 128 pp. illus. bibliography.

> A nicely illustrated introduction to the mysticism of the tree in myth, folklore and religion.

289. Crowley, Aleister. *The Qabalah of Aleister Crowley: Three Texts.* New York: Samuel Weiser, 1973. 50, 155, 69 pp. ISBN 0-87728-222-6.

> Introduction by Israel Regardie. A later edition by Weiser is entitled *777 and Other Cabalistic Writings of Aleister Crowley.* This edition contains *Gematria, Liber 777* and *Sepher Sephiroth.* Crowley's works tend to be difficult to understand and have a contorted writing style. Best for serious students.

290. Encausse, Gerard [pseud. Papus]. *The Qabalah: Secret Tradition of the West.* Wellingborough, Eng.: Thorsons, 1977. 384 pp. illus.

> Studies in Hermetic Tradition, vol. 4. Translated from the French *La Cabbale.* The author has made a special study of the Cabala and its relationship to tarot (see item 766).

291. Firth, Violet Mary [pseud. Dion Fortune]. *The Mystical Qabalah.* London: Benn, 1957; Williams & Norgate, 1935, 1941, 1951. 306 pp. illus.

> A useful overview of a complex subject.

292. Godwin, David. *Godwin's Cabalistic Encyclopedia: a Complete Guide to Cabalistic Magick.* St. Paul: Llewellyn, 1979. 351, 101 pp. illus. bibliography. ISBN 0-87542-293-4.

> A basic guide to mastering gematria (Hebrew numerology) without learning Hebrew. The author borrows heavily from Crowley's works.

Includes definitions, numerical values, dictionaries, and a pronunciation guide.

293. González-Wippler, Migene. *Kabbalah for the Modern World: How God Created the Universe.* New York: Julian Press, 1974. 171 pp. bibliography.

An attempt to pull together Cabalistic theory, Christianity, and other medieval beliefs along with a bit of Jung.

294. Kenton, Warren. *Introduction to the Cabala.* New York: Samuel Weiser, 1972. 196 pp.

A good basic overview.

295. Knight, Gareth. *A Practical Guide to Qabalistic Symbolism.* Cheltenham, Eng.: Helio, 1965; New York: Samuel Weiser, 1972. 2 vols. illus.

An outline for relating the Cabala to daily living.

296. Pick, Bernhard. *The Cabala: Its Influence on Judaism and Christianity.* LaSalle, Ill.: Open Court, 1974. 109 pp. index. bibliography.

An abridgment of the 1913 work published by Open Court.

297. Regardie, Israel. *The Tree of Life: a Study in Magic.* New York: Samuel Weiser, 1969, 1971. 284 pp. illus. bibliography.

A highly regarded work on the mystical system based on the Cabala.

298. Waite, Arthur Edward. *The Holy Kabalah.* New Hyde Park, N.Y.: University Books Reprint, 1960. 636 pp. bibliography.

Solid study by a respected occult expert. Crowley used to jeer at Waite's writing style, but it certainly seems to be a case of the pot calling the kettle black.

Numerology

299. Avery, Kevin Quinn. *The Numbers of Life.* New York: Dolphin Books, 1977, rev. ed. 289 pp. illus. ISBN 0-385-12629-8.

An easy-to-follow set of directions which presents the bad as well as the good in interpreting numbers. Includes information on personality, habits, expressions in life, and problems.

300. Coates, Austin. *Numerology*. Secaucus, N.J.: Citadel Press, 1974; London: Mayflower, 1978. 126 pp. index. illus. ISBN 0-8065-0499-4.

Originally published by Muller (London) in 1974. A very personalized system of numerology developed by someone who claims to have worked independently, drawing only on Oriental systems for his sources. The book is well written and easy to follow.

301. Hitchcock, Helyn. *Helping Yourself with Numerology*. West Nyack, N.Y.: Parker, 1972. 238 pp. illus. ISBN 0-13-386771-4.

A simple approach for beginners. The author presents some "numeroscopes" of famous personalities, in addition to providing how-to-do-it instruction for the use of numerology in daily life.

302. Hopper, Vincent Foster. *Medieval Number Symbolism: Its Sources, Meaning, and Influence on Thought and Expression*. New York: Cooper Square, 1969. 241 pp. ISBN 0-81540-305-4.

Columbia University Studies in English and Comparative Literature. First published in 1938. An explanation of numerology in the Middle Ages.

303. Johnson, Vera Scott, and Wommack, Thomas. *The Secrets of Numbers: a Numerological Guide to Your Character and Destiny*. New York: Dial Press, 1973. 257 pp.

A good introduction to the subject; includes philosophy and principles, directions, and tables.

304. Leek, Sybil. *Numerology*. New York: Collier, 1969. 148 pp. illus.

A knowledgeable witch shares her secrets in this chatty, basic book.

305. Oliver, George. *The Pythagorean Triangle: or, the Science of Numbers*. Minneapolis: Wizards Book Shelf, 1975. 237 pp. illus. bibliographic references. ISBN 0-913510-17-3.

A Secret Doctrine Reference series book. Originally published by Ballantyne (Edinburgh) in 1875.

306. Samuelson, Harding V. *Numerology for the Millions*. Los Angeles: Sherbourne Press, 1970. 187 pp.

For the Millions series. Simple, how-to-do-it approach for the general reader.

307. Stein, Sandra Kovacs. *Instant Numerology: Charting Your Road Map to the Future.* New York: Harper & Row, 1979. 101 pp. bibliography. ISBN 0-06-090706-1.

> Foreword by Kevin Quinn Avery. One of the easiest manuals for beginners to use. Many of the charts were developed by the author.

See also item 224.8

I Ching

308. Douglas, Alfred. *How to Consult the I Ching, the Oracle of Change.* New York: Putnam, 1971. 251 pp. illus.

> Illustrated by David Sheridan. First published in Great Britain with the title *The Oracle of Change.* Based on a 1715 edition of *I Ching,* with the main focus on divination rather than mysticism and magic.

309. *I Ching.* Various editions of the text exist.

> James Legge is probably the most reproduced translator, with editions from the Clarendon Press, Dover, Bantam, Citadel, Wehman, Causeway, and University Books to his credit. First issued in 1899 as volume 16 of *The Sacred Books of the East.*

310. *The I Ching; or, Book of Changes.* Princeton, N.J.: Princeton University Press, 1968. 3d ed. 740 pp.

> Bollingen series. The Richard Wilhelm translation rendered into English by Cary F. Baynes. Foreword by C. G. Jung. Preface to the third edition by Hellmut Wilhelm. Considered by most scholars to be the best English-language version.

311. Reifler, Sam. *The I Ching: a New Interpretation for Modern Times.* New York: Bantam, 1974. 279 pp. illus. ISBN 0-552-68056-7.

> With the help of Alan Ravage. A simplification and modernization.

312. Shchutskii, Iulian Konstantinovich. *Researches on the I Ching.* Princeton, N.J.: Princeton University Press, 1979. 255 pp. index. bibliography. ISBN 0-691-09939-1.

> Translated by William L. MacDonald and Tsuyoshi Hawgawa with Hellmut Wilhelm. Introduction by Gerald Swanson. A scholarly work originally published in Russia in 1960. Deals primarily with studies done in the Far East.

313. Sherrill, W. A., and Chu, W. K., comps. *An Anthology of I Ching*. London: Routledge & Kegan Paul, 1978. 245 pp. index, illus. ISBN 0-7100-8590-7.

> Presents essays on the traditional use of I Ching in divination, geomancy and astrology.

314. Wilhelm, Hellmut. *Heaven, Earth, and Man in the Book of Changes*. Seattle: University of Washington Press, 1977. 230 pp. index. ISBN 0-295-95516-3.

> Publications on Asia of the Institute for Comparative and Foreign Area Studies, no. 28. Original and creative thought on I Ching by a noted scholar and son of the famed translator of the work.

315. Wing, R. L. *The I Ching Workbook*. New York: Doubleday, 1979. 180 pp. ISBN 0-385-12838-X.

> A modernized version of the well-known title. Contains ideas for using and interpreting the hexagrams. Chinese pronunciation is included, along with workbook pages for practice.

5
SECRET SOCIETIES, EXOTIC RELIGIONS, AND MYSTICISM

Illuminati, n. A sect of Spanish heretics of the latter part of the
   sixteenth century; so called because they were light
   weights—cunctationes illuminati.

> Ambrose Bierce,
> *The Devil's Dictionary*

In the occult world, magic sometimes is involved with mystical religions and secret societies. In other words, some practitioners prefer to join efforts with others in order to perform magic and mysticism. It has long been acknowledged by witches that spells, and power generation in general, are more effective when practiced by groups, known as covens. There are those in the past and the present who have agreed with this general idea; thus interest in organizations, lodges, and religions that delve into mysticism from the ancient past, and sometimes from exotic locations, such as Tibet and India, has developed. The search for truth and meaning has taken many interesting twists and turns in occult history and belief.

Some ideas have survived as religious tenets; others as legends or in oral traditions. Some mystics claim insights from spiritual sources, while others interpret words and notions from the past. There is a close relationship between this area of the occult and religions accepted by society and some areas of science, such as psychology. The influence of certain mystical concepts on widely accepted beliefs is evident. For example, the recent interest in charismatic Christian religions and the seriousness with which parapsychology is now considered by scientific researchers illustrate the impact of occult mysticism.

The books in this chapter are divided into the following sections:

- General Works
- Druids and Druidism
- Freemasonry
- Rosicrucianism
- The Golden Dawn
- Theosophy, Spiritualism, and Reincarnation

General Works

316. Cerminara, Gina. *Insights for the Age of Aquarius.* Englewood Cliffs, N.J.: Prentice–Hall, 1973. 314 pp. index. illus. ISBN 0-13-467589-4.

> An approach to the problems of the occult and mystical aspects of religions by means of scientific analysis. A useful overview of the problem of making religion and science compatible.

317. Constant, Alphonse Louis [pseud. Eliphas Lèvi]. *The Book of Splendours by Eliphas Lèvi.* Wellingborough, Eng.: Aquarian Press, 1973; New York: Samuel Weiser, 1973. 191 pp.

> Translated from *Le livre des splendeurs.* Appendix by Papus. Foreword by W. N. Schors. In three parts: the Great Synod, Kabalism, and Freemasonry; legends of Krishna; and lessons on the Kabalah from Lèvi's letters.

318. Darual, Arkon. *A History of Secret Societies.* New York: Pocket Books, 1969. 307 pp. index. illus. ISBN 0-671-77051-9.

> Originally published by Citadel Press in 1961. Sometimes criticized as being inaccurate, this title explores a wide variety of secret societies throughout history, including the Assassins, the Knights Templar, the Sufi, Gnostics, Rosicrucians, the Illuminati, Thugs, tongs, and others.

319. Eliade, Mircea. *From Primitives to Zen: a Thematic Sourcebook of the History of Religions.* New York: Harper & Row, 1967. 644 pp.

> Religious mysticism is examined throughout the world and the ages by a noted scholar.

320. Evans-Wentz, W. Y., ed. *The Tibetan Book of the Dead: or, the Afterdeath Experience on the Bardo Plane.* New York: Oxford University Press, 1960. 249 pp.

> A Galaxy Book. The renowned book on the spiritual journey to be faced after death.

321. Godwin, Joscelyn. *Mystery Religions in the Ancient World.* New York: Harper & Row, 1981; London: Thames & Hudson, 1981; Toronto: Fitzhenry & Whiteside, 1981. 176 pp. index. illus. bibliography. ISBN 0-06-063140-6.

An amply illustrated survey of the Eastern religions that enjoyed popularity in the ancient world, such as the cults of Mithras, Dionysus, and Orpheus, esoteric Christianity and Judaism, and Gnosticism.

322. Hall, Manly Palmer. *An Encyclopedia Outline of Masonic, Hermetic, Quabbalistic, and Rosicrucian Symbolic Philsophy: Being an Interpretation of the Secret Teachings Concealed within the Rituals, Allegories, and Mysteries of All Ages*. Los Angeles: The Philosophical Research Society, 1977. 254 pp. index. illus. bibliography. ISBN 0–89314–539–4.

A reduced facsimile reprint of the 1928 edition published by H. S. Crocker (San Francisco) with the title *Secret Teachings for All Ages*. Considered to be one of Hall's most important works. A good, nicely illustrated survey of major secret fraternal orders.

323. Heckethorn, Charles William. *The Secret Societies of All Ages*. New Hyde Park, N.Y.: University Books, 1965. 2 vols. bibliography.

Although outdated, this reprint of an 1897 edition first written in 1875 is useful as a view of the thinking of the time in which it was written.

324. Jung, Carl Gustav. *Psychology and the Occult*. Princeton, N.J.: Princeton University Press, 1978. 167 pp. illus. bibliography. ISBN 0-691-01791-3.

From the Bollingen series. Translated by R.F.C. Hull. Includes Jung's thoughts on spiritualistic phenomena, the soul and death, psychology and spiritualism, and the future of parapsychology.

325. MacKenzie, Norman Ian. *Secret Societies*. New York: Holt, Rinehart & Winston, 1968; Collier, 1971; Crown, 1967; London: Aldus, 1968. 350 pp. illus. maps.

Discusses the mysteries of Rosicrucianism and Freemasonry.

326. Martin E. J. *The Trial of the Templars*. London: Allen & Unwin, 1928. 94 pp.

An account of the accusations against the subsequent trial of the Templars' supposed secret satanic cult.

327. Melton, J. Gordon. *The Encyclopedia of American Religions*. Wilmington, N.C.: McGrath, 1978. 2 vols. index. bibliographic references. ISBN 0-8434-0643-7.

Descriptions of 1,200 churches, both old and new. Volume two includes information on Swedenborg, spiritualism, theosophy, neopaganism, satanism, ritual magic groups, and others. Historical background and basic beliefs of each group are presented clearly.

328. Queenborough, Lady Edith Starr Miller. *Occult Theocracy.* France: International League for Historical Research, 1933. 2 vols. index. illus. bibliography.

Published posthumously for private circulation only. Includes material on Freemasonry, ancient occult systems, druids, witchcraft, secret societies, and others. A bit jumpy in style, although otherwise quite readable.

329. White, John Warren, ed. *Kundalini: Evolution and Enlightenment.* Garden City, N.Y.: Doubleday / Anchor, 1978. 400 pp.

A description of the school of thought based on the Tantric yogi idea that enormous unleased spiritual energy exists in everyone. Includes material from Eastern mysticism as well as on stigmata and UFOs.

330. Wilgus, Neal. *The Illuminoids: Secret Societies & Political Paranoia.* Albuquerque, N.M.: Sun Books, 1978, 1981. 262 pp.

Introduction by Robert Anton Wilson. A history of all secret societies, not just the Illuminoids of the title. Includes a useful chronology.

See also items 39.4.

Druids and Druidism

331. Kendrick, Sir Thomas Downing. *The Druids: a Study in Keltic Prehistory.* New York: Barnes & Noble, 1928; R. V. Coleman, 1927; London: Methuen, 1927, 1928. 227 pp. illus. maps.

An old but still respected work in the area.

332. MacNeill, Marie. *The Festival of Lughnasa; a Study of the Survival of the Celtic Festival of the Beginning of Harvest.* London: Oxford University Press, 1962. 697 pp. illus. maps. bibliography.

Includes legends in the original Gaelic with English summaries. A detailed examination of an important Celtic festival with druidic characteristics.

333. Piggott, Stuart. *The Druids.* New York: Praeger, 1968; London: Thames & Hudson, 1968; Harmondsworth, Eng.: Penguin, 1974. 236 pp. index. illus. maps. bibliography.

> Ancient Peoples and Places series, volume 63. Factual and legendary information about the druids. The priesthood of druidism is treated thoroughly. Good illustrations. Very readable.

334. Ross, Anne. *Pagan Celtic Britain.* New York: Columbia University Press, 1967; London: Routledge & Kegan Paul, 1967. 433 pp. index. illus. maps. bibliography.

> Basically an archaeological study with great attention to the nature of places of worship. Discusses the changes brought about by the Romans.

335. Spence, Lewis. *The History and Origins of Druidism.* New York: Barnes & Noble, 1950; Samuel Weiser, 1949; London: Rider, 1949. 199 pp. bibliography.

> A noted occult writer and expert examines druidism.

336. Spence, Lewis. *The Mysteries of Britain: Secret Rites and Traditions of Ancient Britain Restored.* New York: Samuel Weiser, 1970. 256 pp.

> First published in 1928. An examination of Celtic mysteries.

See also item 37.5, 224.4.

Freemasonry

337. Duncan, Malcolm C. *Duncan's Masonic Ritual and Monitor: or, Guide to the Three Symbolic Degrees of the Ancient York Rite, and to the Degrees of Mark Master, Past Master, Most Excellent Master, and the Royal Orch.* New York: David McKay, 1976; Fitzgerald, 1866, 1880, 1922. 281 pp. illus. ISBN 0-6795-0626-8.

> A basic manual for Freemasons.

338. Gould, Robert Freke. *History of Freemasonry.* London: Caxton, 1931; New York: Scribner's, 1936. 3 to 6 vols., depending on printing. illus. bibliography.

First published in 1884–87 by John Beacham (New York). Other editions available.

339. Mackey, Albert Gallatin. *The History of Freemasonry: Its Legends and Traditions: Its Chronological History.* New York: Masonic History Co., 1898, 1906. 7 vols. illus.

Lengthy, official history. The skeptical may wish to consult the definition of Freemasons in *The Devil's Dictionary.*

340. Waite, Arthur Edward. *A New Encyclopedia of Freemasonry (Ars Magna Latomorum) and of Cognate Instituted Mysteries: Their Rites, Literature and History.* New York: Weathervane, 1970; New Hyde Park, N.Y.: University Books, 1970; Philadelphia: David McKay, n.d. 2 vols. in one. 458, 488 pp. illus. ISBN 0-517-19148-2.

Introduction by Emmett McLoughlin. Reprint of the edition first published by McKay in 1926. A sympathetic history of the Masons, along with an examination of certain myths about the lodge. A standard work in the field.

Rosicrucianism

341. Allen, Paul Marshall, comp. *A Christian Rosenkreutz Anthology.* Blauvelt, N.Y.: Steinerbooks, 1974; New York: Samuel Weiser, 1974. 702 pp. illus.

An anthology of major Rosicrucian writings throughout history, including works by Thomas Vaughan, Robert Flood, and Rudolf Steiner. Includes a number of facsimile illustrations from the original texts.

342. Hartmann, Franz. *With the Adepts: an Adventure among the Rosicrucians.* London: Rider, 1910; New York: Theosophical Pub. Co., 1910. 2d ed. 174 pp.

Originally published in 1887 as *An Adventure among the Rosicrucians.*

343. Heindel, Max. *The Rosicrucian Mysteries.* Oceanside, Calif.: Rosicrucian Fellowship, 1911. 226 pp. index.

Official publication describing the history of Rosicrucianism and how its principles can lead its followers to a better life.

344. Lewis, Harve Spencer. *Rosicrucian Manual*. San Jose, Calif.: Rosicrucian Press, 1941. 214 pp. illus.

> An official publication.

345. Waite, Arthur Edward. *The Real History of the Rosicrucians*. New York: Rudolf Steiner, 1977. 446 pp. illus.

> First published by Redway (London) in 1887.

346. Yates, Frances Amelia. *The Rosicrucian Enlightenment*. London: Routledge & Kegan Paul, 1972; Paladin, 1975. 315 pp. index. illus. maps. ISBN 0-586-08211-2 (Paladin edition).

> A useful and important book in the field. Scholarly. The text focuses on the early seventeenth century: ". . . a phase in the history of European culture which is intermediate between the Renaissance and the so-called scientific revolution of the seventeenth" (Preface).

See also item 780.

The Golden Dawn

347. Colquhoun, Ithell. *The Sword of Wisdom: MacGregor Mathers and the Golden Dawn*. New York: Putnam, 1975; London: Spearman, 1975. 307 pp. index. illus. ISBN 0-399-11534-8.

> Begins with an autobiographical note by the author whose discovery of the Golden Dawn as a schoolgirl led to later explorations of the occult. Chapters separate the "good" from the "bad and dissident."

348. Howe, Ellic. *The Magicians of the Golden Dawn: a Documentary History of a Magical Order 1887–1923*. New York: Samuel Weiser, 1978; London: Routledge & Kegan Paul, 1972. 306 pp. index. illus. ISBN 0-87728-369.9.

> Includes the relationship of the Golden Dawn to the English Rosicrucian Society. Appendixes include some documents of the society. Information about Yeats, MacGregor Mathers, Waite, Crowley, and others is included. Well researched and nicely written.

349. King, Francis. *Astral Projection, Magic, and Alchemy: Being Hitherto Unpublished Golden Dawn Material by S. L. MacGregor Mathers and Others*. London: Spearman, 1971. 254 pp. ISBN 0-85435-171-X.

Printed lectures presented to the members of the Golden Dawn prior to 1900. A few facsimile magic documents are included.

350. Moore, Virginia. *The Unicorn: William Butler Yeats' Search for Reality.* New York: Macmillan, 1954. 519 pp. bibliography.

Supplies detailed information on the Golden Dawn, as well as autobiographical material on Yeats.

351. Regardie, Israel. *The Golden Dawn: an Account of the Teachings, Rites, and Ceremonies of the Order of the Golden Dawn.* Chicago: Aries Press, 1937–40. 4 vols; St. Paul: Llewellyn, 1969, 1971. 2d ed. 2 vols. illus.

Contains many of the most important rituals and teachings.

352. Torrens, Robert George. *The Golden Dawn: Its Inner Teachings.* New York: Samuel Weiser, 1973. 304 pp.

First published by Spearman (London) in 1969 as *The Inner Teachings of the Golden Dawn.* Published as *Secret Rituals of the Golden Dawn* by Aquarian Press (Wellingborough) in 1973. Original rituals included.

Theosophy, Spiritualism, and Reincarnation

353. Albertson, Edward. *Theosophy for the Millions.* Los Angeles: Sherbourne Press, 1971. 165 pp.

For the Millions series. As such, it is for the general reader. Covers Mme. Blavatsky, the development of theosophy, and some basic tenets of the faith.

354. Blavatsky, Helena P. *The Theosophical Glossary.* Los Angeles: The Theosophy Company, 1952. 389 pp.

A photographic reproduction of the original edition as it was first issued in London in 1892. "Purposes to give information on the principal Sanskrit, Pahlavi, Tibetan, Pali, Chaldean, Persian, Scandinavian, Hebrew, Greek, Latin, Kabalistic and Gnostic words, and Occult terms generally used in Theosophical literature . . ." (Frontispiece).

355. Brandon, Ruth. *The Spiritualists: the Passion for the Occult in the Nineteenth and Twentieth Centuries*. New York: Knopf, 1983. 315 pp. index. illus. bibliography. ISBN 0-39452-740-2.

> A demystification of the spiritualist movement in the U.S. Well researched and written on an easy-to-understand level. Includes European influences.

356. Brennan, James Herbert. *Reincarnation: Five Keys to Past Lives*. Wellingborough, Eng.: Aquarian Press, 1981. 94 pp. index. ISBN 0-85030-275-7.

> Good introductory survey to reincarnation of those who wish to determine if they have lived before their present lives. Not theoretical.

357. Cayce, Hugh Lynn. *Venture Inward*. New York: Harper & Row, 1972; Toronto: Fitzhenry & Whiteside, 1972. 207 pp. ISBN 0-06-087021-4.

> Originally published by Harper & Row (New York) in 1964. Edgar Cayce's son used his father's work and philosophies to present the famous psychic's ideas on meditation, dreams, mediumship, and the like.

358. Delacour, Jean-Baptiste. *Glimpses of the Beyond: the Extraordinary Experiences of People Who Have Crossed the Brink of Death and Returned*. New York: Delacorte, 1973. 216 pp. bibliography.

> Translated from the German *Aus dem Jenseits Zurück* by E. G. Garside, published in 1973. Accounts of those who returned from death.

359. Driscoll, Walter, and the Gurdjieff Foundation of California. *Gurdjieff: an Annotated Bibliography*. New York: Garland, 1984. 350 pp. index. ISBN 0-8240-8972-3.

> Gurdjieff was a Russian mystic whose teachings of Eastern concepts and philosophies were very influential in the early twenteith century and continue to exert an influence today. Includes a list of his writings and materials in English and French. Annotations provided.

360. Ford, Arthur. *Nothing So Strange*. New York: Harper & Row, 1958. 246 pp.

> The autobiography of a famous medium of the twentieth century.

361. Head, Joseph, and Cranston, S. L., eds. *Reincarnations, the Phoenix Fire Mystery: an East-West Dialogue on Death and Rebirth from the Worlds of Religion, Science, Psychology, Philosophy, Art, and Literature, and from Great Thinkers of the Past and Present.* New York: Warner, 1979; Julian Press / Crown, 1977. 620 pp. index. bibliographic notes. ISBN 0-446-97140-5.

A collection of articles pertaining to the book's subtitle.

362. Hick, John Harwood. *Death and Eternal Life.* New York: Harper & Row, 1976. 495 pp. index. bibliography. ISBN 0-06-063901-6.

An international historical survey of various religions and beliefs dealing with death and the afterlife. Scholarly and thoughtful. The author concludes with a strong argument in favor of reincarnation.

363. Kerr, Howard H. *Mediums and Spirit-Rappers and Roaring Radicals: Spiritualism in American Literature, 1850–1900.* Urbana: University of Illinois Press, 1972. 261 pp. ISBN 0-252-00218-0.

A history of American spiritualism and its influence on American society and literature during its growth period.

364. Langley, Noel. *Edgar Cayce on Reincarnation.* New York: Warner, 1967. 286 pp. bibliography.

Edited by Hugh Lynn Cayce. Written by the author of *The Search for Bridie Murphy.* Cayce's thoughts on the afterlife and reincarnation are brought together. An official edition from the Association for Research and Enlightenment, Inc. in Virginia Beach, Virginia.

365. Lodge, Oliver J. *Raymond: or Life and Death with Examples of the Evidence for Survival of Memory and Affection after Death.* New York: George H. Doran, 1916; London: Methuen, 1916. 404 pp. index. illus.

A classic work on the afterlife of a soldier killed in World War I.

366. McHargue, Georgess [pseud.] *Facts, Frauds and Phantasms: a Survey of the Spiritualist Movement.* New York: Doubleday, 1972. 269 pp. illus. bibliography.

Covers the history of spiritualism from Mesmer and the Fox sisters to the present day. Includes information regarding the Catholic Church's stance against spiritualism, fradulent mediums, and the like. An objective, though not particularly sympathetic, view. Glossary provided.

367. Meade. Marion. *Madame Blavatsky: the Woman Behind the Myth.*
New York: Putnam, 1980. 528 pp. index. illus. bibliography.
ISBN 0-399-12376-8.

An objective yet sympathetic portrayal of the founder of theosophy.
Includes material on her writing, as well as her life. Although questions
are raised, the author believes that Mme. Blavatsky was undoubtedly a
sensitive.

368. Moody, Raymond A., Jr., *Life After Life.* Harrisburg, Pa.: Stack-
pole Books, 1976; New York: Bantam, 1976. 125 pp. bibliography.

Originally published by Mockingbird Books (Atlanta) in 1975. A compilation of 50 case studies of individuals who were brought back to life
after having supposedly died, and some secondhand accounts of such
cases. Selected from a pool of 150 cases, the book contains the author's
accounts and conclusions from interviews with these individuals. Also
includes his findings regarding death in the Bible, Swedenborgian
concepts, and others.

369. Moss, Peter, and Keeton, Joe. *Encounters with the Past: How Man
Can Experience and Relive History.* Harmondsworth, Eng.: Penguin,
1981; Garden City, N.Y.: Doubleday, 1980. 233 pp. index. illus.
ISBN 0-14-005587-8.

Originally published by Sidgwick & Jackson (London) in 1979 and
issued with two records. Doubleday edition is published as *Encounters
with the Past: Man's Ability to Relive History.* Keeton has been involved
with hypnotic regression for some years, and this book is an account of
his work and the general nature of hypnosis. A number of case studies
are included.

370. Nelson, Geoffrey K. *Spiritualism and Society.* New York:
Schocken, 1969; London: Routledge, 1969. 307 pp.

Good survey, approached on sociological terms.

371. Osis, Karlis, and Haraldsson, Erlendur. *At the Hour of Death.*
New York: Avon, 1977. 244 pp. ISBN 0-3800-1802-0.

Introduction by Elizabeth Kübler-Ross. The results of interviews with a
thousand doctors and nurses who reported patients' behavior and
comments as they approached death. Two surveys were conducted in
the U.S. and one in India. Certain similarities were found. Proof of
afterlife seems evident to the authors.

372. Pearsall, Ronald. *The Table–Rappers*. London: Michael Joseph, 1972. 258 pp. index. illus. bibliography. ISBN 0-7181-0645-8.

History and account of spiritualism, séances, and table-rapping. Also includes poltergeists, zombies, and information on the theosophical movement.

373. Rauscher, William V., and Spragget, Allen. *The Spiritual Frontiers*. Garden City, N.Y.: Doubleday, 1975. 312 pp. bibliography. ISBN 0-385-07189-2.

Much of this book is a criticism of Arthur Ford. There is a strong focus on parapsychology, and a justification for religious investigations.

374. Ring, Kenneth. *Life at Death: a Scientific Investigation of the Near-Death Experience*. New York: Coward, McCann & Geoghegan, 1980. 310 pp. index. bibliography. ISBN 0-698-11032-3.

Case studies of over a hundred people who experienced near-death situations. Various factors affecting the decision to return to life are explored, along with the author's speculations about the collective experience of the subjects.

375. Roberts, Jane. *Adventures in Consciousness: an Introduction to Aspect Psychology*. Englewood Cliffs, N.J.: Prentice-Hall, 1979. index. illus. ISBN 0-13-013961-0.

A reprinting of the work by the same publisher first issued in 1975. This title tells of the coming of Seth to the author. Seth is a spirit who has appeared many times to Roberts and students in her psychic classes. A number of Seth books have been published.

376. Rogo, D. Scott, and Bayless, Raymond. *Phone Calls from the Dead*. Englewood Cliffs, N.J.: Prentice-Hall, 1979. 172 pp. index. illus. bibliography. ISBN 0-13-664334-5.

Case studies and discussion of telephone calls to the living by spirits, or those still living who claim it was impossible for them to have made reported telephone calls.

377. St. Johns, Adela Rogers. *No Good-byes: My Search into Life beyond Death*. New York: McGraw-Hill, 1981. 205 pp. ISBN 0-07-054450-6.

The well-known author and reporter presents her case for existence after death, based on various experiences in her own life. She also recounts her communications with people on the other side, such as Clark Gable. She believes she lived before in Elizabethan England.

378. Steiner, Rudolf. *An Outline of Occult Science*. Spring Valley, N.Y.: Anthroposophic Press, 1972. ISBN 0-910142-16-2.

> A translation of *Die Geheimwissenschaft im Umriss* by Maud and Henry B. Monges. Revised for this edition by Lisa D. Monges. Originally published as volume 13 in the Bibliographic Survey (1961). A basic work for understanding Steiner, who began as a theosophist and broke away to form the anthroposophical movement.

379. Steiner, Rudolf. *Theosophy: an Introduction to the Supersensible Knowledge of the World and the Destination of Man*. Spring Valley, N.Y.: Anthroposophic Press, 1971. 195 pp. 18th ed. ISBN 0-910142-65-3.

> Translation of *Theosophie, Einfuhrung in uber-sinnliche Welterkenatins und Menschenbestimmung* by Gilbert Church. Contents: the essential nature of man, pre-embodiment of the spirit and destiny, the three worlds, and the path of knowledge.

380. Stevenson, Ian. *Cases of the Reincarnation Type*. Charlottesville: University Press of Virginia, 1975–. irregular serial.

> In the four volumes published as of 1983, Stevenson reports on case studies of reincarnation throughout the world. The volumes are arranged geographically.

381. Stringfellow, William, and Towne, Anthony. *The Death and Life of Bishop Pike*. Garden City, N.Y.: Doubleday, 1976. 466 pp. illus. bibliography. ISBN 0-385-07455-7.

> A careful examination of Pike's papers, writings, and interviews covers his death and contributions during life. Many psychic experiences are included. The political and personal beliefs of the authors intrude on occasion.

382. Swedenborg, Emanuel. *Heaven and Its Wonders and Hell*. New York: Swedenborg Foundation, 1971. 496 pp. index. ISBN 0-87785-068-2.

> Originally published in Latin (London) in 1758. Introduction by Helen Keller. A classic work by the founder of the Swedenborgian movement. Includes a discussion on the nature of souls and the existence of souls after death.

383. Webb, James. *The Harmonious Circle: an Exploration of the Lives and Work of G. I Gurdjieff, P. D. Ouspensky, A. R. Orage, Maurice Nicoll,*

Jean Toomer, Rodney Collin-Smith, J. B. Bennett and Others. New York: Putnam, 1978. 608 pp. index. illus. bibliography.
ISBN 0-339-11465-3.

A good survey of the development and basic beliefs of Gurdjieff and his followers. Considered to be objective and thorough, as well as well written. Includes a biography of Gurdjieff.

See also items 37.1, 37.6, 37.8, 37.9, 37.12, 37.16, 37.21, 37.22, 37.23, 37.25, 37.28, 37.29, 37.30, 37.31, 37.32, 861, 885, 889.

6
PSYCHICS AND PSYCHICAL RESEARCH

> *Clairvoyant*, n. A person, commonly a woman, who has the
> power of seeing that which is invisible to her patron—
> namely, that he is a blockhead.
>
> Ambrose Bierce,
> *The Devil's Dictionary*

In the latter part of the nineteenth century, a number of spiritualist
and related areas became the subject of research. "Legitimate" scientists scoffed at this research for the most part. In the early years, most
investigations of psychical and paranormal occurrences were handled
by societies, such as the Society for Psychical Research (British) and
its American counterpart, the ASPR. The investigators, often called
"ghost hunters," were accused of being gullible and of not using
proper scientific care in conducting investigations. Sometimes they
were accused of being charlatans themselves.

In the twentieth century these investigations have continued,
and a few brave academicians, notably J. B. Rhine in the days
between the two world wars, conducted and published the results of
controlled scientific experiments in the psychical area. The field has
been slow to gain recognition, however. Even though today there is
more acceptance of parapsychology as a legitimate field for scientific
investigation, it continues to be subjected to considerable scrutiny
and doubt. At least there appears to be acknowledgment that scientific controls have been tightened. With the increased number of
people working in the field, replication and double-checking have
become possible.

In recent decades there has been the added titillation of learning
that Russian scientists have been working in the psychic area—some,
it is suspected, for military purposes. Psychics have been employed
by police departments to help solve crimes (with varying degrees of
success). The young poeple who were in the forefront of the "Age of
Aquarius" in the late 1960s have become part of the establishment,
yet many have retained some of their ideas and willingness to believe

in things beyond the normal range of acceptance. These, and other factors, have combined to make pyschical research almost legitimate, and psychics are thought more often to be gifted rather than freaks.

The psychic world now has a number of branches for study and consideration as a result of investigation, research, and study. This chapter is divided into the following sections:

- Reference Sources
- General Works
- Out-of-the-Body Experiences
- Psychokinesis
- Clairvoyance and Dowsing
- Auras and the Kirlian Effect
- Telepathy
- Altered States of Consciousness

Reference Sources

384. *Advances in Parapsychological Research*. New York: Plenum Press, 1977-1981; Jefferson, N.C.: McFarland, 1984–. biennual. index. bibliographies. ISSN 0195-9867.

> Edited by Stanley Krippner. The first two volumes of the series comprise a historical survey of developments in the field. Ongoing volumes cover current research. The 1977 volume is subtitled *Psychokinesis*, and the 1979 volume is subtitled *Extrasensory Perception*. Volume four covers methodological advances, psychokinesis, psi theories, healing, psychology implications, and criticisms.

385. Ashby, Robert H. *The Guidebook for the Study of Psychical Research*. London: Rider, 1972, 157 pp; New York: Samuel Weiser, 1972. 190 pp. ISBN 0-87728-188-2.

> Contents include the nature of psychical research, a bibliography for beginning students, a bibliography for advanced students, procedures for sitting with a medium, resources available to the student, and important figures in psychical research. "Intended for the person interested in Extrasensory Perception (ESP) and related topics who determines to investigate psychical research." (Preface).

386. *Catalogue of the Library of the [British] Society for Psychical Research*. Boston: G. K. Hall, 1976. 341 pp. ISBN 0-8161-0008-X.

Reproductions of title and author cards from a noted special library. Although not that great in number (apparently 7,000 volumes), these are the essential works in the field.

387. Finch, W. J., and Finch, Elizabeth. *Who's Who in the Psychic World*. Phoenix: Esoteric Publs. / Psychic Register International, 1973. 240 pp.

A dated, though still useful, listing of individual psychics and psychical scholars.

388. Goss, Michael, comp. *Poltergeists: an Annotated Bibliography of Works in English, circa 1880–1975*. Methuchen, N.J.: Scarecrow Press, 1979. 389 pp. indexes. ISBN 0-81081-181-2.

Covers books, periodical articles, reviews, specilized and / or research papers, and correspondence, as well as encyclopedia articles. Nice introduction to the history of literature on the subject. Citations are arranged by author. Annotations are given. Includes materials on ghosts and haunted houses. Geographical and general indexes.

389. King, Clyde S., comp. *Psychic and Religious Phenomena Limited: a Bibliographic Index*. Westport, Conn.: Greenwood Press, 1978. 245 pp. bibliography. ISBN 0-313-20616-3.

Arranged in two parts. Part I lists books, newspapers, and periodicals divided into the following classes: phenomena concerning visions at the moment of death, observations of the departing soul, dreams related to death and behavior of animals in the presence of death, astral projections, natural and spontaneous mystical experiences, mystical experiences induced by chemical, mechanical or physical means, psychic music, and psychic voices. Part II is a listing of books.

390. McConnell, Robert A. *ESP Curriculum Guide*. New York: Simon & Schuster, 1971. 128 pp. index. illus. bibliography. ISBN 0-671-21007-6.

For secondary-school and college teachers who wish to plan and teach a course on ESP. Includes a syllabus and ideas for how-to-do-it exercises.

391. Morris, Robert L., ed. *Perspectives in Psychical Research*. New York: Arno Press, 1976. 34 vols.

A series of important reprints in the field. Original place and date of publication cited for each. Includes the following:

391.1. Carrington, Hereward. *Laboratory Investigations into Psychic Phenomena.* Philadelphia, 1939. ISBN 0-405-07021-7.

391.2. Colquhoun, J. C. *Report of the Experiments on Animal Magnetism: Made by a Committee of the Medical Section of the French Royal Academy of Sciences, Read at the Meetings of the 21st and 28th of June, 1831; Translated, and Now for the First Time Published with an Historical and Explanatory Introduction, and an Appendix.* Edinburgh, 1833. ISBN 0-405-07022-5.

391.3. Coover, John Edgar. *Experiments in Psychical Research at Leland Stanford Junior University.* Stanford, Calif., 1917. illus. ISBN 0-405-07023-3.

391.4. Cumberland, Stuart. *A Thought-Reader's Thoughts: Being the Impressions and Confessions of Stuart Cumberland.* London, 1888. ISBN 0-405-07024-1.

391.5. Doyle, Sir Arthur Conan. *The History of Spiritualism.* New York, 1926. illus. ISBN 0-405-07025-X.

391.6. Driesch, Hans. *Psychical Research: the Science of the Super-Normal.* London, 1933. ISBN 0-405-07026-8.

391.7. Ehrenwald, Jan. *New Dimensions of Deep Analysis: a Study of Telepathy in Interpersonal Relationships.* New York, 1955. ISBN 0-405-07027-6.

391.8. Esdaile, James. *Natural and Mesmeric Clairvoyance: with the Practical Application of Mesmerism in Surgery and Medicine.* London, 1852. ISBN 0-405-07028-4.

391.9. Fukurai, T. *Clairvoyance and Thoughtography.* London, 1931. illus. ISBN 0-405-07929-2.

391.10. Garrett, Eileen J. *My Life as a Search for the Meaning of Mediumship.* New York, 1939. ISBN 0-405-07030-6.

391.11. Geley, Gustave. *Clairvoyance and Materialisation: a Record of Experiments.* London, 1927. illus. ISBN 0-405-07031-4.

391.12. Gregory, Williams *Animal Magnetism: or, Mesmerism and its Phenomena.* London, 1909. 5th ed. ISBN 0-405-07032-2.

391.13. Gudas, Fabian, ed. *Extrasensory Perception.* New York, 1961. ISBN 0-405-07033-0.

391.14. Haddock, Joseph W. *Somnolism and Psycheism: or, the Science of the Soul and the Phenomena of Nervation as Revealed by*

Vital Magnetism or Mesmerism, Considered Physiologically and Philosophically; with Notes of Mesmeric and Psychical Experience. London, 1851. 2d ed. illus. ISBN 0-405-07034-9.

391.15. Hibbert-Ware, Samuel. *Sketches of the Philosophy of Apparitions: or, an Attempt to Trace Such Illusions to Their Physical Causes.* Edinburgh, 1824. ISBN 0-405-07035-7.

391.16. Mulholland, John. *Beware Familiar Spirits.* New York and London, 1938. ISBN 0-405-07036-5.

391.17. Murchison, Carl, ed. *The Case for and against Pychical Belief.* Worcester, Mass., 1927. illus. ISBN 0-405-07037-3.

391.18. Myers, Frederic William Henry. *Human Personality and Its Survival of Bodily Death.* London and New York, 1954. 2 vols. ISBN 0-405-07038-1.

391.19. Podmore, Frank. *The Newer Spiritualism.* London, 1910. ISBN 0-405-07041-1.

391.20. Podmore, Frank. *Studies in Psychical Research.* New York and London, 1897. ISBN 0-405-07042-X.

391.21. Price, Harry. *Fifty Years of Psychical Research: a Critical Study.* London and New York, 1939. illus. ISBN 0-405-07043-8.

391.22. Price, Harry, and Dingwall, Eric J. *Revelations of a Spirit Medium.* London and New York, 1922. index. bibliography. ISBN 0-405-07044-6.

391.23. Prince, Walter Franklin. *The Enchanted Boundary: Being a Survey of Negative Reactions to Claims of Psychic Phenomena, 1820–1930.* Boston, 1930. ISBN 0-405-07045-4.

391.24. Richet, Charles. *Thirty Years of Psychical Research: Being a Treatise on Metapsychics.* New York, 1923. illus. ISBN 0-405-07046-2.

391.25. Roll, William G. *Theory and Experiment in Psychical Research.* New York, 1975. illus. ISBN 0-405-07047-0.

391.26. Salter, W. H. *ZOAR: or the Evidence of Psychical Research Concerning Survival.* London, 1961. ISBN 0-405-07048-9.

391.27. Saltmarsh, Herbert Francis. *Evidence of Personal Survival from Cross Correspondence.* London, 1938. ISBN 0-405-07049-7.

391.28. Saltmarsh, Herbert Francis. *Foreknowledge.* London, 1938. ISBN 0-405-06990-1.

391.29. Sidgwick, Eleanor Mildred. *Phantasms of the Living: Cases of Telepathy Printed in the Journal of the Society for Psychical Research during Thirty-Five Years;* and Gurney, Edmund; Myers, Frederic W. H., and Podmore, Frank. *Phantasms of the Living?* New York, 1962. ISBN 0-405-06991-X.

391.30. Thomas, John F. *Beyond Normal Cognition: an Evaluative and Methodological Study of the Mental Content of Certain Trance Phenomena.* Boston, 1937. ISBN 0-405-06992-8.

391.31. Tyrrell, George Nugent Merle. *Science and Psychical Phenomena.* New York and London, 1938. ISBN 0-405-06993-6. (See item 457.)

391.32. Von Schrenck Notzing, A. *Phenomena of Materialisation: a Contribution to the Investigation of Mediumistic Teleplastics.* London and New York, 1920. illus. ISBN 0-405-06995-2.

391.33. Wallace, Alfred Russel. *Miracles and Modern Spiritualism.* London, 1896. rev. ed. ISBN 0-405-06996-0.

391.34. Warcollier, Rene. *Experimental Telepathy.* Boston, 1938. illus. ISBN 0-405-06997-9.

392. Naumov, E. K., and Vilanskaya, L. V. *Bibliographies on Parapsychology (Psycho-energetics) and Related Subjects.* Arlington, Va.: Joint Publications Research Service, 1972 distributed by NTIS. 101 pp.

Originally published in Moscow in 1971.

393. Pleasants, Helene. *Biographical Dictionary of Parapsychology with Directory and Glossary 1964–1966.* New York: Garrett / Helix, 1964. 371 pp. bibliography.

Historical and contemporary coverage. Nearly five hundred individuals arranged alphabetically. Originally published by the National Laboratory of Psychical Research (London) in 1929 as *Biographical Dictionary of Psychical Research, Spiritualism, Magic, Psychology, Legerdemain and Other Methods of Deception, Charlatanism, Witchcraft and Technical Works for the Scientific Investigation of Alleged Abnormal Phenomena Circa 1450 A.D. to 1929 A.D.* A supplement to this was issued in 1935.

394. Rao, K. Ramakrishna, ed. *The Basic Experiments in Parapsychology.* Jefferson, N.C.: McFarland, 1984. 272 pp. index. bibliography. ISBN 0-89950-084-6.

Explains the sixteen most significant basic experiments in parapsychology.

395. Regush, Nicholas, with Regush, June. *The New Consciousness Catalog*. New York: Putnam, 1979. 159 pp. illus. ISBN 0-399-11923-X.

A sensible, albeit too brief, catalog and directory modeled after the *Whole Earth Catalog*. Organized into five main parts: the life flow of microcosm-macrocosm, exploring states of consciousness, psychic research sources, methods of conscious development, and dimensions of healing. Suggests books to read on various subjects, such as auras, acupuncture, biofeedback, Kirlian electrophotography, and pyramid power. Includes lists of slide sets, tapes, and journals.

396. *Research in Parapsychology, [year]: Abstracts and Papers from the [number] Annual Convention of the Parapsychological Association, [year]*. Metuchen, N.J.: Scarecrow Press 1972–. annual. index. illus. bibliographies. ISSN 0093-4793.

Different editors, including J. D. Morris, William G. Roll, R. L. Morris, Richard Broughton, John Beloff, and Rhea White. Continues the *Proceedings of the Parapsychological Association*. An excellent overview of current research interests in the field. The 1983 annual contains two new sections on newly completed work and research in progress. Some complete texts are included, along with a number of abstracts. The 1982 volume covers the joint conference of the Society for Psychical Research and the Parapsychological Association with broader coverage than that found in the other annuals.

397. Rogo, D. Scott. *Parapsychology: a Century of Inquiry*. New York: Dell, 1976; Taplinger, 1975. 317 pp. index. bibliography.

A good historical survey and good starting point, even though it was considered flawed in the eyes of some critics primarily on the grounds of containing generalities.

398. Sargent, Carl, and Eysenck, Hans J. *Know Your Own Psi-Q: Probe Your ESP Powers*. New York: World Almanac, 1983; London: Michael Joseph, 1983. 192 pp. illus. ISBN 0-345-31305-4.

A series of tests devised to help score ESP talents, such as those using cards, dice, and pictures. A chapter on computer programs is included.

399. White, Rhea A. *Surveys in Parapsychology: Reviews of the Literature, with Updated Bibliographies*. Metuchen, N.J.: Scarecrow Press, 1976. 484 pp. ISBN 0-8108-0906-0.

A competent, useful volume by an acknowledged expert in parapsychological literature. Selected from previously published articles in respected journals.

400. White, Rhea A., and Dale, Laura A. *Parapsychology: Sources of Information.* Metuchen, N.J.: Scarecrow Press, 1973. 303 pp. indexes. bibliographies. ISBN 0-8108-0617-7.

> Compiled under the auspices of the American Society for Psychical Research. Annotated list of 282 books. Discusses parapsychology in encyclopedias, parapsychological organizations, parapsychological periodicals, and scientific recognition of parapsychology. Major topics covered are telepathy, clairvoyance, precognition, and psychokinesis. Also covered are altered states of consciousness, anpsi (psi in animals), anthropology and psi phenomena, automatisms, criticisms, experimental psychical research, hauntings and poltergeists, histories and historical works, interdisciplinary studies, mediums and sensitives, out-of-the-body experiences, philosophy and the psi experience, precognition and retrocognition, psychiatry and psi phenomena, psychical research in general, psychokinesis, psychology and psi phenomena, reference books, religion and psi phenomena, spiritualism, spontaneous psi phenomena, survival, tests for psi, and unorthodox healing. Includes addresses of lesser-known publishers and a glossary. Indexes by name, subject, and title. According to the publisher, a new edition is in preparation.

401. Wolman, Benjamin B., ed. *Handbook of Parapsychology.* New York: Van Nostrand Reinhold, 1977. 967 pp. indexes. illus. bibliography. ISBN 0-442-29576-6.

> Laura A. Dale, Gertrude R. Schmeidler, and Montague Ullman are associate editors. A fine anthology consisting of the following sections: history of parapsychology, research methods in parapsychology, perception—communication and parapsychology, parapsychology and physical systems, parapsychology and altered states of consciousness, parapsychology and healing, survival of bodily death, parapsychology and other fields, parapsychological models and theories, and Soviet research in parapsychology. Suggested readings at ends of chapters. Glossary. Name and subject indexes. "It is also a handbook for change . . ." (Introduction).

General Works

402. Angoff, Allan, ed. *The Psychic Force: Essays in Modern Psychical Research from the "International Journal of Parapsychology."* New York: Putnam, 1970. 345 pp. index. bibliographic references.

> Glossary of terms included. Essays on modern psychical research. Topics include the following: general articles on parapsychology, mes-

merism and hynosis, sleep and dreams, visions and hallucinations, medicine and parapsychology, twins and extrasensory perception, telepathy, religion and parapsychology, creativity as a psychic force, reincarnation, survival, and communication with the dead.

403. Bartlett, Laile. *Psi Trek: a World-Wide Investigation into the Lives of Psychic People and the Researchers Who Test Such Phenomena as: Healing, Prophecy, Dowsing Ghosts, and Life After Death.* New York: McGraw-Hill, 1981. 337 pp. index. bibliography. ISBN 0-07-003915-1.

An investigation by a sociologist of various psi centers. A good introduction to what is going on in the field, although the presentation seems a bit disorganized at times.

404. Beloff, John, ed. *New Directions in Parapsychology.* London: Elek Science, 1974; Metuchen, N.J.: Scarecrow Press, 1975. 174 pp. index. bibliographic references.

Postscript by Arthur Koestler. Glossary included. Contains material on instrumentation in the parapsychology laboratory and an up-to-date survey of psychical research.

405. Beloff, John. *Psychological Sciences: a Review of Modern Psychology.* New York: Barnes & Noble, 1973. 361 pp. index. bibliography. ISBN 0--6490-359-1.

A comparison of parapsychology with the other, more accepted branches of psychology.

406. Bentov, Itzhak. *Stalking the Wild Pendulum: on the Mechanics of Consciousness.* New York: Bantam, 1978; Dutton, 1977. 155 pp. illus. ISBN 0-553-20768-7.

The author presents the theory that the universe is not static but oscillating, which would account for various paranormal phenomena, such as telepathy and auras.

407. Boswell, Harriet A. *Master Guide to Psychism.* West Nyack, N.Y.: Parker, 1969. 223 pp.

A how-to-do-it manual for developing psychic powers, it covers séances, human auras, premonition and precognition, psychokinesis and telekinesis, automatism, reincarnation, astral projection, Ouija boards, possession and obsession, developing psychometry powers, psychic photography, and telepathy.

408. Bowles, Norma and Hynds, Fran. *Psi Search*. San Francisco: Harper & Row, 1978. 168 pp. index. illus. bibliography. ISBN 0-06064-083-9.

> Written with the assistance of Joan Maxwell. Includes psi in the laboratory, traditional associations, and possible applications.

409. Braude, Stephen E. *ESP and Psychokinesis: a Philosophical Examination*. Philadelphia: Temple University Press, 1979. 283 pp. index. bibliography. ISBN 0-87722-163-4.

> Philosophical Monographs series. A fine, scholarly introduction to the whole area of parapsychology by a philosophy professor.

410. Burt, Sir Lodowic Cyril. *E.S.P. and Psychology*. New York: Halstead, 1975. 179 pp. index. bibliographic notes. ISBN 0-47012-531-4.

> Edited by Anita Gregory. A selection of writings by an early researcher in the field. Includes material on Jung.

411. Carrington, Hereward. *Modern Psychical Phenomena: Recent Researches and Speculations*. New York: Dodd, Mead, 1919. 331 pp. illus.

> Divided into three main parts: the relationship of psychical phenomena to evolution, psychology, biology, and ethics; recent experiments and theories; and recent research in crystal vision and crystal gazing.

412. Carrington, Hereward. *The World of Psychic Research*. New York: A. S. Barnes, 1973; London: Thomas Yoseloff, 1973. 190 pp. index. ISBN 0-49801-299-9.

> Originally published as *Invisible World* by Beechhurst Press (New York) in 1946. A classic collection of essays on various subjects by a highly respected scholar in the field.

413. Christopher, Milbourne. *ESP, Seers, & Psychics: What the Occult Really Is*. New York: Thomas Y. Crowell, 1970. 268 pp. index. bibliography. ISBN 0-69026-815-7.

> Contents include astrology, extrasensory perception, ESP in animals, predicting the future, thought reading, dowsing, poltergeists, haunted houses, the great mediums, and fire walking.

414. Donnelly, Katherine Fair. *The Guidebook to ESP and Psychic Wonders*. New York: David McKay, 1978. 176 pp. index. bibliographies. ISBN 0-679-50805-8.

A personalized introduction to telepathy, precognition, clairvoyance, psychic healing, aura reading, psychometry, psychokinesis, and spiritualism.

415. Douglas Alfred. *Extra-Sensory Powers: a Century of Psychical Research.* London: Victor Gollancz, 1976; New York: Overlook Press, 1977. 392 pp. index. illus. bibliography. ISBN 0-575-02137-3.

An accurate and scholarly presentation on the subject, beginning with the early days of research into spiritualism to present-day sophisticated, scientific investigation in parapsychology.

416. Drury, Nevill. *Don Juan, Mescalito and Modern Magic: the Mythology of Inner Space.* London: Routledge & Kegan Paul, 1978. 229 pp. index. illus. bibliography. ISBN 0-710-08582-6.

An espousal of Western trance experiences, including arguments in favor of psychedelics, inner voyages, out-of-the-body experiences, and trances over Eastern methods, such as yoga. A weakness is the lack of distinction between drug / chemical experiences and those trances brought about by mythical and / or magical systems.

417. Ehrenwald, Jan. *The ESP Experience: a Psychiatric Validation.* New York: Basic Books, 1978. 308 pp. index. illus. bibliography. ISBN 0-465-02056-9.

Divided into five major sections: origins, psychodynamics, psychopathy, theory, and uses of parapsychology. Individual chapters stress various paranormal phenomena, such as poltergeists, Uri Geller, and so on. Medical focus.

418. Emmons, Charles F. *Chinese Ghosts and ESP: a Study of Paranormal Beliefs and Experiences.* Metuchen, N.J.: Scarecrow Press, 1982. 297 pp. illus. bibliography. ISBN 0-8108-1492-7.

An interesting study of public opinion in Hong Kong regarding ghosts and ESP.

419. Gauld, Alan, comp. *The Founders of Psychical Research.* London: Routledge & Kegan Paul, 1968. 387 pp.

A well-written, biographical approach to the early days of psychical research. The compiler was the editor of *SPR Journal.*

420. Gooch, Stan. *The Paranormal.* New York: Harper & Row, 1978. 313 pp. index. bibliography. ISBN 0-06011549-1.

Includes essays on paranormal matters, e.g., dreams, ghosts, reincarnation, Kirlian auras, psychic healing, and ESP in animals. Nontechnical writing.

421. Goodman, Jeffrey. *Psychic Archaeology: Time Machine to the Past.* New York: Berkley, 1977. 223 pp. index. illus. bibliography. ISBN 0-399-11843-8.

Originally published by Putnam in 1977. A good overview of the use of psychics in archaeology. Certain sensitives apparently have been successful in locating promising sites for excavations.

422. Greenhouse, Herbert B. *Premonitions: a Leap into the Future.* New York: Bernard Geis, 1971; London: Turnstone, 1972; New York: Warner, 1973. 302 pp. index.

An introduction to the concept of precognition. Many anecdotes and case histories.

423. Gris, Henry, and Dick, William. *The New Soviet Psychic Discoveries: a First-Hand Report on the Latest Breakthroughs in Russian Parapsychology.* London: Sphere, 1980; Souvenir Press, 1979; New York: Warner, 1979. 304 pp. index. ISBN 0-7221-4085-1.

Originally published by Prentice-Hall (Englewood Cliffs, N.J.) in 1978. Examples of the work going on in the psychic field in Russia.

424. Haynes, Renee. *The Seeing Eye, the Seeing I: Perception, Sensory and Extra-Sensory.* New York: St. Martin's, 1976; London: Hutchinson, 1976. 224 pp. index. bibliographic references.

A book designed to help the reader look beyond the accepted range of vision. Includes cases and anecdotes. Easier to read than many books in this area.

425. Heywood, Rosalind. *Beyond the Reach of Sense.* New York: Dutton, 1961. 224 pp. index.

Originally published by Chatto & Windus (London) in 1959 under the title *The Sixth Sense.* A revised edition is available from Penguin (Harmondsworth, Eng.). A good, basic introduction to parapsychology.

426. Hintze, Naomi A., and Pratt, J. Gaither. *The Psychic Realm: What Can You Believe?* New York: Random House, 1975. 269 pp. index. bibliography. ISBN 0-394-49538-1.

A novelist and a parapsychologist present joint discussions on ESP, astral projection, psi in animals, possession, precognition, altered states of consciousness, psychic surgery, faith healing, ghosts, mediums, reincarnation, resurrection, and dreams. For each topic, Hintze describes an actual occurrence and Pratt explains it.

427. Holroyd, Stuart. *Psi and the Consciousness Explosion.* New York: Taplinger, 1977; London: Bodley Head, 1977. 234 pp. index. bibliographic references. ISBN 0-8008-6556-1.

The author presents a strong case for using prayer, meditation, and belief to restore one's spiritual dimensions. Many examples, international in scope, are included.

428. Inglis, Brian. *Natural and Supernatural: a History of the Paranormal from Earliest Times to 1914.* London: Abacus, 1979. 579 pp. index. bibliography. ISBN 0-349-11826-4.

Originally published by Hodder & Stoughton (London) in 1977. A useful and unusual (since it covers an earlier period than most histories in this field) survey of paranormal phenomena as they were viewed by different societies through history. A sequel, *Science and Parascience* (London: Hodder & Stoughton, 1984), covers the modern period.

429. Irwin, Harvey J. *Psi and the Mind: an Information Processing Approach.* Metuchen, N.J.: Scarecrow Press, 1979. 193 pp. index. bibliography. ISBN 0-8108-1258-4.

An examination of psi skills and how they work, viewed as information-processing systems in the mind. Emphasis is on the parallel process of memory.

430. Jacobson, Nils O. *Life Without Death? On Parapsychology, Mysticism & the Question of Survival.* New York: Delacorte, 1971. 339 pp. index. ISBN 0-85500-026-0.

Translated from the Swedish *Liv efter Döden?* by Sheila La Farge. A Swedish psychologist looks at parapsychology, including speaking in tongues and voices from space. Case studies are provided.

431. Johnson, Raynor C. *The Imprisoned Splendor.* New York: Harper & Row, 1953. 424 pp. index. bibliography.

An important and widely cited work. A synthesis of science, physical research, philosophy, and religion.

432. Knight, David C. *The ESP Reader*. Secaucus, N.J.: Castle Books, 1969. 432 pp.

This edition was published in arrangement with Grosset & Dunlap. An anthology of classic articles from the field.

433. Koestler, Arthur. *The Roots of Coincidence*. New York: Random House, 1972; Vintage, 1973; London: Hutchinson, 1972. 149 pp. index. bibliography. ISBN 0-394-48038-4.

Postscript by Renee Haynes. An argument in favor of the existence of ESP.

434. Krippner, Stanley. *Human Possibilities: Mind Exploration in the USSR and Eastern Europe*. New York: Anchor Press / Doubleday, 1980. 348 pp. index. bibliography. ISBN 0-385-12805-3.

Information gathered firsthand by the author on many trips. Includes information on Kirlian photography, bioenergetics, psychic healing, holistic medicine, psychology, hypnosis, dowsing, electromagnetic fields, and Russian folk healing.

435. Ludwig, Jan, ed. *Philosophy and Parapsychology*. Buffalo, N.Y.: Prometheus Books, 1978. 454 pp. bibliography. ISBN 0-87975-075-8.

A balanced collection of pieces, including works by philosophers, psychologists, parapsychologists, and skeptics. The articles span a period from 1949 to 1954. Many of the works are considered classics.

436. MacKenzie, Andrew. *The Unexplained*. London: Andrew Barker, 1966. 176 pp.

Published by Abelard-Schuman (New York) in 1970 with the subtitle *Some Strange Cases in Psychical Research*. Barker edition has an introduction by H. H. Price.

437. Mauskopf, Seymour H., and McVaugh, Michael R. *The Elusive Science: Origins of Experimental Psychical Research*. Baltimore: Johns Hopkins University Press, 1980. 388 pp. index. illus. bibliographic references. ISBN 0-8018-2331-5.

Afterword by J. B. and L. E. Rhine. A history of parapsychology, with emphasis on the history of research in the field. Very pro-Rhine.

438. Mishlove, Jeffrey. *Psi Development Systems*. Jefferson, N.C.: McFarland, 1983. 304 pp. index. bibliography. ISBN 0-89950-035-8.

Explores all kinds of systems purporting to enhance psychic abilities.

439. Moore, R. Laurence. *In Search of White Crows: Spiritualism, Parapsychology and American Culture*. New York: Oxford University Press, 1977. 310 pp. bibliography. ISBN 0-19-502259-9.

> Contents include the history and development of spiritualism in nineteenth-century America, and a review of psychical research. Thoughtful, scholarly approach. "A book about people who believe in white crows" (Preface).

440. Motoyama, Hiroshi. *Science and the Evolution of Consciousness: Chakras, Ki, and Psi*. Brookline, Mass.: Autumn Press, 1978, distributed by Random House. 149 pp. illus. bibliographic references. ISBN 0-394-73634-6.

> With Rande Brown. Introduction by William A. Tiller. Foreword by E. Stanton Makey. Afterword by Harold Sherman. The author discusses the measurement of vital forces which emanate from living beings.

441. Murphy, Gardner. *Challenge of Psychical Research: a Primer of Parapsychology*. Westport, Conn.: Greenwood Press, 1979; New York: Harper & Row, 1961. 297 pp. index. illus. ISBN 0–313–21048–9.

> With the collaboration of Laura A. Dale. An important work divided into sections on spontaneous (uncontrolled) cases, experimental telepathy, experimental clairvoyance, precognition, psychokinesis, and survival. A basic text.

442. Nash, Carroll B. *Science of Psi: ESP and PK*. Springfield, Ill.: Charles C. Thomas, 1978. 299 pp. bibliography. ISBN 0-398-03803-1.

> An excellent beginning text. Includes a glossary. Expecially good for statistical information.

443. Ornstein, Robert Evan, ed. *The Nature of Human Consciousness: a Book of Readings*. New York: Viking Press, 1973. 514 pp. illus. ISBN 0-670-50480-7.

> Classic articles on psychology, parapsychology, esoteric psychologies, Sufism, and biological rhythms.

444. Ostrander, Sheila, and Schroeder, Lynn. *Psychic Discoveries behind the Iron Curtain*. Englewood Cliffs, N.J.: Prentice-Hall, 1970. 443 pp. index. illus. bibliography.

> Introduction by Ivan T. Sanderson. An excellent overview of various psychic happenings and experiments in Communist countries.

445. Owen, Robert Dale. *Footfalls on the Boundary of Another World.* Philadelphia: J. B. Lippincott, 1860. 528 pp. index. bibliography.

Preface explains that the author, son of socialist and spiritualist Robert Owen, became interested in the occult while serving as minister to Naples for the U.S. State Department. Contains sections on the nature of the impossible, sleep and dreams, hauntings, apparitions, and death.

446. Panati, Charles. *Supersenses: Our Potential for Parasensory Experience.* Anchor Press / Doubleday, 1976; New York: Quadrangle / New York Times Book Co., 1974. 341 pp. index. illus. bibliography. ISBN 0-385-11192-4.

A fine overview of research methodologies in the field, and laboratory and statistical analysis. Discusses experiments in telepathy, precognition, clairvoyance, psychokinesis, psychic healing, dream ESP, astral projection, hypnosis and ESP, mysticism, and psi.

447. Randall, John L. *Parapsychology and the Nature of Life.* New York: Harper Colophon, 1977. 256 pp. index. illus. bibliography. ISBN 0-06-090571-9.

Originally published by Harper & Row (New York) in 1975. Good discussion of the development of parapsychology and its growing acceptance in science.

448. Rhine, Joseph Banks. *Extrasensory Perception.* Boston: Bruce Humphries, 1934. 240 pp. illus. bibliographic references.

First published for the Boston Society for Psychic Research in 1934. Foreword by William McDougall. Introduction by Walter Franklin Prince. A classic work in the field by one of the noted early researchers. Rhine's first book which discusses his famous research at Duke University.

449. Rhine, Louisa Ella. *The Invisible Picture: a Study of Psychic Experiences.* Jefferson, N.C.: McFarland, 1981. 267 pp. index. bibliography. ISBN 0-89950-015-3.

The report of Rhine's lifework on spontaneous, psychic phenomena (uncontrolled by experimental boundaries). A fine analysis of a great deal of anecdotal material. "It is a factual account of a decades-long study of a large number of personal experiences that seemed to be psychic" (Preview).

450. Rogo, D. Scott. *In Search of the Unknown: the Odyssey of a Psychical Investigator.* New York: Taplinger, 1976. 190 pp. ISBN 0-8008-4194-8.

> A sprightly, interesting autobiography of a psychic investigator. Many anecdotes and case studies. Practical advice on encouraging the occurrence of ESP.

451. Schmeidler, Gertrude R., and McConnell, R. A. *ESP and Personality Patterns.* New Haven, Conn.: Yale University Press, 1958; Westport, Conn.: Greenwood Press, 1973. 110 pp. index. bibliography.

> The findings of the well-known sheep and goat experiments are discussed here, along with information on Rorschach tests.

452. Schul, Bill. *The Psychic Power of Animals.* New York: Fawcett, 1976. 213 pp.

> Reports of what would be considered paranormal behavior in animals.

453. Smith, Eleanor Touhey. *Psychic People.* New York: Bantam, 1969; William Morrow, 1968. 197 pp. bibliography.

> Chapters on Jean-Baptiste Vianney, Frederick Bligh Bond, Joan Grant, Daniel Home, Amanda Theodosia Jones, Mollie Fancher, Hester Dowden, Helene Smith, Edeltraud Fulda, Leonora Piper, Mrs. John H. Curran, Eileen Garrett, Emanuel Swedenborg, Caryll Houselander, Henry Gross, Fredericka Hauffe, Geraldine Cummins, Cheiro, and Sidney Dickinson.

454. Smith, Susy. *ESP.* New York: Pyramid Books, 1962. 189 pp.

> A good survey, although now dated, written in layman's language.

455. Targ, Russell, and Puthoff, Harold E. *Mind-Reach: Scientists Look at Psychic Ability.* New York: Dell, 1978; Delacorte / E. Friede, 1977; London: Jonathan Cape, 1977; Paladin, 1978. 230 pp. index. illus. bibliographic references. ISBN 0-440-55665-1.

> Introduction by Margaret Mead. Foreword by Richard Bach. A journalistically written report of the parapsychological research at Stanford Research Institute in the early 1970s.

456. Tart, Charles T. *PSI: Scientific Studies of the Psychic Realm.* New York: Dutton, 1977. 241 pp. indexes. bibliography. ISBN 0-525-47472-2.

A philosophical exploration of Tart's research and that of others in the past few decades. Includes information on most psi phenomena.

457. Tyrrell, George Nugent Merle. *Science and Psychical Phenomena and Apparitions.* New Hyde Park, N.Y.: University Books, 1961. 371, 168 pp. index.

Includes an appendix of cases. A reprint of two earlier works first published in 1938. The foreword by Laura A. Dale to *Science and Psychical Phenomena* (see 391.31) and the preface by H. H. Price to *Apparitions* are included.

458. Vasil'ev, Leonid Leonidovich. *Experiments in Distant Influence: Discoveries by Russia's Foremost Parapsychologist.* New York: Dutton, 1976; London: Wildwood House, 1976. illus. bibliographic references. ISBN 0-525-47421-8.

Original English edition published by the Institute for the Study of Mental Images (Church Crookham, England) in 1963 with the title *Experiments in Mental Suggestion.* Edited by Anita Gregory. Russian title: *Eksperimental'nye Issledovaniia Myslennogo Vnusheniia.*

459. Watkins, William Jon. *The Psychic Experiment Book.* Englewood Cliffs, N.J.: Prentice-Hall, 1980. 283 pp. illus. bibliography. ISBN 0-13-73198-1.

A series of over a hundred experiments to try in a variety of areas; biofeedback, meditation, mental imagery, psychic healing, etc.

460. Wheatley, James M. O., and Edge, Hoyt L., eds. *Philosophical Dimensions of Parapsychology.* Springfield, Ill.: Charles C. Thomas, 1976. 483 pp.

A collection of papers and articles on the philosophy of parapsychology.

461. White, John Warren, and Krippner, Stanley eds. *Future Science: Life Energies and the Physics of Paranormal Phenomena.* Garden City, N.Y.: Doubleday / Anchor Press, 1977. 598 pp. illus. bibliography. ISBN 0-385-11203-3.

Organized into six major parts: "X" energy, occult forces of life, geometry of the paranormal, from psychics to metaphysics, new technology, and social dimensions. Most of the articles were gathered from a few journals in the field. Scholarly.

462. Yeterian, Dixie. *Casebook of a Psychic Detective*. New York: Stein & Day, 1981. 208 pp. index.

> Accounts (including lots of dialogue) of cases the author has been involved with through the years. Melodramatic, but she knows how psychics may apply their gifts.

See also items 38.7, 39.7, 39.8, 39.20.

Out-of-the-Body Experiences

463. Black, David. *Ekstasy: Out-of-the-Body Experiences*. Indianapolis: Bobbs-Merrill, 1975. 243 pp. index. bibliography.
ISBN 0-672-51972-0.

> Divided into four parts: introduction, laboratory experiments, theories, and conclusions. The author interviewed psychics and psychic researchers and visited a number of research centers to gather information for this book.

464. Green, Celia. *Out-of-the-Body Experiences*. New York: Ballantine Books, 1968. 170 pp. index.

> Foreword by H. H. Price. The author is director of the Institute of Psychophysical Research in Oxford, England. One of the first works on this important subject.

465. Mitchell, Janet Lee. *Out-of-the-Body Experiences: a Handbook*. Jefferson, N.C.: McFarland, 1981. 140 pp. index. bibliography.
ISBN 0-89950-031-5.

> Foreword by Gertrude Schmeidler. A convincing case for OBE, presented by a researcher in the field who believes that the number of anecdotal reports of the phenomenon throughout history alone is important proof of its existence.

466. Monroe, Robert A. *Journeys Out of the Body*. Garden City, N.Y.: Anchor Press, 1977. updated ed. 280 pp. ISBN 0-385-00861-9.

> Originally published by Doubleday (Garden City, N.Y.) in 1971. A personal account by an OBE traveler.

467. Rogo, D. Scott, ed. *Mind beyond the Body: the Mystery of ESP Projection*. Harmondsworth, Eng. and New York: Penguin, 1978. 365 pp. bibliographic references. ISBN 0-14-004590-9.

Divided into four parts dealing with descriptions of OBEs, laboratory investigations, reports from subjects, and possible theories.

Psychokinesis

468. Clark, Adrian V. *Psycho-Kinesis: Moving Matter with Mind*. West Nyack, N.Y.: Parker, 1973. 218 pp. bibliographic references.

A space scientist uses case studies to illustrate how to obtain fame, fortune, power, love, and friendship by means of psychokinesis.

469. Hasted, John B. *The Metal-Benders*. London: Routledge & Kegan Paul, 1981. 279 pp. index. illus. bibliographic references. ISBN 0-7100-0597-0.

A technical account of the author's experiments in the area. Heavy concentration on physics.

470. Owen, Iris M. *Conjuring up Philip: an Adventure in Psychokinesis*. New York: Harper & Row, 1976; Pocket Books, 1977. 217 pp. bibliography. ISBN 0-06-013279-5.

The author was assisted by Margaret Sparrow. An account of a group experiment (by the Toronto Society for Psychical Research) in which an entity named Philip either was created or materialized.

471. Panati, Charles, ed. *The Geller Papers: Scientific Observations on the Paranormal Powers of Uri Geller*. Boston: Houghton Mifflin, 1976. 317 pp. illus. bibliographic references. ISBN 0-395-24351-3.

A collection of articles dealing with "checks" on Geller's abilities. Some appeared first in popular periodicals.

472. Robinson, Diana. *To Stretch a Plank: a Survey of Psychokinesis*. Chicago: Nelson-Hall, 1980. 277 pp. indexes. bibliography.ISBN 0-88229-404-0.

Nicely written, easy-to-understand book on the history of and current scene in PK.

See also item 39.20.

Clairvoyance and Dowsing

473. Barrett, Sir William, and Besterman, Theodore. *The Divining Rod: an Experimental and Psychological Investigation.* New Hyde Park, N.Y.: University Books, 1968. 336 pp. index illus. bibliography.

> Originally published by Methuen (London) in 1926. Foreword by Leslie Shepard in the University Books reprint edition. Scholarly and thorough treatment of the subject. Focuses primarily on Britain, with an appendix on American aspects.

474. Bird, Christopher. *The Divining Hand: the Art of Searching for Water, Oil, Minerals, and Other Natural Resources and Anything Lost, Missing, or Badly Needed.* New York: Dutton, 1979. 340 pp. index. illus. bibliography. ISBN 0-525-09373-7.

> Illustrated by Thomas Heston. Covers the history of dowsing during the past five centuries, as well as current practices. Includes speculation on how it may work.

475. Hitching, Francis. *Dowsing: the Psi Connection.* Garden City, N.Y.: Anchor Books, 1978. 306 pp. index. bibliography. ISBN 0-385-12125-3.

> The history and tradition of dowsing throughout the world. The author suggests that dowsing is a psychic talent that can be developed with practice. Includes exercises for this purpose.

476. LeShan, Lawrence L. *The Medium, the Mystic and the Physicist, toward a General Theory of the Paranormal.* New York: Viking Press, 1974; London: Turnstone, 1974. 299 pp. bibliographic references. ISBN 0-670-46566-6.

> More recent edition published by Turnstone in 1980 with the title *Clairvoyant Reality: towards a General Theory of the Paranormal.* In three sections: similarities between clairvoyance, mysticism, and physics; psychic healing; and probable advances in psychic healing.

Auras and the Kirlian Effect

477. Butler, Walter Ernest. *How to Read the Aura.* London: Aquarian Press, 1971, distributed by Samuel Weiser. 64 pp. ISBN 0-87728-090-8.

Paths to Inner Power series. Contents: what is the aura?, the structure of the aura, the circuit of force, the emotional-mental aura, and developing auric sight.

478. Johnson, Kendall. *The Living Aura: Radiation Field Photography and the Kirlian Effect*. New York: Hawthorne Books, 1976. 178 pp. index. illus. ISBN 0-8015-4312-6.

Foreword by Thelma Moss. A discussion of procedures, and many examples by the first American to reproduce the Kirlian effect.

479. Stanford, Ray. *What Your Aura Tells Me*. Garden City, N.Y.: Doubleday, 1977. 151 pp. ISBN 0-385-07060-9.

A very personal account by a psychic who describes what he sees in auras and what they may mean.

Telepathy

480. Carrington, Whately. *Telepathy: an Outline of Its Facts,Theory, and Implications*. London: Methuen, 1945. 170 pp. index. bibliography.

An important work in the field.

481. Seal, S. G., and Bateman, F. *Modern Experiments in Telepathy*. London: Faber & Faber, 1954; New Haven, Conn.: Yale University Press, 1954. 425 pp. index.

An overview of telepathic experimentation. Interesting for the period covered.

Altered States of Consciousness

482. Aaron, Bernard, and Osmond, Humphrey. *Psychedelics: the Uses and Implications of Hallucinogenic Drugs*. Garden City, N.Y.: Doubleday, 1970. 512 pp. index. bibliography.

A collection of essays on the nature of the experience, anthropological considerations, effects of psychedelics on religion, psychedelic effects on mental functioning, non-drug analogues to the psychedelic state, therapeutic applications, and the sociology of psychedelics in the current scene.

483. Belo, Jane. *Trance in Bali.* Westport, Conn.: Greenwood Press, 1977, 1960. 284 pp. illus. ISBN 0-8371-9652-3.

Preface by Margaret Mead. Reprint of an edition published by Columbia University Press. An ethnological study of religious trance in Bali, Indonesia.

484. Dingwall, Eric J., ed. *Abnormal Hypnotic Phenonmena: a Survey of Nineteenth-Century Cases.* New York: Barnes & Noble, 1968; London: J. & A. Churchill, 1967. 4 vols. illus.

Contents: volume 1—France, edited by E. J. Dingwall; volume 2—Belgium and the Netherlands, Germany, and Scandinavia, edited by G.Zorab, L. Moser, and E. Bjelfvenstan; volume 3—Russia and Poland, Italy, Spain, Portugal, and Latin America, edited by L. Zielinski, L. Leppo, and E. J. Dingwall; and volume 4—United States of America and Great Britain, edited by Alan Angoff and E. J. Dingwall.

485. Donahoe, James J. *Enigma: Psychology, the Paranormal, and Self-Transformation.* Oakland, Calif.: Bench Press, 1979. 199 pp. index. bibliography. ISBN 0-916534-09-X.

Glossary included. An exploration of dreams as a paranormal experience.

486. Jung, Carl Gustav, ed. *Man and His Symbols.* Garden City, N.Y.: Doubleday, 1964; London: Aldus Books, 1964. 727 pp. index. illus. bibliographic notes.

Final editing was done after Jung's death by M. L. von Franz. Explains in relatively simple terms to the general reader the symbolism Jung saw in dreams. Contents include a general chapter on dreams, by Jung; the influence of ancient myths, by Joseph L. Henderson; the process of individuation, by M. L. von Franz; symbolism in the visual arts, by Aniela Jaffe; and symbols in an individual analysis, by Jolande Jacobi.

487. Miller, Gustavus Hindman. *10,000 Dreams Interpreted.* Chicago: M. A. Donahue, 1931. 617 pp. index.

A standard reference on the meaning of dreams, arranged in dictionary format.

488. Robinson, Lady Stearn, and Corbett, Tom. *The Dreamer's Dictionary.* New York: Warner, 1974; London: Souvenir Press, 1974; Coronet, 1975. 382 pp. ISBN 0-446-30610-X.

Dictionary arrangement of 3,000 items and their meanings in dreams. Descriptions are briefer than in the Miller title (item 487), and generally provide more positive interpretations.

489. Shapin, Betty, and Coly, Lisette, eds. *PSI and States of Awareness: Proceedings of an International Conference Held in Paris, France, August 24–26, 1977.* New York: Parapsychology Foundation, 1978. 278 pp. illus. bibliographic references. ISBN 0-912328-30-4.

The text of 14 conference papers, approximately half on laboratory research.

490. Ullman, Montague, Krippner, Stanley, and Vaughan, Alan. *Dream Telepathy.* New York: Macmillan, 1973; London: Turnstone, 1973; Baltimore: Penguin, 1974. 300 pp. index. illus. bibliography. ISBN 0-85500-012-0.

A solid contribution to the literature. Includes spontaneous telepathic dreams, experimental studies at the dream lab (Menninger Dream Laboratory, Brooklyn, where Ullman was director), research implications, and a number of appendixes with additional information on dream research.

See also items 39.5, 553.

7
GHOSTS, POLTERGEISTS, AND HAUNTINGS

GHOSTS, n. There is one insuperable obstacle to a belief in
   ghosts. A ghost never comes naked: he appears either in a
   winding-sheet or "in his habit as he lived." To believe in
   him, then, is to believe that not only have the dead the
   power to make themselves visible after there is nothing
   left of them, but that the same power inheres in textile
   fabrics.

Ambrose Bierce,
The Devil's Dictionary

Ghosts long have been the subject of fascination for many people.
Those concerned with spiritualism (see chapter 5) have considered
such apparitions as proof of life beyond death and / or as links with
another plane of existence. Parapsychologists (see chapter 6) have
viewed abnormal activity of this sort as a suitable subject for scientific
investigation, primarily that of the phenomena known as poltergeists. However, research and scientific investigation in these areas
have only existed for the past century.

There is a long tradition of ghost stories, and the appeal of the
haunted house cannot be denied. The majority of Americans view
such tales indulgently for the most part, relegating ghost stories to
the realm of escapist literature and remembrances of childhood
shiverings. However, many people do believe in the existence of
ghosts; in fact, recent polls have shown that approximately 20 percent
of the English believe in ghosts. Haunted houses are sought in Britain
and real estate prices go up when a house is rumored to be haunted.
In America, of course, more people think of the horrors of Amityville
than the charms of the Canterville ghost when considering purchase
of a possibly haunted house. Local folklore abounds with ghost
stories and tales of haunted houses. Those interested in ghostly
phenomena in particular regions should turn to materials usually
located in local historical societies and public libraries.

Material in this chapter is divided as follows:

General Works

491. Bardens, Dennis. *Ghosts and Hauntings.* New York: Taplinger, 1965; Ace Books, 1973. 255 pp. illus.

> A good collection of true ghost stories.

492. Bayliss, Raymond. *Animal Ghosts.* New Hyde Park, N.Y.: University Books, 1970. 188 pp. bibliography.

> Foreword by Robert Crookall. Ghosts of dogs, horses, and other beasts.

493. Brown, Raymond Lamont. *Phantom Soldiers.* New York: Drake Publications, 1975. 184 pp. index. illus. maps. bibliography. ISBN 0-87749-777-X.

> True tales of hauntings and ghosts from the military. Mostly British cases (includes some European and one American). "The selection of material herein collected is first of all taken from the narrative of people of unimpeachable integrity . . ." (Introduction).

494. Brown, Raymond Lamont. *Phantoms of the Sea: Legends, Customs and Superstitions.* New York: Taplinger, 1973; London: Patrick Stephens, 1972. 192 pp. illus. bibliography.

> Sailors' superstitions and seafaring folklore, as well as disappearances such as the *Mary Celeste.*

495. Brown, Raymond Lamont. *Phantoms of the Theater.* Nashville: Thomas Nelson, 1977; London: Satellite Books, 1978. 154 pp. bibliography. ISBN 0-905186-64-8.

> European and American theatrical hauntings. Most of the ghosts are of deceased actors. Includes information on ghosts in dramatic works.

496. Fodor, Nandor. *On the Trail of the Poltergeist.* New York: Citadel Press, 1958. 222 pp. illus.

The learned and respected occult expert discusses the phenomenon of the poltergeist.

497. Gauld, Alan, and Cornell, A. D. *Poltergeists*. London: Routledge & Kegan Paul, 1979. 406 pp. index. illus. bibliography. ISBN 0-7100-0185-1.

Descriptions of cases involving poltergeists. These have been analyzed in light of various poltergeist theories and classified according to type.

498. Gettings, Fred. *Ghosts in Photographs: the Extraordinary Story of Spirit Photography*. New York: Harmony Books, 1978. 152 pp. illus. bibliographic references. ISBN 0-517-52930-0.

Text explains the history and development of spirit photography. Many examples, such as the famous photo of Mrs. Lincoln with the spirit of the assassinated president standing behind her with his hands on her shoulders, are provided. Includes a discussion of quacks.

499. Green, Andrew. *Ghost Hunting: a Practical Guide*. St. Albans, Eng.: Mayflower, 1976; Garnstone, 1973. 159 pp. illus. bibliography. ISBN 0-583-12500-X.

A professional ghost hunter shares techniques and ideas. For amateurs who may wish to conduct field investigations.

500. Green, Celia, and McCreery, Charles. *Apparitions*. London: Hamilton, 1975. 218 pp. index. bibliography. ISBN 0-241-89182-5.

Institute of Psychophysical Research Proceedings. Case studies of true ghost stories collected in recent years. The authors draw some conclusions, in addition to reporting the eyewitness accounts.

501. Haining, Peter. *A Dictionary of Ghost Lore*. Englewood Cliffs, N.J.: Prentice-Hall, 1984. 225 pp. index. illus. ISBN 0-13-210477-6.

A Reward Book. Published by Robert Hale (London) as *A Dictionary of Ghosts*. Dictionary format. International scope with British bias. Informal, popular style of writing. Index of names and places. Covers mediums, authorities, and victims, as well as ghosts. Not reviewed as favorably as Haining's works in the black magic and witchcraft areas.

502. Haining, Peter. *Ghosts: the Illustrated History*. New York: Macmillan, 1975; London: Sidgwick & Jackson, 1974. 126 pp. illus.

Pictorial account of famous ghosts and hauntings.

503. Hippisley, Coxe, and Dacres, Anthony. *Haunted Britain: a Guide to Supernatural Sites Frequented by Ghosts, Witches, Poltergeists and Other Mysterious Beings.* New York: McGraw-Hill, 1973; London: Hutchinson, 1973; Pan, 1975. 201 pp. index. illus. maps. bibliography. ISBN 0-330-24328-4.

> A geographical approach to the ghosts of Great Britain. An excellent travel guide for the occult tourist.

504. Lang, Andrew. *The Book of Dreams and Ghosts.* Hollywood, Calif.: Newcastle, 1972; New York: Causeway Books, 1974; San Bernardino, Calif.: Borgo Press, 1980. 301 pp. illus. ISBN 0-87877-010-0.

> First published in 1897. A collection of true tales of ghosts, haunted houses, and psychic occurrences by the noted folklorist and fairy-tale author / compiler.

505. MacKenzie, Andrew. *A Gallery of Ghosts: an Anthology of Reported Experience.* New York: Taplinger, 1973. 160 pp. ISBN 0-8008-3122-5.

> A charming account of the author's experiences with ghostly happenings.

506. O'Donnell, Elliott. *Elliott O'Donnell's Casebook of Ghosts.* New York: Taplinger, 1969. 287 pp. illus.

> Ghostly happenings, some poltergeist in nature.

507. Playfair, Guy Lyon. *This House is Haunted: the True Story of a Poltergeist.* New York: Stein & Day, 1980; London: Sphere, 1981. 290 pp. illus. ISBN 0-8128-2732-5.

> First published by Souvenir Press (London) in 1980 as *This House is Haunted: an Investigation of the Enfield Poltergeist.* "I don't know what a poltergeist is, and nor does anybody else" (Preface).

508. Rogo, D. Scott. *The Poltergeist Experience: Investigations into Ghostly Phenomena.* New York and Harmondsworth, Eng.: Penguin, 1979. 301 pp. index. bibliographic references. ISBN 0-14-00-4995-9.

> An international survey of poltergeist activity. Some historical background included. Author does a good job of synthesizing common characteristics.

509. Roll, William George. *The Poltergeist*. Metuchen, N.J.: Scarecrow Press, 1976; New York: Doubleday, 1972. 208 pp. illus. ISBN 0-8108-0984-2.

An overview of the subject.

510. Salter, W. H. *Ghosts and Apparitions*. London: G. Bell, 1938. 138 pp.

Psychic Experiences series. Glossary included.

511. Sitwell, Sacheverell. *Poltergeists: an Introduction and Examination Followed by Chosen Instances*. New York: University Books, 1959. 418 pp.

Introduction (including poem) by Edith Sitwell. Decorations by Irene Hawkins. Silhouettes by Cruikshank. A general discussion of poltergeists followed by specific cases, such as the Epworth phenomenon, written by John Wesley in 1716; Willington Mill, by John Practer (1835); Tedworth drummer, by Joseph Glanvil (1661); Hinton Ampner haunting, by Mrs. Ricketts (1771); Calvados Castle, by Camille Flammarion (1875); German poltergeists, by Catherine Crow (covers 1773–1849); and later nineteenth century cases by other authors.

512. Thompson, Charles John Samuel. *The Mystery and Lore of Apparitions: with Some Accounts of Ghosts, Spectres, Phantoms and Boggarts in Early Times*. Detroit: Gale Research, 1974. reprint. 331 pp. illus.

Originally published by Frederick A. Stokes (New York) in 1931. Includes hauntings from ancient Greece, Rome, and the Orient to the present time. Emphasis is on European hauntings.

513. Turner, James. *Unlikely Ghosts*. New York: Taplinger, 1969. 218 pp. ISBN 0-8008-79406.

A collection of true ghost stories.

See also items 39.14, 457, 586.4, 880.

English Ghosts

514. Alexander, Marc. *Haunted Castles*. London: Muller, 1974. 352 pp. illus.

Ghosts in one of their favorite sites.

515. Alexander, Marc. *Haunted Churches and Abbeys of Britain.* London: A. Barker, 1978. 178 pp. index. illus. maps. ISBN 0-213-16677-1.

Ghosts in sanctified locations somehow seem to be scarier.

516. Alexander, Marc. *Phantom Britain: This Spectre'd Isle.* London: Muller, 1975. 256 pp. index. illus. map.

An account of English ghosts and hauntings. An overview of some of Britain's best-known haunts.

517. Chambers, Aidan. *Great British Ghosts.* London: Pan, 1974. 125 pp. illus. ISBN 0-330-24070-6.

Piccolo True Adventures series. Illustrated by Barry Wilkinson. Traditional, picturesque ghosts from Victorian times to the modern day in locales such as bowling alleys. A children's book, but useful for adults as well. The author also has written *Ghosts That Haunt You, Ghosts after Ghosts,* and *Ghosts and Hauntings.*

518. Christian, Roy. *Ghosts and Legends.* North Pomfret, Vt.: David & Charles, 1976. 156 pp.

Strongly folkloric in nature. Mainly ghosts connected with ruined historic piles and other traditional locales.

519. Forman, John. *Haunted East Anglia.* London: Fontana, 1976; Robert Hale, 1974. 224 pp. index. illus. ISBN 0-00-634009-1.

Superstitions and folklore, plus ghosts.

520. Green, Andrew. *Our Haunted Kingdom.* London: Wolfe Publications, 1973. 367 pp. illus. bibliography.

Over 350 authenticated hauntings and / or case histories recorded in the United Kingdom over the past twenty-five years.

521. Green, Andrew. *Phantom Ladies.* Folkestone, Eng.: Bailey & Swinfen, 1977. 151 pp. illus. bibliography. ISBN 0-561-00295-9.

Ghost Hunters' Library. A guide to true ghost happenings in Great Britain, arranged geographically by county.

522. Hallam, Jack. *Ghosts' Who's Who.* North Pomfret, Vt.: David & Charles, 1977. 157 pp. illus. map. bibliography. ISBN 0-7153-7452-4.

A biographical dictionary of English ghosts. Includes not only "people" but also animals. Legends, as well as documented cases, are included.

523. Holzer, Hans W. *The Great British Ghost Hunt.* Indianapolis: Bobbs-Merrill, 1975; London: W. H. Allen, 1976. 207 pp. illus. ISBN 0-672-51846-7.

The author communes with various well-known ghosts in England and Scotland with the help of a medium.

524. Moss, Peter. *Ghosts over Britain: True Accounts of Modern Hauntings.* London: Sphere, 1976; Elm Tree, 1977. 156 pp. ISBN 0-7221-6192-1.

Sixty true ghost and poltergeist tales, gathered specifically for this book.

525. Price, Harry. *The Most Haunted House in England: Ten Years' Investigation of Borley Rectory.* Bath, Eng.: Chivers, 1980. 255 pp. index. illus. map. ISBN 0-85594-075-1.

Originally published by Longman's Green (London) in 1940. A well-documented account of hauntings and their investigation. The house burned and is no longer available for examination. (See item 875 for a debunking view of Price.)

526. Underwood, Peter. *A Gazetteer of British Ghosts.* New York: Walker, 1975, 1971; London: Souvenir Press, 1971; Pan, 1973; Fontana, 1974. 255 pp. illus. ISBN 0-8027-0471-9.

Dictionary arrangement of ghostly spots. Indexed by county. Mostly English sites are covered.

527. Whitaker, Terence W. *Lancashire's Ghosts and Legends.* London: Granada, 1980. 224 pp. index. illus. ISBN 0-583-13546-3.

An account of some scary, occult-type phenomena and ghost legends of the area.

528. Whitaker, Terence W. *Yorkshire's Ghosts and Legends.* London: Granada, 1983. 223 pp. index. illus. ISBN 0-583-13592-7.

Foreword by Gerald Main. Traditional ghost stories of northern England.

Irish, Scottish, and Welsh Ghosts

529. Holzer, Hans W. *The Lively Ghosts of Ireland*. Indianapolis: Bobbs-Merrill, 1967. 182 pp. illus.

> A nice assortment of haunted Irish locales.

530. Reynolds, James. *More Ghosts in Irish Houses*. New York: Farrar, Straus, 1956. 276 pp. illus.

> A sequel to *Ghosts in Irish Houses*. About two dozen true Irish ghost stories.

531. Underwood, Peter. *A Gazetteer of Scottish and Irish Ghosts*. London: Souvenir Press, 1973; New York: Walker, 1975. 252 pp. index. illus. ISBN 0-8027-0471-9.

> A companion volume to item 526. Similar format and arrangement.

532. Underwood, Peter. *Ghosts of Wales*. London: Corgi, 1980; Swansea, Wales; C. Davies, 1978. 234 pp. illus. ISBN 0-552-11315-8.

> The Welsh, as well as other Celts, long have been reputed to be very fey. Their ghosts are every bit as mysterious and scary as others.

American Ghosts

533. Anson, Jay. *The Amityville Horror*. Englewood Cliffs, N.J.: Prentice-Hall, 1977; London: W. H. Allen, 1978. 201 pp. ISBN 0-13-32599-6.

> A best-selling book made into a blockbuster movie, this purports to be the true story of a house haunted by restless spirits on Long Island. The sequels, *The Amityville Horror II* and *The Amityville Horror—the Final Chapter*, by John G. Jones, continue the story of the house's inhabitants, who are beset even after leaving the house of horrors.

534. Bartell, Jan Bryant. *Spindrift; Spray from a Psychic Sea*. New York: Hawthorn Books, 1974. 245 pp.

> A true story of a haunted townhouse in Greenwich Village. The writing style is a bit florid and dramatic. "What is detailed herein is presented as it was lived through" (Author's Note).

535. Bell, Charles Bailey. *The Bell Witch: a Mysterious Spirit.* Nashville: Lark Bindery, 1934. 228 pp. illus.

> Reprinted by Charles Elder (Nashville) in 1972 under the title *A Mysterious Spirit.* An account of one of America's best-known poltergeists from the early nineteenth century, who supposedly still causes much grief for the descendants of the Bell family.

536. Clyne, Patricia Edwards. *Ghostly Animals of America.* New York: Dodd, Mead, 1977. 192 pp. illus. ISBN 0-396-07465-0.

> Illustrated by Ted Lewin. Little-known stories of mysterious animal spirits roaming the New World.

537. Holzer, Hans. *Ghosts of the Golden West.* Indianapolis: Bobbs-Merrill, 1968. 220 pp. illus.

> Issued by Swallow Press (Chicago) in 1980 as *Westghosts: the Psychic World of California.* Illustrated by Catherine Buxhoeveden. Accounts of "true" hauntings on the West Coast.

538. Holzer, Hans. *The Ghosts That Walk in Washington.* Garden City, N.Y.: Doubleday, 1971. 232 pp. illus.

> Famous Washington ghosts, including the tales of Lincoln and other dead presidents.

539. Holzer, Hans. *Haunted Hollywood.* Indianapolis: Bobbs-Merrill, 1974. 133 pp. ISBN 0-672-51739-6.

> Movie stars and other actors take on ghostly form.

540. Holzer, Hans. *The Phantoms of Dixie.* Indianapolis: Bobbs-Merrill, 1972. 210 pp. illus.

> Old plantation houses and gloomy swamps provide wonderful backgrounds for a variety of ghosts.

541. Owen, Alan Robert George. *Psychic Mysteries of the North: Discoveries from the Maritime Provinces and Beyond.* New York: Harper & Row, 1975. 243 pp. index. illus. bibliographic references. ISBN 0-601-3266-3.

> Published in Canada under the title *Psychic Mysteries of Canada.* Includes general psychic occurrences, as well as ghost stories and poltergeist activities. Most examples are Canadian.

542. Smith, Susy. *Ghosts around the House.* New York: World, 1970. 191 pp. bibliography.

A sequel to her *Prominent American Ghosts.* Includes one Canadian ghost, as well as tales centered on the infamous Dakota apartment building in New York, the Bell Witch, and other stories.

543. Turner, James. *Ghosts in the South West.* North Pomfret, Vt.: David & Charles, 1973. 165 pp. illus. ISBN 0-7153-6283-1.

Even the empty spaces of the desert provide fruitful grounds for ghosts and folklore legends.

544. Webb, Richard. *Great Ghosts of the West.* Los Angeles: Nash, 1971. 278 pp.

Chatty, supposedly true ghost stories from California, the Mojave Desert, and the Sierra Nevadas. Ghosts are grouped according to personality traits, such as noncommittal ghosts and talkative ghosts.

545. Winer, Richard, and Osborn, Nancy. *Haunted Houses.* New York: Bantam, 1979. 244 pp. index. illus. bibliography.

Sixteen "true" ghost stories, including the tale of James Dean's death car. Sensationalist writing. The first in a series including *More Haunted Houses,* by Richard Winer and Nancy Osborn Ishmael (New York: Bantam, 1981), and *Houses of Horror,* by Richard Winer (New York: Bantam, 1983).

8
PRIMITIVE MAGIC AND BELIEFS

Curse, v.t. Energetically to belabor with a verbal slap-stick. This
is an operation which in literature, particularly in the
drama, is commonly fatal to the victim. Nevertheless, the
liability to a cursing is a risk that cuts but a small figure in
fixing the rates of life insurance.

Ambrose Bierce,
The Devil's Dictionary

Magic has been popular and had many fervent believers throughout
the world at various times. Even today, magic is employed as part of
religious practices and customs in certain parts of the world. Anthropological studies have uncovered many such beliefs, exerting their
influence in various magical systems.

As with other worldwide phenomena, certain similarities can be
observed in a number of these so-called primitive, magical practices.
For example, the idea that certain persons are endowed with the
power to communicate with gods, and share that power with others,
has resulted in a strong shamanistic philosophy in various cultures.
The belief that some gods exhibit human foibles is another common
belief. The idea that the gods can be placated and appealed to
through gifts is yet another such notion.

One fascinating belief system in this area is that of santería, the
formation of a hybrid religion combining the old gods of the West
African, predominantly Yoruban, religion with the Christian saints of
new masters. The continued practice of these syncretic religions has
provided some of the most popular occult fascinations, such as
voodoo.

The material in this chapter is organized into the following sections:

- General Works
- African Roots
- Santería

General Works

546. Baldwin, Gordon C. *Schemers, Dreamers, and Medicine Men: Witchcraft and Magic among Primitive People.* New York: Four Winds Press, 1970. 176 pp. index. bibliography.

Glossary included. General overview. Contains accounts of mana, divination, numbers, ghosts, witches, shamans, and magic in primitive societies.

547. Campbell, Joseph. *The Historical Atlas of World Mythology.* New York: Harper & Row, 1984–. multivol.

Van der Marck Editions. Volume one of this critically acclaimed new work is entitled *The Way of the Animal Power* (ISBN 0-912383-00-3). It recounts the mythic origins of the cosmos and time itself.

548. Campbell, Joseph. *The Masks of God: Primitive Mythology.* New York: Viking Press, 1960; Harmondsworth, London, Eng.: Penguin, 1962. 4 vols.

A classic work on myths and their meanings. Volume one concerns itself with primitive mythology; volume two with Oriental mythology; volume three with occidental mythology; and volume four with creative mythology.

549. Castaneda, Carlos. *The Eagle's Gift.* New York: Simon & Schuster, 1981. 316 pp. ISBN 0-671-23087-5.

The most recent of Castaneda's best-selling works. Although his work is considered fanciful rather than factual by many, the author's influence cannot be denied. Earlier works include *The Second Ring of Power* (New York: Simon & Schuster, 1977), *Tales of Power* (New York: Pocket Books, 1976), and *The Teachings of Don Juan* (New York: Pocket Books, 1974), etc. These books explore the supposed teachings of an old Yaqui Indian to Castaneda, including trances, mystical journeys, and hallucinations induced by peyote. These books have been especially revered by college students.

550. DeMille, Richard. *Castaneda's Journey: the Power and the Allegory.* Santa Barbara, Calif.: Capra Press, 1976. 205 pp.

Despite the author's belief that Castaneda's works are fictional rather than anthropological, he touts them as valuable allegories.

551. Drury, Nevill. *The Shaman and the Magician: Journeys between the Worlds*. London: Routledge & Kegan Paul, 1982. 129 pp. index. illus. bibliography. ISBN 0-71009-100-0.

Foreword by Michael Harner. An exploration ". . . for common denominators between shamanism and contemporary western occultism" (foreword).

552. Eliade, Mircea. *Shamanism*. London: Routledge & Kegan Paul, 1972; New York: Pantheon Books, 1951; Princeton, N.J.: Princeton University Press, 1964.

Princeton University Press edition, Bollingen series 76. Originally published in French, it has been enlarged and revised. Earlier editions have the subtitle *Archaic Techniques of Ecstacy*. A masterful treatment of the subject.

553. Furst, Peter T., ed. *Flesh of the Gods: the Ritualistic Use of Hallucinogens*. New York: Praeger, 1972; London: Allen & Unwin, 1972. 304 pp.

An anthology of the best available anthropological accounts of drugs used in religious experiences.

554. Halifax, Joan. *Shamanic Voices: a Survey of Visionary Narratives*. New York: Dutton, 1979. 268 pp. illus. bibliography. ISBN 0-525-47525-7.

A collection of shamanic visions from the twentieth century. Stresses initiation rather than healing rituals, and the context in which shamans work.

555. Harner, Michael J. *The Way of the Shaman: a Guide to Power and Healing*. New York: Bantam, 1982; Harper & Row, 1980. 214 pp. index. illus. bibliography. ISBN 0-553-20693-1.

A modern shaman shares his secrets in this how-to-do-it book. The author does not profess to understand why shamanism works, but endorses its practice anyway.

556. Jensen, Adolf Ellegard. *Myth and Cult among Primitive Peoples*. Chicago: University of Chicago Press, 1963. 349 pp.

Translated by Marianna Tax Choldin and Wolfgang Weissleder from *Mythos und Kult bei Naturvolkern*. Scholarly.

557. Larsen, Stephen. *The Shaman's Doorway: Opening the Mythic Imagination to Contemporary Consciousness.* New York: Harper & Row, 1976. 244 pp. illus. ISBN 0-06-064929-1.

> A follower of Campbell, Larsen explores the role of myth throughout civilization, including its relationship with reality. Theoretical.

558. Lieban, Richard Warren. *Cebuano Sorcery: Malign Magic in the Philippines.* Berkeley: University of California Press, 1977, 1967. 163 pp. index. illus. bibliography. ISBN 0-520-03420-1.

> Primarily a study of the effects of magical belief on behavior.

559. Mair, Lucy. *Witchcraft.* New York: McGraw-Hill, 1969. 255 pp.

> World University Library. An anthropological study of witchcraft and magic in primitive societies today.

See also item 224.7.

African Roots

560. Bascom, William Russell. *Sixteen Cowries: Yoruba Divination from Africa to the New World.* Indianapolis: Indiana University Press, 1980. 790 pp. bibliography. ISBN 0-25335-280-0.

> The story of the migration of an African belief to the Western Hemisphere.

561. Evans-Pritchard, Edward E. *Witchcraft, Oracles and Magic among the Azande.* Oxford: Clarendon Press, 1976, distributed by Oxford University Press. abridged ed. 265 pp. index. bibliography. ISBN 0-19-874029-8.

> Abridged and introduced by Eva Gillies. Originally published in 1937 with a forward by Prof. C. G. Seligman. An anthropological study of evil in the Azande culture. A very influential work.

562. Marwick, Max G. *Sorcery in Its Social Setting: a Study of the Northern Rhodesian Cewa.* Manchester, Eng.: Manchester University Press, 1965. 339 pp. illus. maps. bibliography.

> An English anthropologist studies witchcraft in Africa.

563. Middleton, John, and Winter, E. H., eds. *Witchcraft and Sorcery in East Africa.* New York: Praeger, 1963. 302 pp. illus. bibliographies.

> Foreword by E. E. Evans-Pritchard. A collection of pieces on sorcery in the old British East African colonies.

564. Swanson, Guy E. *The Birth of the Gods: the Origin of Primitive Beliefs.* Ann Arbor: University of Michigan Press, 1960. 260 pp.

> An exploration of the apparent need of early man to develop and worship supernatural entities.

Santería

565. Bramly, Serge. *Macumba: the Teachings of Maria-José, Mother of the Gods.* New York: St. Martin's, 1977. 214 pp. illus. ISBN 0-312-50338-5.

> Translated by Meg Bogin from *Macumba, forces noires du Bresil,* published by Editions Seghers (Paris) in 1975. Glossary included. The author's account of interviews with the leader of a popular urban congregation in Rio de Janeiro.

566. Chesi, Gert. *Voodoo: Africa's Secret Power.* Austria: Perlinger, 1980. 275 pp. illus. ISBN 3-85399-013-4.

> Translated from *VOODOO: Afrikas geheine Macht.* Coffee-table-book format. Explores the syncretic evolution of the Yoruba religion in West Africa with Christianization attempts by colonists.

567. Deren, Maya. *The Voodoo Gods.* St. Albans, Eng.: Paladin, 1976. 318 pp. index. illus. map. bibliography. ISBN 0-586-08243-3.

> Introduction by Joseph Campbell. Originally published by Thames & Hudson (London) as *Divine Horsemen.* (This version is available as a paperback from Dell, published in 1972.) A careful study, based on considerable field work.

568. González-Wippler, Migene. *Santería: African Magic in Latin America.* Bronx, N.Y.: Original Products, 1981; New York: Julian Press, 1973. 181 pp. index. bibliography. ISBN 0-385-09696-8.

> Glossary included. Discusses the historical background of the Yorubas. Includes a good chart of the syncretic mix, e.g., Oggun, god of iron and war corresponding to St. Peter.

569. Haskins, James. *Voodoo and Hoodoo: Their Tradition and Craft as Revealed by Actual Practitioners.* New York: Stein & Day, 1978. 226 pp. index. illus. bibliography. ISBN 0-8128-2431-8.

> An overview of voodoo in its original African form, its changes into hoodoo in the New World, and its influence on other, more widely accepted religions.

570. Haskins, James. *Witchcraft, Mysticism, and Magic in the Black World.* New York: Doubleday, 1974. 156 pp. index. maps. bibliography. ISBN 0-385-02878-4.

> Includes African roots. Focuses on three legendary voodoo figures: Marie Laveau, High John the Conqueror, and Tituba of Salem Village.

571. Huxley, Francis. *The Invisibles: Voodoo Gods in Haiti.* New York: McGraw-Hill, 1966; London: Rupert Hart-Davis, 1966. 247 pp. illus.

> Glossary of Haitian plants. A personalized account of the investigation of a syncretic belief in Haiti.

572. Langguth, A. J. *Macumba: White and Black Magic in Brazil.* New York: Harper & Row, 1975. 273 pp. ISBN 0-06-012503-9.

> A U.S. writer discovers Brazilian rites and magic.

573. Leacock, Seth, and Leacock, Ruth. *Spirits of the Deep: a Study of an Afro-Brazilian Cult.* Garden City, N.Y.: Doubleday, for The American Museum of Natural History, 1972. 404 pp. illus. index. bibliography.

> Glossary. An account of Batuque in Belem by an American anthropologist and his wife, a historian.

574. Metraux, Alfred. *Voodoo in Haiti.* New York: Schocken, 1972, 1959. 400 pp. illus.

> Beliefs, folklore, and religious rites of Haitian voodoo, probably the best known of the syncretic religions.

575. Pelton, Robert W. *The Complete Book of Voodoo.* New York: Putnam, 1972. 254 pp. illus.

> The author has written a number of books on voodoo, including *Voodoo Signs and Omens* and *Voodoo Secrets from A to Z.* A how-to-do-it approach.

576. St. Clair, David. *Drum and Candle.* Garden City, N.Y.: Double-day, 1971. 304 pp. illus.

> An anecdotal discussion of santería by a popular writer. Includes personal accounts. "These people have managed to stay pure and natural and close to Nature in such a way that the secrets of Nature are revealed to them" (p. 254).

See also item 372.

9
MYTHS, LEGENDS, AND FOLKLORE

Mythology, n. The body of a primitive people's beliefs concerning its origin, early history, heroes, deities and so forth, as distinguished from the true accounts which it invents later.

Ambrose Bierce,
The Devil's Dictionary

One of the areas that endures with persistence in the realm of mysteries is that of myths, legends, and folklore. It is the world of fairy tales, peopled by admirable heroes, evil sorceresses, fire-breathing dragons, and howling werewolves. Not always considered part of the occult, these tales of magic once may have been part of religions. Certainly, some were devised in earlier days as explanations of life's mysteries. Some, such as Greek and Roman myths about the constellations in the sky, may have been created for entertainment as much as educational purposes. Whatever their background, these wonderful stories may have been accepted as truth at one time, and still have fascination today. Why else does the story of Dracula still have the power to hold listeners spellbound? The universal appeal of these stories, in which magic and mystery is ever present, cannot be denied.

For larger-than-life heroes only evil magic is a suitable adversary, and only foul sorcery can bring defeat and death. Perhaps these heroes may not be dead; in Great Britain it is said that Arthur only sleeps in Avalon, and that he will return to save the kingdom in its hour of greatest need. There is a seductive appeal, as well as logic, to such tales. Good and evil are differentiated clearly, and portrayed in striking detail.

Whether or not people actually believe them, these notions remain popular. Because of their mystical elements, they are part of the occult today.

Material in this chapter is organized into the following sections:

- General Works
- Lost Worlds

- Stone Structures
- Fairies and Other Mythical Beings
- Monsters and Mythical Beasts
- Man into Beast
- Vampires

General Works

577. Ashe, Geoffrey, ed. *The Quest for Arthur's Britain*. New York: Praeger, 1968; London: Pall Mall, 1968; Paladin, 1968; Granada, 1971. 282 pp. index. illus. maps. bibliography.

> A careful exploration of the King Arthur legend, with accounts of excavations at Cadbury, Tintagel, Glastonbury, and other sites. Includes a discussion of the influence of the legend as a theme in British imagination and literature.

578. Barber, Richard. *A Companion to World Mythology*. New York: Delacorte, 1979. 312 pp. index. illus. maps. ISBN 0-440-00750-X.

> Illustrated by Pauline Baynes. Dictionary arrangement. Includes indexes of myths, topics, minor characters, and real names and places.

579. Briggs, Katharine Mary. *A Dictionary of British Folktales in the English Language, Incorporating the F. J. Norton Collection*. London: Routledge & Kegan Paul, 1970–71; Bloomington: Indiana University Press, 1970. 2 vols. index. bibliographies. ISBN 0-253-31715-0.

> A lucid discussion of the divisions of folk tales into categories, such as narratives and legends. Relies on the Stith Thompson Motif-Index (see item 597).

580. Bulfinch, Thomas. *Bulfinch's Mythology: the Age of Fable, the Age of Chivalry, Legends of Charlemagne*. New York: Avenel, 1978, distributed by Crown. 2d ed. 957 pp. index. illus. maps. ISBN 0-517-274159.

> Illustrated by Elinore Blaisdell. Many editions of this work exist. First published as three separate works: *The Age of Fable* (1855), *The Age of Chivalry* (1858), and *Legends of Charlemagne* (1863). Mythology is connected with literature in this collection. Major chapters cover classic myths, Nordic myths, King Arthur, the Mabinogeon, Beowulf, Cuchulainn, Hereward the Wake, Robin Hood, and Charlemagne. An example of Victorian scholarship in the area of myth and folklore.

581. Campbell, Joseph. *The Hero with a Thousand Faces*. Princeton, N.J.: Princeton University Press, 1968. 2d ed. 416 pp. illus. bibliography.

> First published in 1949. An exploration of the hero legend in its various guises in various cultures.

582. Cavendish, Richard, ed. *Legends of the World: a Cyclopedia of the Enduring Myths, Legends, and Sagas of Mankind*. New York: Schocken, 1982. 433 pp. index. illus. bibliography. ISBN 0-8052-3805-0.

> Illustrated by Eric Fraser. An international survey of myths and legends, many associated with religions, which have survived to the present. In four sections: the Far East, the Middle East, the West, and Africa and the Americas (also Oceania and Australia). Articles cover such diverse subjects as Buddha, Zoroaster, Sufi saints, Solomon, Cuchulainn, El Cid, Robin Hood, Mwindo, the Virgin of Guadalupe, and the snake-people. A useful, comparative survey of legendary themes, such as outlaws and bandits, is found in the back of the volume, along with a list of contributors.

583. Davidson, Hilda Roderick Ellis. *Gods and Myths of Northern Europe*. Baltimore: Penguin, 1964. 251 pp. bibliography.

> A Pelican Book. A quick, handy source to Norse mythology.

584. Davidson, Hilda Roderick Ellis. *Pagan Scandinavia*. London: Thames & Hudson, 1967; New York: Praeger, 1967. 214 pp. index. illus. maps. bibliography.

> Ancient People and Places series. Traces the rise and decline of various religious cults in Scandinavia from earliest known times to the Christian period.

585. Eastman, Mary Huse. *Index to Fairy Tales, Myths, and Legends*. Boston: Faxon, 1926, 1937–52. 3 vols. supps.

> First published by the Boston Book Co. (Boston) in 1915 in 311 pages. The Faxon edition is in 610 pages with supplements. The work has been updated by Norma Ireland and published as *Index to Fairy Tales 1949–1972; Including Folklore, Legends, and Myths in Collections* (Westwood, Mass.: Faxon, 1973). An index to fairy tales and legends in various anthologies.

586. *The Enchanted World*. Alexandria, Va.: Time-Life Books, 1984–. ? vols. illus. bibliographies.

Chief series consultant, Tristram Potter Coffin. Series editor, Ellen Phillips. A series of handsomely illustrated coffee-table books on mythic and occult themes. Includes the following:

586.1. *Wizards and Witches.* ISBN 0-8094-5209-9.

586.2. *Fairies and Elves.* ISBN 0-8094-5212-X.

586.3. *Dragons.* ISBN 0-8094-5208-1.

586.4. *Ghosts.* ISBN 0-8094-5216-2.

586.5. *Legends of Valor.* ISBN 0-8094-5220-0.

586.6. *Dwarfs.* ISBN 0-8094-5225-1.

586.7. *Magical Beasts.* ISBN 0-8094-5230-8.

586.8. *Night Creatures.* ISBN 0-8094-5234-0.

586.9. *Giants and Ogres.* ISBN 0-8094-5238-0.

586.10. *Spells and Bindings.* ISBN 0-8094-5242-1.

586.11. *Water Spirits.* ISBN 0-8094-5246-4.

586.12. *Humble Heroes.* ISBN 0-8094-5250-2.

586.13. *Fabled Kingdoms.* ISBN 0-8094-5254-5.

586.14. *Fall of Camelot.*

586.15. *Christmas Book.*

587. Frazer, Sir James George. *The Golden Bough: a Study in Magic and Religion.* New York: St. Martin's, 1955. 13 vols.

First published in 1907–15 in twelve volumes by Macmillan (London). An aftermath volume published later is now included in the set. Different abridged and illustrated editions exist. Most are published by Macmillan, St. Martin's, or the New American Library. Contents: volumes 1–2, The Magic Art and the Evolution of Kings; volume 3, Taboo and the Peril of the Soil; volume 4, The Dying God; volumes 5–6, Adonis, Athis, Osiris, Studies in Oriental Religion; volumes 7–8, Spirits of the End of the World; volume 9, The Scapegoat; volumes 10–11, Balder the Beautiful, The Fire Festivals of Europe; volume 12, Bibliography and Index; volume 13, Aftermath.

588. *Funk and Wagnalls Standard Dictionary of Folklore, Mythology and Legend.* New York: Funk & Wagnalls, 1973. 1,236 pp.

Editor, Maria Leach; associate editor, Jerome Fried. Dictionary / encyclopedia format. The standard work in the field, first published in two volumes in 1949–50.

589. Graves, Robert. *The White Goddess: a Historical Grammar of Poetic Myth.* New York: Farrar, Straus & Giroux, 1966. amended and enl. ed. 511 pp. illus. index.

Also published by Vintage (New York) in 1958 and Faber & Faber (London) in 1959. An exploration of certain pervasive mythic themes in folklore and history.

590. Gray, Louis Herbert. *The Mythology of All Races.* New York: Cooper Square, 1964. 13 vols. illus. maps. bibliographies.

First published in 1916–32 by the Archaeological Institute of America. Contents: volume 1, Greek and Roman; volume 2, Eddic; volume 3, Celtic; volume 4, Finno-Ugric, Siberian; volume 5, Semitic; volume 6, Indian and Iranian; volume 7, Armenian and African; volume 8, Chinese and Japanese; volume 9, Oceanic; volume 10, North American; volume 11, Latin American; volume 12, Egyptian and Indo-Chinese; volume 13, Index.

591. Jenkins, Elizabeth. *The Mystery of King Arthur.* London: Michael Joseph, 1975. 224 pp. index. illus. bibliography. ISBN 0-698-10676-8.

Close to being a coffee-table book. Mostly pictures. Includes the progress of the legend up to Tennyson's *Idylls of the King*.

592. Jung, Emma, and Von Franz, Marie Louis. *The Grail Legend.* London: Hodder & Stoughton, 1971; New York: Putnam, for C. G. Jung Foundation for Analytical Psychology, 1970. 452 pp. index. illus. bibliography.

Translated by Andrea Dykis from *Die Graalslegende in psychologischer Sicht*. An exploration by Jung's widow and one of his disciples of various medieval symbols, including the grail, the sword, the stone, the lance and the vessel.

593. Loomis, Roger Sherman. *Arthurian Literature in the Middle Ages: a Collaborative History.* Oxford: Clarendon Press, 1959. 574 pp. bibliography.

A scholarly work on the medieval version of the King Arthur legend.

594. MacDonald, Margaret Read, ed. *Storyteller's Sourcebook*. Detroit: Gale Research, 1982. 818 pp. index. ISBN 0-8103-0471-6.

> A Neal-Schuman Book. An index to over 700 published collections of folktales. Subject, motif, and title access. Ethnic / geographic index included.

595. Reiss, Edmund, et al. *Arthurian Legend and Literature: an Annotated Bibliography*. New York: Garland, 1984–. ? vols. ISBN 0-8240-9123-X.

> Volume 1, *The Middle Ages* (Reference Library of the Humanities, vol. 415). A sourcebook for additional research.

596. Seznec, Jean. *The Survival of the Pagan Gods; the Mythological Tradition and Its Place in Renaissance Humanism and Art*. New York: Pantheon Books, 1953; Princeton, N.J.: Princeton University Press, 1951; New York: Harper Torchbooks, 1961. 376 pp. illus. bibliography.

> Translated by Barbara F. Sessions from *Survivance des dieux antiques*. A scholarly study of the endurance of myth in various forms.

597. Thompson, Stith. *Motif-Index of Folk-Literature: a Classification of Narrative Elements in Folktales, Ballads, Myths, Fables, Mediaeval Romances, Exempla, Fabliaux, Jest-Books and Local Legends*. Bloomington: Indiana University Press, 1955–58. rev. ed. 6 vols.

> First published in 1932–36. A classified index to various themes located in all types of folklore.

598. Vitaliano, Dorothy. *Legends of the Earth: Their Geologic Origins*. Secaucus, N.J.: Lyle Stuart, 1973. 318 pp. index.

> An interesting, albeit somewhat confusing, exploration of the influence of geologic origins on myths and folklore.

See also item 224.1.

Lost Worlds

599. Berlitz, Charles Frambach. *Mysteries from Forgotten Worlds*. New York: Dell, 1973. 225 pp. illus. maps. bibliography.

> Photographs, drawings, and field archaeology reports by J. Manson Valentine. Speculates on the communication between various prehis-

toric civilizations and the lost world of Atlantis. Berlitz's later book, *Atlantis: the Eighth Continent* (New York: Putnam, 1984), was not well reviewed.

600. Charroux, Robert. *Forgotten Worlds: Scientific Secrets of the Ancients and Their Warning for Our Time.* New York: Walker, 1973. 288 pp.

> Translated by Lowell Blair from *Le livre des mondes oubrés.* Originally published in 1971 in France. Published under the title *Lost Worlds: Scientific Secrets of the Ancients* in 1974. Accounts of Atlantis, strange stone constructions, Easter Island, and even UFOs.

601. Churchward, James. *The Lost Continent of Mu.* London: Spearman, 1959; Futura, 1974; Sudbury, Eng.: Spearman, 1934. 286 pp. illus. maps.

> First published by Rudge (New York) in 1926. A well-known, sometimes discounted, report of the existence of the lost continent of Mu.

602. de Camp, Lyon Sprague. *Lost Continents: the Atlantis Theme in History, Science and Literature.* New York: Dover, 1970. 348 pp. index. illus. maps. bibliography. ISBN 0-486-22668-9.

> Originally published by Gnome Press in 1954. Describes lost / destroyed worlds, including Atlantis, Lemuria, and other fabled isles.

603. Donnelly, Ignatius. *Atlantis: the Antediluvian World.* Blauvelt, N.Y.: Rudolf Steiner, 1973. 2d ed. 355 pp. illus.

> Reprint of an 1882 work. This edition was printed originally in 1971. Introduction by Paul M. Allen. Contents: the history of Atlantis, the deluge, the civilizations of the Old World and New compared, the mythologies of the Old World, a recollection of Atlantis, and the colonies of Atlantis. A sequel, *Ragnarok, the Age of Fire and Gravel,* is available.

604. Ebon, Martin. *Atlantis: the New Evidence.* New York: Signet, 1977. 154 pp. illus. bibliography. ISBN 0-451-07271-1.

> An interesting theory, based on the premise that Atlantis is situated in the Aegean Sea. Includes thoughts of mystics such as Edgar Cayce to back up the argument.

605. Ferro, Robert, and Grumley, Michael. *Atlantis: the Autobiography of a Search.* Garden City, N.Y.: Doubleday, 1970. 168 pp. maps.

A psychic and real journey to find the lost continent as prophesied by Edgar Cayce.

606. Hayes, Christine. *Red Tree: Insight into Lost Continents Mu and Atlantis, as Revealed to Christine Hayes.* San Antonio, Tex.: Naylor, 1972. 176 pp. ISBN 0-8111-0465-6.

Thoughts on the lost continents.

607. Mertz, Henriette. *Atlantis: Dwelling Place of the Gods.* Chicago: Henriette Mertz, 1976. 189 pp. illus. maps. bibliography.

Argument for the placement of ancient Atlantis in the southwest of the United States.

608. Michell, John F. *The View over Atlantis.* New York: Ballantine Books, 1969, 1972; London: Garnstone, 1972; Abacus, 1973. rev. ed. 211 pp. index. illus. bibliography. ISBN 0-85511-020-1.

Suggests that the earth is covered with a vast, worldwide ruin of an ancient civilization.

609. Muck, Otto. *The Secret of Atlantis.* New York: Pocket Books, 1979; Times Books, 1978. 290 pp. index. illus. bibliographic references. ISBN 0-671-82392-2.

Translated by Fred Bradley from the German edition, published by Econ Verlag (Dusseldorf) in 1976. A thorough examination of Atlantis' existence and destruction.

610. Ramage, Edwin S., ed. *Atlantis: Fact or Fiction?* Bloomington: Indiana University Press, 1978. 210 pp. index. maps. bibliography.

Contributors include J. Rufus Fears, S. Casey Fredericks, John V. Luce, Edwin S. Ramage, Dorothy B. Vitaliano, and Herbert E. Wright, Jr. Papers presented at a panel discussion sponsored by the Department of Classical Studies at Indiana University. Examines the existence of Atlantis from historical, geographical, literary, and mythological points of view.

611. Spence, Lewis. *Atlantis in America.* Detroit: Singing Tree, 1972; Secaucus, N.J.: Lyle Stuart, 1926. 213 pp. illus.

Originally published in 1925. A good overview of the tradition of Atlantis.

612. Spence, Lewis. *The Occult Sciences in Atlantis*. New York: Samuel Weiser, 1970; London: Aquarian Press, 1970. 136 pp. references.

Further arguments for the existence of Atlantis.

613. Wellard, James. *The Search for Lost Worlds: an Exploration of the Lands of Myth and Legend Including Atlantis, Sheva, and Avalon*. London: Pan, 1975. 176 pp. illus. bibliography. ISBN 0-330-24253-9.

A good overview of the various theories and legends of lost continents, islands, and other lands.

See also item 39.15.

Stone Structures

614. Aldersmith, Herbert, and Davidson, David. *The Great Pyramid: Its Divine Message; and Original Co-ordination of Historical Documents and Archaeological Evidence*. London: Williams & Norgate, 1948. 568 pp. illus. maps.

First published in 1924. An eleventh edition is available from Pyramid Records. An early account of the mystical properties of the Egyptian pyramids.

615. Atkinson, Richard John Copeland. *Stonehenge*. London: Hamilton, 1956; New York: Macmillan, 1956; Harmondsworth, Eng.: Penguin, 1960. 210 pp. illus. bibliography.

A good, basic, and conventional view of Stonehenge.

616. Bord, Janet, and Bord, Colin. *Mysterious Britain*. Garden City, N.Y.: Doubleday, 1973; London: Granada, 1973. 262 pp. illus. bibliography.

Discusses stone circles and lines, as well as monuments. Includes material on ley lines, which depict ancient sites as being arranged deliberately in straight-line relationships.

617. Burl. Aubrey. *The Stone Circles of the British Isles*. New Haven, Conn.: Yale University Press, 1976. 431 pp. index. illus. bibliography.

An objective, scholarly examination of a number of theories regarding the stone circles to be found in Britain. Particular attention is paid to Stonehenge and Avebury.

618. Dos Passos, John. *Easter Island: Island of the Enigmas.* Garden City, N.Y.: Doubleday, 1971. 150 pp. illus. maps.

> A synopsis of descriptions by early explorers regarding the Easter Island sculptures. Includes Dos Passos's ideas on the subject.

619. Hadingham, Evan. *Circles and Standing Stones: an Illustrated Exploration of Megalith Mysteries of Early Britain.* Garden City, N.Y.: Doubleday, 1976; London: Walker, 1975. 247 pp. index. illus. maps. bibliography.

> Considers the stone circles and monoliths of Britain as possible astronomical observatories. Includes travel directions. Also covers Brittany. Scholarly approach.

620. Hawkins, Gerald S. *Beyond Stonehenge.* New York: Harper & Row, 1973. 319 pp. index. illus. bibliography. ISBN 0-060-11786-9.

> An enthusiastic endorsement of the astronomical function of the stone megaliths in Britain and elsewhere. Very personalized account. A sequel, in a sense, to the author's *Stonehenge Decoded*, published in 1965 by Doubleday.

621. Hitching, Francis. *Earth Magic.* New York: William Morrow, 1977; Pocket Books, 1978. 330 pp. index. illus. bibliography. ISBN 0-688-03157-9.

> A learned study of stone circles, megaliths, ley lines, etc., in Europe and America.

622. King, Serge V. *Pyramid Energy Handbook.* New York: Warner, 1979, 1977. 190 pp. illus. bibliography. ISBN 0-446-92029-0.

> A practical, simple approach to using pyramid power.

623. Mendelssohn, Kurt. *The Riddle of the Pyramids.* New York: Praeger, 1974. 224 pp. illus. bibliography.

> A study of the Mexican and Egyptian pyramids by a physicist who concludes that the process of building the structures was their purpose, not the end result.

624. Morrison, Tony. *Pathway to the Gods: the Mystery of the Andes Lines.* New York: Harper & Row, 1979. 208 pp. illus. maps. ISBN 0-06-613057-1.

> Incorporating the work of Gerald S. Hawkins. An examination of the earth-work lines dating from pre-Columbian Nazca days.

625. Niel, Fernard. *The Mysteries of Stonehenge.* New York: Avon, 1975. 208 pp. illus. ISBN 0-380-00473-9.

Avon's Mysteries series. Translation by Lowell Blair of *Stonehenge: Le temple mysterieux de la préhistorie,* published by R. Laffont (Paris) in 1974.

626. Schul, Bill, and Pettit, Ed. *The Psychic Power of Pyramids.* Greenwich, Ct.: Fawcett, 1976. 224 pp. index. illus. bibliography. ISBN 0-449-90001-0.

The secret powers that pyramids hold can be harnessed by individuals who observe certain properties of the psychic powers involved.

627. Tompkins, Peter. *The Magic of Obelisks.* New York: Harper & Row, 1981. 470 pp. index. illus. ISBN 0-06-014899-3.

The role of obelisks in pyramid magic. Includes an account of pyramidology and the fascination it held for Napoleon, Golden Dawn magicians, and others.

628. Tompkins, Peter. *Mysteries of the Mexican Pyramids.* New York: Harper & Row, 1976. index. illus. bibliography. ISBN 0-06-014324-X.

Historical account of the construction and rediscovery of the Mexican pyramids by various explorers. Speculations on the nature and origins of the pyramids. Heavy emphasis on undocumented mysticism.

629. Tompkins, Peter. *Secrets of the Great Pyramid.* New York: Harper & Row, 1971; London: Allen Lane, 1973. 416 pp. illus. bibliography. ISBN 0-060-14327-4.

An in-depth study of the great, Cheops', pyramid at Giza. The author tries to prove that the pyramid is a record in itself of ancient Egyptian mathematical and astronomical data. A good overview of the various theories on pyramids.

630. Toth, Max, and Nielsen, Greg. *Pyramid Power.* New York: Warner Destiny, 1974, 1976. 257 pp. index. illus. bibliography. ISBN 0-446-89278-5.

In two parts: the archaeologists' pyramids, and the power of the pyramids today for those who believe and use such psychic powers. Includes an exploration of these mystic powers.

631. Trento, Salvatore Michael. *The Search for Lost America: Mysteries of the Stone Ruins in the United States.* Harmondsworth, Eng. and

New York: Penguin, 1979; New York: Contemporary Books, 1978.
248 pp. index. illus. bibliography. ISBN 0-14-005226-7.

> A discussion of ancient stone structures / ruins in the U.S. by an
> archaeologist.

632. Waisbard, Simone. *The Mysteries of Machu Picchu.* New York:
Avon, 1979. 304 pp. illus. bibliography ISBN 0-380-43687-6.

> Avon's Mysteries series. Translated from the French *Machu Picchu: cité
> perdue des Incas,* published by Editions R. Laffont in 1974. Description of
> the history and mysticism of the ancient Incas as discovered and
> speculated on in one of their lost cities.

633. Watkins, Alfred. *The Old Straight Track: Its Mounds, Beacons,
Motes, Sites, and Markstones.* London: Methuen, 1925, 1933, 1948;
Sphere, 1925. 234 pp. index. illus. maps.

> The originator of the ley lines supposition regarding ancient sites in
> Britain discusses his ideas.

Fairies and Other Mythical Beings

634. Briggs, Katharine Mary. *An Encyclopedia of Fairies: Hobgoblins,
Brownies, Bogies, and Other Supernatural Creatures.* New York: Pan-
theon Books, 1976. 481 pp. illus. index. bibliography.
ISBN 0-394-40918-3.

> Originally published as *A Dictionary of Fairies* by Allen Lane (London)
> in 1976. Includes an index of types and motifs of fairies. Dictionary
> format. Briggs has been president of the British Folklore Society.

635. Doyle, Sir Arthur Conan. *The Coming of the Fairies.* New York:
Samuel Weiser, 1972. 196 pp. illus.

> Originally pubished in 1921. The account of the famous Cottingley
> fairies, including the photographs later admitted to be fakes by one of
> the claimants. At the time it was considered as proof of fairy existence
> by many.

636. Huygen, Wil. *Gnomes.* New York: Abrams, 1976. 200 pp. illus.
ISBN 0-810-90965-0.

> Illustrated by Rien Roortvliet. Originally published by Unieboek B.V. in
> 1976 as *Leven en werken van de kaboutes.* The coffee-table book on gnomes

which became a best-seller and launched Abrams's series on mythical beings. The scanty text is fanciful rather than scholarly. A number of spin-offs have been published, such as *Giants*, devised by David Larkin.

637. Keightley, Thomas. *The World Guide to Gnomes, Fairies, Elves and Other Little People.* New York: Avenel, 1978, distributed by Crown. 560 pp. index. illus. ISBN 0-519-26313-0.

> Originally published in 1878 by G. Bell (London) as *The Fairy Mythology*. Includes an appendix of some Irish fairy legends, and verses by the author. A geographic arrangement covering the fairy myths of the Orient, Scandinavia, northern islands, Germany, Switzerland, Great Britain, the Celts and Cymry, southern Europe, eastern Europe, Africa, and the Jews.

638. Larkin, David. ed. *Fairies.* New York: Abrams, 1978; London: Souvenir Press, 1978. unpaged. illus. ISBN 0-8109-0901-4.

> Also published in 1979 by Peacock Press / Bantam Books (New York) and by Pan (London). Description and illustration by Brian Frond and Alan Lee. Another coffee-table book by Abrams. Gnomes are not included in the account of little people provided here.

639. Wilson, Peter Lamborn. *Angels.* New York: Pantheon Books, 1980; London: Thames & Hudson, 1980. 200 pp. index. illus. bibliography. ISBN 0-394-51355-X.

> Profusely illustrated account of angels. Emphasis is on the Christian tradition, but information on angels in other cultures, such as the Jewish, Eskimo, and Oriental cultures, also is included.

Monsters and Mythical Beasts

640. Borges, Jorge Luis. *The Book of Imaginary Beings.* New York: Avon, 1970; London: Penguin, 1973. 256 pp.

> With Margarita Guerrero. Revised, enlarged, and translated by Norman Thomas di Giovanni in collaboration with the author. First published in Mexico (1957) with the title *Menual de zoologia fantastica*. Second, enlarged edition first published in Buenos Aires in 1967. A discussion of the beasts of legends, including not only dragons and unicorns but lesser-known South African beasties as well. Encyclopedia format.

641. Byrne, Peter. *The Search for Bigfoot: Monster, Myth or Man.* Washington, D.C.: Acropolis Books, 1975. 263 pp. illus. ISBN 0-874-91159-1.

> Foreword by Robert Rives. An official report from the Bigfoot Information Center in Oregon. An account of eyewitness sightings.

642. Campbell, Elizabeth Montgomery, and Solomon, David. *Search for Morag.* New York: Walker, 1973; London: Tom Stacey, 1972. 192 pp. illus. bibliography. ISBN 0-8027-0422-0.

> Describes sightings in Loch Morar of a beast rather like Nessie.

643. Clark, Jerome, and Coleman, Loren. *Creatures of the Goblin World.* Highland Park, Ill.: Clark, 1984. 186 pp. bibliography.

> Originally published by Warner as *Creatures of the Outer Edge* in 1978. Contains accounts of mystery animals, Bigfoot, manimals, phantom cats and dogs, and phantasms.

644. Costello, Peter. *In Search of Lake Monsters.* London: Garnstone, 1974; New York: Coward, McCann & Geoghegan, 1974; Albans, Eng.: Panther, 1975. 400 pp. index. illus. bibliography. ISBN 0-8551-1400-2.

> Overview of possible lake monsters from all over the world. Includes three chapters on Nessie.

645. Dinsdale, Tim. *Project Water Horse: the True Story of the Monster Quest at Loch Ness.* London: Routledge & Kegan Paul, 1975. 213 pp. index. illus. maps. bibliography. ISBN 0-7100-8029-8.

> First-hand account of many years of searching for Nessie. Author also has written *The Story of the Loch Ness Monster,* published by Wingate (London) and Target (London), both in 1973.

646. Eberhard, George M. *Monsters: a Guide to Information on Unaccounted-for Creatures, Including Bigfoot, Many Water Monsters, and Other Irregular Animals.* New York: Garland, 1982. 358 pp. index. ISBN 0-8240-9213-9.

> Fictional monsters excluded. Accounts of cryptozoology. Contains 4,500 entries for English-language books, pamphlets, and journal articles.

647. Ingersoll, Ernest. *Dragons and Dragon Lore*. New York: Payson & Clark, 1928. 203 pp. index. illus. bibliography.

> Introduction by Henry Fairfield Osborn. Examines dragons as objects of worship, fear, and superstition throughout Eastern and Western cultures. "I feel confident that the present work will arouse a widespread interest among students of animal form and history on the one hand, and or folk-lore, primitive religion and mythology on the other" (Introduction).

648. Ley, Willy. *Exotic Zoology*. New York: Capricorn Books, 1966. 468 pp. index.

> Excerpts from the author's earlier books: *The Lungfish, the Dodo, and the Unicorn; Dragons in Amber;* and *Salamanders and Other Wonders.* Considers mythic and prehistoric beasts, oceanic mysteries, and the like.

649. McCloy, James F., and Miller, Fay, Jr. *The Jersey Devil*. Wallingford, Penn.: Middle Atlantic Press, 1976. 121 pp. illus.

> An account and history of the mysterious Jersey Devil, which has been seen in New Jersey for centuries.

650. Nigg, Joe. *The Book of Gryphons*. Cambridge, Mass.: Applewood books, 1982. 111 pp. illus. bibliography. ISBN 0–918222–37–0.

> Profusely illustrated history of the gryphon. Contents: master of two worlds; sacred to the sun; saints, demons and knights; fabulous and regal and in modern times.

651. Sable, Martin Howard. *Exobiology: a Research Guide*. Brighton, Mich.: Green Oak Press, 1978. 324 pp. index. ISBN 0-931600-00-6.

> An international listing of material published over three centuries. Includes sources on flying saucers and other matters related to possible life on other planets.

652. Shepard, Odell. *The Lore of the Unicorn*. New York: Avenel, 1982, distributed by Crown. 312 pp. index. illus. bibliographic notes. ISBN 0-517-37156-1.

> First published in 1930. Includes many legends of the unicorn.

653. Tchernine, Odette. *In Pursuit of the Abominable Snowman*. New York: Taplinger, 1971. 184 pp. illus. maps. ISBN 0-8008-4187-5.

Originally published in 1970 as *Yeti*. A survey of the search for the Bigfoot-type monsterman. Contains information regarding Russian efforts.

See also items 39.2, 586.3, 586.7.

Manimals

654. Baring-Gould, Sabine. *The Book of Werewolves: Being an Account of a Terrible Superstition*. New York: Causeway Books, 1973. 266 pp. ISBN 0-88356-008-9.

First published in 1865. Author was an English parson and noted folklorist. Information on lycanthropy in ancient Greece and Rome, Scandinavia, the Middle Ages, France, and Galicia; also covers mythological origins and legends.

655. Beatty, Kenneth James. *Human Leopards*. New York: AMS Press, 1978. 139 pp. illus.

Manimals, people who turn into various animals, have had great appeal. Is it any wonder that people are reputed to turn themselves into giant cats?

656. Copper, Basil. *The Werewolf in Legend, Fact and Art*. New York: St. Martin's, 1977; London: Robert Hale, 1977. 240 pp. index. illus. selected filmography. bibliography. ISBN 0-312-86222-9.

Good, solid overview of the subject.

657. Kriss, Marika. *Werewolves, Shapeshifters, and Skinwalkers*. Los Angeles: Sherbourne Press, 1972. 143 pp. illus. ISBN 0-8202-0152-9.

For the Millions series. A brief introduction to legends concerning humans who become beasts.

658. O'Donnell, Elliott. *Werwolves*. New York: Longone, 1965. 292 pp.

A history of the werewolf metamorphosis belief. Accounts of werewolves in Great Britain, France, Germany, Austria-Hungary, the Balkans, Spain, the Lowlands, Denmark, Norway and Sweden, Iceland, Lapland-Finland, and Russia and Siberia.

See also items 39.1., 890.

Vampires

659. Copper, Basil. *The Vampire—in Legend, Fact, and Art.* London: Robert Hale, 1973; Corgi, 1975; New Hyde Park, N.Y.: Citadel Press, 1975. 208 pp. index. illus. bibliography. ISBN 0-7091-3585-8.

> A good, readable overview. Includes coverage of the vampire in legend, literature, film, and theater.

660. Glut, Donald F. *The Dracula Book.* Metuchen, N.J.: Scarecrow Press, 1975. 388 pp. index. illus. ISBN 0-8108-0804-8.

> Introduction by Christopher Lee. Contains an account of Vlad the Impaler and other historic prototypes of the vampire. Also covers Stoker's novel and various versions of the legend in books, movies, on the stage, radio, and television, and in comics.

661. McNally, Raymond T., and Florescu, Radu. *In Search of Dracula: a True History of Dracula and Vampire Legends.* Greenwich, Conn.: New York Graphic Society, 1972; London: New English Library, 1973; New York: Galahad, 1975. 223 pp. illus. maps. bibliography.

> A full, personal account of the search for Dracula in modern-day Romania. Gives an account of Vlad the Impaler, probably the model for the Dracula legend.

662. Masters, Anthony. *The Natural History of the Vampire.* New York: Putnam, 1972; London: Rupert Hart-Davis, 1972. 259 pp. index. illus. bibliography. ISBN 0-399-10931-5.

> An overview of the legends and origins of vampires along with their practices. Covers the vampire in literature and as viewed by Christianity. Interesting anecdotes. Includes a look at vampirism as a current cult.

663. Riccardo, Martin V. *Vampires Unearthed: the Vampire and Dracula Bibliography of Books, Articles, Movies, Records and Other Materials.* New York: Garland, 1982. 143 pp. ISBN 0-8240-9128-0.

> The Unexplained, the Mysterious, and the Supernatural series. Over 1,000 English-language items. Arranged in four sections: fiction, drama and media, nonfiction, and organizations and journals.

664. Ronay, Gabriel. *The Truth about Dracula.* New York: Stein & Day, 1972. 180 pp. index. illus. maps. ISBN 0-8128-1524-6.

A good introductory survey of the vampire legend. Accounts of Vlad the Impaler, Countess Elisabeth Bathory, and the fascination for the legend in German literature, movies, and Nazi myths.

665. Summers, Montague. *The Vampire, His Kith and Kin*. New Hyde Park, N.Y.: University Books, 1960; London: Routledge, 1928. 356 pp.

Summers turns his thorough examination and scholarly approach to legends of the vampire.

10
ANCIENT ASTRONAUTS, DISAPPEARANCES, AND UFOs

> *Proof,* n. Evidence having a shade more of plausibility than of
> unlikelihood. The testimony of two credible witnesses as
> opposed to that of only one.
>
> > Ambrose Bierce,
> > *The Devil's Dictionary*

Legends not only have been created in ancient and "ignorant"
cultures, they have continued to be formed in modern times. Materials in this chapter treat some of the most common of these modern
legends: the presence of ancient gods, or spacemen, from alien
creatures on earth; disappearances into mysterious voids, most notably the Bermuda Triangle; and UFO sightings and encounters.

These modern legends have had persistent followings. In fact,
Gallup polls reveal that the majority of Americans now believe in
UFOs. Accounts of experiences with flying saucers are popular in
tabloids such as the *National Enquirer*. Such modern legends are
sometimes the framework for false reports—rumors—of happenings
such as cattle mutilations in the American West.

In some ways, the most intriguing aspect of these modern
legends is their indication of the continuous human fascination with
the unusual, and the penchant for giving unknown phenomena
unusual and yet somehow believable explanations. This illustrates
well how the legends and myths of past ages may have originated.
Also, it is a testimony to the willingness of humans to consider new
ideas and explanations for puzzles.

Local and regional folklore provides many such stories of unusual and bizarre happenings and notions. Tales of dogs howling on
the anniversary dates of weird happenings, countless modern ghost
stories, and strange animal behavior are a part of this occult continuum.

This chapter covers only a few widespread modern legends. It is
divided into the following sections:

- General Works
- Bermuda Triangle
- UFOs

General Works

666. Blumrich, Josef F. *Spaceships of Ezekiel*. London: Corgi, 1974; New York: Bantam, 1974. 179 pp. index. illus. bibliography. ISBN 0-552-09556-7.

> Translation of *Da Trat sich der Himmel auf*, published by Econ-Verlag (Dusseldorf, Germany) in 1974. The author initially was skeptical of von Daniken's theories of ancient astronauts but agrees with him after investigation (see also item 709).

667. Daniken, Erich von. *Chariots of the Gods? Unsolved Mysteries of the Past*. London: Souvenir Press, 1969; Corgi, 1971. New York: Putnam, 1970. 190 pp. index. illus. maps. bibliography. ISBN 0-552-08800-5.

> Translated by Michael Heron from *Erinnerungen an die Zukunft*, published by Econ-Verlag (Dusseldorf, Germany) in 1968. The first of von Daniken's works which introduced the modern legend of ancient astronauts. Other works by the author include *Gold of the Gods, Gods from Outer Space, Miracle of the Gods, Signs of the Gods*, and *Von Daniken's Proof*.

668. Daniken, Erich von. *In Search of Ancient Gods: My Pictorial Evidence for the Impossible*. New York: Putnam, 1973. 224 pp. illus. bibliography. ISBN 0-399-11346-0.

> Translated by Michael Heron; first published in Germany. Slight text with many illustrations supporting the author's theory of ancient visitors to earth.

669. Drake, Walter Raymond. *Gods and Spacemen in the Ancient East*. London: Sphere, 1973. 240 pp. index. bibliography. ISBN 0-7221-3044-9.

> Originally published as *Spacemen in the Ancient East* by Spearman (London) in 1968. An examination of the East in order to demonstrate the influence of extraterrestrial life on earth. The author covers the occident in his *Gods and Spacemen in the Ancient West*.

670. Landsburg, Alan, and Landsburg, Sally. *In Search of Ancient Mysteries*. London: Corgi, 1974. 197 pp. index. illus. bibliography. ISBN 0-552-09588-5.

> Foreword by Rod Serling. Supports the idea 'that human intelligence has been learned from extraterrestrials throughout the ages.

671. Mooney, Richard Edwin. *Colony—Earth*. New York: Stein & Day, 1974; London: Souvenir Press, 1974; St. Albans, Eng.: Panther, 1975. 251 pp. index. ISBN 0-8128-1658-7.

> Argues that earth was colonized by extraterrestrials. Many unusual theories are included.

672. Sanderson, Ivan Terence. *Invisible Residents: a Disquisition upon Certain Matters Maritime, and the Possibility of Intelligent Life under the Waters of This Earth*. London: Tandem, 1974; New York: World, 1970. 254 pp. index. illus. bibliography. ISBN 0-426-13880-5.

> A fascinating theory which espouses the notion of the existence of an underwater civilization.

673. Steiger, Brad. *Gods of Aquarius: UFO's and the Transformation of Man*. London: Panther, 1980; Sphere, 1977; W. H. Allen, 1977. 304 pp. index. illus. ISBN 0-586-04538-4.

> First published by Harcourt Brace Jovanovich (New York) in 1976. Asserts that human civilization is in a transitional phase and is passing into a new age when information will be provided by extraterrestrials and a variety of other occult beings.

674. Steiger, Brad. *Mysteries of Time and Space*. Englewood Cliffs, N.J.: Prentice-Hall, 1974. 240 pp. illus. ISBN 0-13-609040-0.

> Special archaeological research by Ron Calais. Suggests that certain technological advances occurred because of assistance from extraterrestrial sources.

675. Temple, Robert Kyle Grenville. *The Sirius Mystery*. New York: St. Martin's, 1975. 244 pp. index. illus. bibliography.

> A scholarly work which theorizes that extraterrestrial knowledge is a part of some branches of Eastern mysticism.

676. Thiering, Barry, and Castle, Edgar. *Some Trust in Chariots: Sixteen Views on Erich von Daniken's "Chariots of the Gods?"* Folkestone, Eng.: Bailey & Swinfen, 1973. 128 pp. illus.

Originally published in Australia in 1972. An interesting overview of opinions of von Daniken's work.

677. Umland, Craig, and Umland, Eric. *Mysteries of the Ancients: Early Spacemen and the Mayas.* London: Souvenir Press, 1975; New York: Walker, 1974. 186 pp. index. illus. maps. bibliography. ISBN 0-285-62162-9.

Presents the theory that ancient astronauts were on earth as miners and became stranded and evolved into the founders of Mayan culture.

See also items 39.17, 888.

The Bermuda Triangle

678. Alexander, Marc. *The Man Who Exorcised the Bermuda Triangle: the Reverend Dr. Donald Omand, Exorcist Extraordinary.* South Brunswick, N.J.: A. S. Barnes, 1980. 203 pp. illus. ISBN 0-498-02467-9.

Introduction by Colin Wilson. An account of the exorcism of the Bermuda Triangle by a noted British exorcist.

679. Berlitz, Charles Frambach, and Valentine, J. Manson. *The Bermuda Triangle.* Garden City, N.Y.: Doubleday, 1974; New York: Avon, 1975. 207 pp. illus. bibliography.

An overview of the disappearances within the Triangle and the various theories advanced about them. Reaches no conclusions. A good introduction to the subject.

680. Cochrane, Hugh. *Gateway to Oblivion: the Great Lakes' Bermuda Triangle.* New York: Avon, 1980; Garden City, N.Y.: Doubleday, 1979. 158 pp. index. illus. maps. bibliography. ISBN 0-380-54817-8.

A variation on the Bermuda Triangle mystery. "It is a strange place where ships, planes, and people vanish into thin air, where weird fogs and gloves of light abound, where ominous waters shroud sinister events" (Frontispiece).

681. Ebon, Martin, ed. *The Riddle of the Bermuda Triangle.* New York: Signet, 1975. 193 pp.

An anthology of opinions on the subject, pro and con.

682. Jeffrey, Adi-Kent Thomas. *The Bermuda Triangle.* New York: Warner, 1975; Lahaska, Penn.: New Hope, 1973. 189 pp. illus. maps. ISBN 0-446-59961-1.

> Excellent introduction to the subject. Consists of a general chapter followed by case studies of disappearances. Good for the casual reader.

683. Kusche, Lawrence David. *The Bermuda Triangle Mystery Solved.* New York: Harper & Row, 1975; Warner, 1975. 256 pp. index. illus. maps. ISBN 0-06-012475-X.

> Author points out that there is probably no one explanation for the disappearances in the Bermuda Triangle area and believes that it is a manufactured mystery.

684. Kusche, Lawrence David. *The Disappearance of Flight 19.* New York: Harper & Row, 1980; Barnes & Noble, 1981. 211 pp. index. illus. bibliography. ISBN 0-06-012477-6.

> An account of the most famous case of a disappearance in the Bermuda Triangle in modern times.

685. Winer, Richard. *The Devil's Triangle.* New York: Bantam, 1974. 222 pp. index. illus. bibliography.

> A popularized account of the mysterious oceanic disappearances in the triangle area.

UFOs

686. Bowen, Charles ed. *Humanoids.* London: Futura, 1974; Spearman, 1969. 256 pp. illus. maps.

> Accounts by scientists concerning recent UFO reports.

687. Briazack, Norman J., and Mennick, Simon. *The UFO Guidebook.* Secaucus, N.J.: Citadel, 1978. 246 pp. bibliography. ISBN 0-8065-0763-2.

> Encyclopedia format. Over 400 terms are defined. "The goal of this guidebook is to collate the language and the terminology dealing with UFO's" (Introduction).

688. Catoe, Lynn E. *UFOs and Related Subjects: an Annotated Bibliography.* Detroit: Gale Research, 1978. 392, 12 pp. index. bibliography. ISBN 0-8103-2021-5.

Prepared by the Library of Congress, Science and Technology Division for the Air Force Office of Scientific Research, Office of Aerospace Research. Bound together with Kay Rogers's *Unidentified Flying Objects*. Introduction by Leslie Shepard. Catoe gives over 1,600 references to book and journal articles. Rogers adds some 200 items. Contents are arranged by subjects, such as abductions, ancient records, occupants, photography, seduction, extraterrestrial life, selected fiction, and the like.

689. Clark, Jerome, and Coleman, Loren. *The Unidentified: Notes Toward Solving the UFO Mystery.* New York: Warner, 1975. 272 pp. ISBN 0-4467-8735-3.

An exploration of the theory originated by Jung that UFOs probably are no more than a manifestation of a collective unconscious. Presents both sides of the controversy.

690. Fitzgerald, Randall. *The Complete Book of Extraterrestrial Encounters.* New York: Collier, 1979. 200 pp. index. bibliography. ISBN 0-02-095500-6.

A helpful overview of UFO literature, with summaries of writings from the various published sources. Arranged in five sections: ancient astronauts, UFOs and UFO occupants, contactees and abductees, debunkers and skeptics, and contacting extraterrestrial intelligence.

691. Flammonde, Paris. *The Age of Flying Saucers: Notes on a Projected History of Unidentified Flying Objects.* New York: Hawthorn Books, 1971. 288 pp. illus. bibliography.

Author compares the current UFO craze to witchcraft as a sociopsychological phenomenon. He is working on a more definitive version of this thesis.

692. Fowler, Raymond E. *UFO's: Interplanetary Visitors: a UFO Investigator Reports on the Facts, Fables, and Fantasies of the Flying Saucer Conspiracy.* Englewood Cliffs, N.J.: Prentice-Hall, 1974. 364 pp. index. illus. ISBN 0-13-935569-3.

Foreword by J. Allen Hynek. Appendix contains summary descriptions of eyewitness accounts based on the local sample used in the author's study. An objective analysis which concludes that the UFO accounts are real and a puzzle.

693. Fuller, Curtis G., ed. *Proceedings of the First International UFO Congress*. New York: Warner, 1980. 429 pp. index. ISBN 0-446-95159-5.

> The congress was held in Chicago in 1977. The editors of *Fate* aided with the editing. Glossary included. Researchers and experts on UFOs provided papers.

694. Hobana, Ian, and Weverbergh, Julien. *UFO's from Behind the Iron Curtain*. London: Souvenir Press, 1974; Corgi, 1975; New York: Bantam, 1975. 308 pp. illus. maps. bibliography. ISBN 0–552–10023–4.

> An exploration of UFO accounts from Communist countries.

695. Hymers, R. L. *Encounters of the Fourth Kind*. Van Nuys, Calif.: Bible Voice, 1976. 132 pp.

> First published as *U.F.O.'s and Bible Prophecy*. Viewers of the movie *Close Encounters of the Third Kind* are aware of the first three kinds of encounters with UFOs. The fourth, according to the author, is possession by satanic demons.

696. Hynek, Joseph Allen. *UFO Experience: a Scientific Equiry*. Chicago: Henry Regnery, 1971; London: Abelard-Schuman, 1974; Corgi, 1974. 336 pp. index. illus.

> A criticism of the Condon Report, which was a strong denial of UFOs compiled under the direction of Edward Condon and published by the New York Times Company (New York) in 1969.

697. Hynek, Joseph Allen, and Vallee, Jacques. *The Edge of Reality: a Progress Report on Unidentified Flying Objects*. Chicago: Henry Regnery, 1975. 288 pp. index. ISBN 0-8092-8209-7.

> Interviews with UFO witnesses.

698. Jacobs, David Michael. *The UFO Controversy in America*. Bloomington: Indiana University Press, 1975. 363 pp. index. bibliography. ISBN 0-253-19006-1.

> Foreword by Joseph Allen Hynek. Author culled newspapers for reports of UFO sightings and has paraphrased them. Covers the periods 1896–1897 and 1947–1974. U.S. sightings only. Scholarly.

699. Jung, Carl Gustav. *Flying Saucers: a Modern Myth of Things Seen in the Skies.* Princeton, N.J.: Princeton University Press, 1978; London: Routledge & Kegan Paul, 1977, 1959. 138 pp. illus. bibliographic references. ISBN 0-691-01822-7.

> Bollinger series. Translated by R. F. C. Hull from *Ein Moderner Mythus,* Jung's analysis of the effect of seeing saucers (whether real or imagined) on the human psyche.

700. Keyhoe, Donald Edward. *Aliens from Space: the Real Story of Unidentified Flying Objects.* Garden City, N.Y.: Doubleday, 1973; St. Albans, Eng.: Panther, 1975. 322 pp. index. ISBN 0-385-06751-8.

> The author presents the argument that UFOs are from a highly developed civilization, and that the U.S. government is suppressing this truth.

701. Keyhoe, Donald Edward. *Flying Saucers from Outer Space.* London: Tandem, 1973. 256 pp. index. ISBN 0-426-12159-7.

> Originally published by Holt (New York) in 1953. The first work to treat UFOs seriously.

702. Klass, Philip J. *UFOs: the Public Deceived.* Buffalo, N.Y.: Prometheus Books, 1983. 310 pp. index. illus. ISBN 0-879-75201-4.

> Focuses on the rumored government cover-up of UFOs. Provides details on a number of case studies of sightings. This is a skeptical view of the entire phenomenon.

703. Rasmussen, Richard Michael. *The UFO Literature: a Comprehensive Annotated Bibliography of Works in Englsh.* Jefferson, N.C.: McFarland, 1985. 263 pp. index. ISBN 0–89950–136–2.

> An annotated listing of over 1,000 items dealing with UFOs, with special interest magazines and pamphlets as well as books. Includes a chapter on the history of UFO literature.

704. Sable, Martin Howard. *UFO Guide: 1947–67: Containing International Lists of Books and Magazine Article[s] on UFO's Flying Saucers, and about Life on Other Planets; World-wide Directories of Flying Saucer Organizations, Professional Groups and Research Centers Concerned with Space Research and Astronautics, a Partial List of Sightings, and an International Directory of Flying Saucer Magazines.* Beverly Hills, Calif.: Rainbow Press, 1967. 100 pp.

The title says it all.

705. Sachs, Margaret. *The UFO Encyclopedia*. New York: Putnam, 1980; London: Corgi, 1981. 416 pp. illus. bibliography. ISBN 0-399-12365-2.

> Dictionary format. Some fairly lengthy articles with bibliographies. Includes an appendix with addresses of UFO groups, periodicals, bookstores, and other useful information.

706. Sagan, Carl, and Page, Thornton, eds. *UFO's—a Scientific Debate*. Ithaca, N.Y.: Cornell University Press, 1972; New York: Norton, 1974. 310 pp. index. illus. bibliography. ISBN 0-8014-0740-0.

> Papers presented at a 1969 symposium sponsored by the American Association for the Advancement of Science in Boston. Various authors present a strong case for scientific investigation in the UFO area.

707. Steiger, Brad, ed. *Project Blue Book*. New York: Ballantine Books, 1976. 423 pp. illus.

> Excerpts from the famous USAF Project Blue Book. Other works are cited.

708. Story, Ronald D., ed. *The Encyclopedia of UFO's*. Garden City, N.Y.: Doubleday, 1980; London: New English Library, 1980. 440 pp. illus. bibliography. ISBN 0-385-11681-0.

> An excellent work containing over 300 articles and good photographs. Considered essential for UFO research. Includes biographies.

709. Tansley, David V. *Omens of Awareness: Startling Parallels between UFO Phenomena and the Expanding Consciousness of Man*. Suffolk: Spearman, 1977; London: Abacus, 1979. 318 pp. illus. bibliography. ISBN 0-854-35134-5.

> Author discusses J. F. Blumrich's *Spaceships of Ezekiel*. "What has emerged combines various aspects of the esoteric teachings which are the basis of all religion, with certain areas of the UFO experience" (Foreword).

710. Vallee, Jacques. *The Invisible College: What a Group of Scientists Has Discovered about UFO Influences on the Human Race*. New York: Dutton, 1975. 216 pp. index. illus. bibliography. ISBN 0-525-13470-0.

> Informal communication exchanges regarding UFOs.

711. Vesco, Renato. *Intercept—but Don't Shoot: the True Story of the Flying Saucers.* New York: Grove Press, 1971. 338 pp. bibliographic references.

> Translation by D. D. Paige of *Intercettateli senza soarare.* Author presents the idea that UFO's may have been developed during the World War II.

See also items 39.17, 651.

11
PROPHECY AND FORTUNE-TELLING

Future, n. That period of time in which our affairs prosper, our
friends are true and our happiness is assured.

Ambrose Bierce,
The Devil's Dictionary

The ability to foretell the future always has fascinated mankind. If one
cannot affect future events by prayer or magic with any certainty, the
next best thing is at least to find out what is destined to happen. From
ancient times to the present, human beings have been intrigued with
the future, whether future events have been ascertained through
scientific methods or through mystical psychic insights.

There always have been various kinds of prophecy and predictions. Great religious mystiques are associated with some systems,
while others have become little more than parlor games. Also, there
always have been accompanying charlatans who have used trickery
to con the gullible.

As with some other areas of the occult, a number of different
fields reveal certain aspects of prophecy and fortune-telling. Examination of the ancient classics uncovers references to oracles and
sibyls; history provides a number of examples of prophets treated as
witches and emissaries of the devil; and parapsychology speculates
on the actual process of precognition.

A wide variety of materials are availabale on prophecy and
fortune-telling, from weighty, scholarly tomes to slight pamphlets
with clumsy illustrations.

The books described in this chapter are subdivided as follows:

- General Works
- Crystal Gazing
- Palmistry
- Phrenology
- Tarot

General Works

712. Alexander, Paul Julius. *The Oracle of Baalbek: the Tiburtine Sibyl in Greek Dress.* Washington, D.C.: Dumbarton Oaks Center for Byzantine Studies, 1967. 151 pp. illus. Distributed by J. J. Augustin.

> Dumbarton Oaks Studies. Scholarly study of an ancient soothsayer. Includes both Greek and English texts.

713. Bevan, Edwyn Robert. *Sibyls and Seers: a Survey of Some Ancient Theories of Revelation and Inspiration.* Folcroft, Penn.: Folcroft Library Editions, 1976; Norwood, Penn.: Norwood Editions, 1977; Philadelphia: R. West, 1978. 189 pp. index. bibliography. ISBN 0-841-41750-4.

> Originally published by G. Allen & Unwin (London) in 1928. A brief introduction to notable prophets throughout history.

714. Clark, Ian F. *The Tale of the Future: from the Beginning to the Present Day: an Annotated Bibliography of Those Satires, Ideal States, Imaginary Wars and Invasions, Political Warnings and Forecasts, Interplanetary Voyages and Scientific Romances—All Located in an Imaginary Future Period—That Have Been Published in the United Kingdom between 1644 and 1970.* London: The Library Association, 1972. 2d ed. 196 pp. index. illus.

> First edition published in 1961. The majority of titles are science fiction rather than nonfiction. Entries are chronologically listed by date of publication. Annotations included.

715. *Cosmopolitan's Guide to Fortune-Telling.* New York: Cosmopolitan Books, 1977. 287 pp. illus. bibliography. ISBN 0-87851-111-3.

> Foreword by Helen Gurley Brown. How-to-do-it information with happy love-life applications.

716. Covina, Gina. *The Ouija Book.* New York: Simon & Schuster, 1981; London: Robert Hale, 1981. 158 pp. illus. ISBN 0-7091-8983-4

> Discusses the historical development of Ouija, along with telling how to use the board and planchette. Gives attention to both explanations of Ouija: (1) as a device for communication with spirits, and (2) as a means for revelation of the subconscious.

717. Criswell, Jeron. *Criswell's Forbidden Predictions Based on Nostradamus and the Tarot.* Atlanta: Drake House / Hallux, 1972. 128 pp. SBN 8375-6769-6.

Criswell, himself a predictor, interprets the tarot and Nostradamus in a sensationalized fashion.

718. Deutch, Yvonne, ed. *Fortune Tellers.* London: Marshall Cavendish, 1974; New York: Black Watch, 1974. 128 pp. illus.

Gold Hand Book series. Compiled by Françoise Strachan. Amply illustrated. Includes chapters on divination, numerology, palmistry, runes, crystal gazing, tarot, tasseography, and dowsing.

719. Dickinson, Peter. *Chance, Luck & Destiny.* Boston: Little, Brown, 1976; London: Victor Gollancz, 1975. 254 pp. illus. ISBN 0-575-01865-8.

An introduction to the subject of fortune-telling and the laws of chance.

720. Dixon, Jeane. *My Life and Prophecies: Her Own Story as Told to Rene Noorbergen.* New York: William Morrow, 1969. 373 pp. ISBN 0-816-16004-X.

The famous predictor's life, with many anecdotes and testimonials to her own Christian faith.

721. Fisher, Joe. *Predictions.* New York: Van Nostrand Reinhold, 1980; London: Sidgwick & Jackson, 1981. 224 pp. illus. maps. bibliography. ISBN 0-442-23375-2.

Illustrated by Peter Commins. Good survey for general readers. Covers Christian saints and Nostradamus, as well as modern prophets.

722. Fontenrose, Joseph. *Delphic Oracle: Its Responses and Operations, with a Catalog of Responses.* Berkeley: University of California Press, 1978. 494 pp. ISBN 0-520-03360-4.

A scholarly, thorough reconstruction of the probable statements of the famed oracle of ancient Greece.

723. Garrison, Omar. *The Encyclopedia of Prophecy.* Secaucus, N.J.: Citadel Press, 1978. 225 pp. illus. ISBN 0-8065-0559-1.

Includes prophets, Armageddon theories, and visions of the future by various groups, such as the druids.

724. Gattey, Charles Neilson. *They Saw Tomorrow: Seers and Sorcerers from Delphi till Today.* London: Granada, 1980; Harrap, 1977. 288 pp. index. illus. select bibliography. ISBN 0-586-04527-9.

> Those with sensational lives were selected. Includes the Pythia of Delphi, Nostradamus, Dr. Dee, the Brahan Seer, Cagliostro, Mlle. Lenormand, Cheiro, Krafft (Hitler's astrologer), and some modern prophets such as Jeane Dixon.

725. Gibson, Walter Brown, and Gibson, Litzka R. *The Complete Illustrated Book of Divination and Prophecy.* Garden City, N.Y.: Doubleday, 1973. London: Souvenir Press, 1974. 336 pp. illus.

> Illustrated by Murray Keshner. A superficial but attractive coffee-table-book approach to popular forms of fortune-telling. Glossary of terms included.

726. Halliday, W. R. *Greek Divination: a Study of Its Methods and Principles.* Chicago: Argonaut, 1913, 1967. 309 pp. index. bibliography.

> The Argonaut Library of Antiquities. Appendix lists bird names, e.g., swans, followed by a list of those seeing (or turning into) swans in visions. Good overview with many references to Greek myths. Scholarly.

727. Holzer, Hans. *The Prophets Speak: What the Leading Psychics Say about Tomorrow.* Indianapolis: Bobbs-Merrill, 1971. 201 pp.

> Includes predictions by Carolyn Chapman, Virginia Cloud, Betty Dye, John Gaudry, Irene Hughes, Jimmy Jacobs, Sybil Leek, and others.

728. King, Bruce [pseud. Zolar]. *Everything You Want to Know about Fortune Telling with Cards; Karma System, Gypsy System, Professional System, Palmistry.* New York: Arco, 1973. 222 pp.

> A good, readable introduction to various fortune-telling systems.

729. Kirchenhoffer, H., trans. *The Book of Fate, Formerly in the Possession of Napoleon, Late Emperor of France; and Now First Rendered into English, from a German Translation, of a Ancient Egyptian Manuscript, Found in the Year 1801, by M. Sonini, in One of the Royal Tombs, Near Mount Libycus, in Upper Egypt.* London: Anglo-American Authors' Association, n.d. 32 double pp. illus.

> Often referred to as *Napoleon's Book of Fate,* this edition includes a long translator's preface along with the description of the system and a fold-out horological chart.

730. Laver, James. *Nostradamus; or, the Future Foretold.* Maidstone, Eng.: George Mann, 1973; London: Collins, 1942. 265 pp. ISBN 0-7041-0010-X.

Good introduction to the work of Nostradamus.

731. Leek, Sybil. *The Sybil Leek Book of Fortunetelling.* London: W. H. Allen, 1970; New York: Macmillan, 1969. 144 pp. illus. ISBN 0-491-00444-3.

The media personality witch tells how to master a variety of fairly simple fortune-telling techniques.

732. MacKenzie, Andrew. *Riddle of the Future.* London: A. Barker, 1974. 172 pp.

An introduction to the history and methods of prediction.

733. Macrae, Norman, ed. *Highland Second-Sight: with Prophecies of Coinneach Odhar and the Seer of Petty.* Folcroft, Penn.: Folcroft Library Editions, 1977. 202 pp. ISBN 0-8414-2305-9.

Introduction by William Morrison. Originally published by G. Souter (Dingwall, Scotland) in 1908. Good account of the phenomenon, including specific predictions by individuals.

734. Nostraedame, Michel de [Nostradamus]. *Predictions.* Various editions.

The noted prophet's works, originally published in Lyon, France, in 1955. Probably the best currently available edition first was published 40 years ago, Jean-Charles de Fontbrune's *Nostradamus: Countdown to Apocalypse* (New York: Holt, Rinehart & Winston, 1980, ISBN 0-03-064177-2). It was translated by Alexis Lykiard and contains a preface by Liz Greene. This version follows the same pattern throughout: discussion of the quatrain in its original form, the author's interpretation, and the history of events which might fit the stanza. Another study, edited by Liberte E. LeVert (Glen Rock, N.Y.: Firebell Books, 1979), has been praised highly.

735. Paracelsus. *The Prophecies of Paracelsus: Occult Symbols and Magic Figures with Esoteric Explanations, by Theophrastus Paracelsus of Hohenheim, and The Life and Teachings of Paracelsus, by Franz Hartmann.* Blauvelt, N.Y.: Rudolf Steiner, 1973. 86, 220 pp. illus.

This edition is a reprint of an edition published by G. Redway (London) in 1887 with the title *The Life of Philippus Theosophrastus, Bombast of*

Hohenheim Known by the Name Paracelsus. A translation of *Prognosticatio eximii doctoris Theophrasti Paracelsi.*

736. Pelton, Robert W. *Your Future, Your Fortune.* Greenwich, Ct.: Fawcett, 1973. 176 pp.

> Different methods of prediction are included, such as geomancy, fingernails, postage stamps, sealing wax, coffee grounds, astrology, etc.

737. Prieditis, Arthur A. *Fate of the Nations.* St. Paul: Llewellyn, 1973. 422 pp. ISBN 0-87542-624-7.

> Studies the prophecies of Nostradamus and compares them with the works of other psychics. Focuses on national futures.

738. Rakoczi, Basil Ivan. *Fortune Telling: a Guide to Foreseeing the Future.* London: MacDonald, 1970. 128 pp. illus. bibliography.

> Published by Harper & Row (New York) in 1973 under the title *Foreseeing the Future.* Describes tarot, meditation, palmistry, crystal gazing, the planchette, and other means of divination.

739. Robb, Stewart. *Nostradamus on Napoleon, Hitler and the Present Crisis.* New York: Scribner's, 1941. 218 pp. illus.

> A popular account of Nostradamus and how it applies to the career of Napoleon and, probably Hitler. A good example of the occult interest that seems to arise in times of national crisis.

740. Sonetheil, Ursula [pseud. Mother Shipton]. *Mother Shipton's Prophecies: the Earliest Editions.* Maidstone, Eng.: George Mann, 1978. 78 pp. illus. ISBN 0-7041-0062-2.

> Originally published by Heywood & Son (Manchester, Eng.) in 1882. The prophecies of a famous sixteenth century English witch. Since she predicted the end of the world in 1881, she seems not to be as highly regarded today as Nostradamus, whose day of Armageddon is yet to come.

741. Theobald, Robert, ed. *Futures Conditional.* Indianapolis: Bobbs-Merrill, 1972. 356 pp. illus. bibliography. ISBN 0-672-61217-8.

> Contents: How People Think about the Future, Choosing Your View of the Future, Refining Your View of the Future, and Basic Tools for Your Future.

742. Vaughan, Alan. *The Edge of Tomorrow. How to Foresee and Fulfill the Future.* New York: Coward, McCann & Geoghegan, 1981. 288 pp. ISBN 0-698-11090-0.

> A how-to-do-it book on predicting by the former editor of *Psychic* magazine. An earlier book, *Patterns of Prophecy*, by the author concentrates more on the theories of prophecy.

743. Wallechinsky, David; Wallace, Amy; and Wallace, Irving. *The People's Almanac Presents the Book of Predictions.* New York: William Morrow, 1980. 513 pp. index. illus. ISBN 0-688-00024-X.

> Includes glossary. In three parts: forecasts by experts on events involving life, instructive foresights of psychics, and personalities and predictions in past times.

744. Ward, Margaret. *Gong Hee Fot Choy: Meaning "Greeting of Riches": a Fortune-Telling Game with Lessons from a Chinese Matchmaker in Numerology and Astrology.* Reno, Nev.: Medley Manufacturing, 1948. 80 pp. chart.

> Front cover design by YIM. Frequently reprinted, and easy to locate in many bookstores. System based on playing cards. "Your sons and your daughters shall prophesy, and your young men shall see visions and your old men shall dream dreams.—Joel 2–8" (title page).

See also items: 39.3, 259.

Crystal Gazing

745. Besterman, Theodore. *Crystal-Gazing: a Study in the History, Distribution, Theory and Practice of Scrying.* New Hyde Park, N.Y.: University Books, 1965. 183 pp. index. bibliography.

> Library of the Mystic Arts series. Historical, international overview by the noted English bibliographer. Legends and literature are included, as well as the process of scrying.

746. Delmonico, Damyan. *I was Curious—a Crystal Ball Gazer.* Philadelphia: Dorrance, 1972. 73 pp. illus.

> A personalized, how-to-do-it approach. Contains advice on how to interpret.

747. Melville, John. *Crystal Gazing and Clairvoyance*. New York: Samuel Weiser, 1970. 92 pp. illus.

> Use of the crystal as a means for seeing what is happening in other places and times.

Palmistry

748. Brandon-Jones, David. *Practical Palmistry*. London: Rider, 1981. 268 pp. illus. bibliography. ISBN 0-09-144831-X.

> An introduction to palmistry.

749. Brockman, Marcel. *The Complete Encyclopedia of Practical Palmistry*. Englewood Cliffs, N.J.: Prentice-Hall, 1972. 187 pp. illus. ISBN 0-13-159988-7.

> A how-to-do-it book including sample readings.

750. Gettings, Fred. *The Book of the Hand: an Illustrated History of Palmistry*. London: Hamlyn, 1965. 213 pp. index. illus.

> Includes information on cheirognomy as well as palmistry. Coffee-table-book format. Good historical information.

751. Hamon, Count Louis [pseud. Cheiro]. *Cheiro's Language of the Hand: a Complete Practical Work on the Science of Cheirognomy and Chiromancy, Containing the System and Experience of Cheiro*. New York: Arco 1962. 27th ed. 224 pp. illus.

> One of the master palmist's helpful guides to his art. The interpretations are particularly interesting.

752. Hoffman, Elizabeth P. *Palm Reading Made Easy*. New York: Essandess, 1971. 119 pp. illus. bibliography. SBN 671-10545-0.

> A practical, how-to-do-it paperback.

753. Hutchinson, Beryl Butterworth. *Your Life in Your Hands: Interpreting the Patterns on Your Palm*. London: Spearman, 1967. 254 pp. illus.

> A practical introduction to palmistry.

754. Niles, Edith. *Palmistry: Your Fate in Your Hands.* New York: Allograph, 1969. 223 pp. illus.

Good how-to-do-it overview.

755. Squire, Elizabeth Daniels. *The New Fortune in Your Hand.* New York: Fleet Press, 1960. 227 pp. index. illus. bibliography.

Includes discussion of the historical development of palmistry, as well as instructions on how to read hands.

756. Steinbach, Marten. *Medical Palmistry: Health and Character in the Hand.* Secaucus, N.J.: University Books, 1975; New York: New American Library, 1976. 188 pp. illus.

An overview of the current trend to incorporate palmistry into holistic medicine.

757. Valcourt-Vermont, Edgar de [pseud. Comte C. St. Germain]. *The Practice of Palmistry for Professional Purposes.* San Bernardino, Calif.: Borgo Press, 1980; Hollywood, Calif.: Newcastle, 1973. 461 pp. illus.

Originally published as two volumes in 1879. Dictionary of palmistry terms and techniques with many illustrations showing line relationships.

Phrenology

758. Davies, John D. *Phrenology: Fad and Science: a 19th Century American Crusade.* Hamden, Conn.: Archon Books, 1971. 203 pp. illus. bibliography. ISBN 0-208-00952-3.

Originally published by Yale University Press (New Haven, Conn.) in 1955. Covers historical development and the impact of phrenology on nineteenth century American social thought.

759. De Giustino, David. *Conquest of the Mind: Phrenology and Victorian Social Thought.* London: Croom Helm, 1975; Totowa, N.J.: Rowan & Littlefield, 1975. 248 pp. index. bibliography.

Croom Helm Social History series. A study of the work of George Combe, leader in phrenology.

760. Stern, Madeleine Bettina. *Heads and Headlines: the Phrenological Fowlers.* Norman: University of Oklahoma Press, 1971. 348 pp. illus. bibliography.

> A family biography of the Fowlers, who led the phrenology movement in the U.S. during its heyday.

761. Wells, Samuel Roberts. *How to Read Character: a New Illustrated Handbook of Phrenology and Physiognomy for Students and Examiners with a Descriptive Chart.* Rutland, Vt.: Tuttle, 1971. 191 pp. illus.

> Originally published by Samuel R. Wells (New York) in 1871.

Tarot

762. Balin, Peter. *The Flight of the Feathered Serpent.* Venice, Calif.: Wisdom Garden, 1978. 183 pp. illus. bibliographic references. ISBN 0-914794-32-9.

> Discusses the Xultan deck designed by the author / illustrator, which is tied to Mayan civilization, mystic secrets, and design motifs.

763. Crowley, Aleister. *The Book of Thoth: a Short Essay on the Tarot of the Egyptians Being the Equinox Volume III No. V by the Master Therion.* New York: Samuel Weiser, 1969. 287 pp. illus.

> Illustrations by Frieda Harris (who designed the Thoth tarot deck under the supervision of Crowley). Heavy mystical emphasis with the usual attendant difficulty of understanding Crowley's writing. Not for the beginner.

764. Douglas, Alfred. *The Tarot: the Origins, Meanings & Uses of the Cards.* New York: Taplinger, 1972; Harmondsworth, Eng.: Penguin, 1974, 1976. 249 pp. index. illus. bibliography. ISBN 0-800-87547-8.

> Illustrated by David Sheridan. Excellent overview of the subject. Includes information on the use of tarot as a gateway to meditation.

765. Dummett, Michael. *Game of Tarot: from Ferrara to Salt Lake City.* London: Duckworth, 1980, dist. by U.S. Games Systems. 600 pp. index. illus. ISBN 0-7156-1014-7.

> Assisted by Sylvia Mann. The author, skeptical of the power of tarot, nevertheless has produced an excellent book on the history and various versions of tarot. Scholarly. Does not provide interpretations.

766. Encausse, Gerard [pseud. Papus]. *The Tarot of the Bohemians: the Most Ancient Book in the World.* North Hollywood, Calif.: Wilshire Book Co., 1970. 355 pp. index. illus. bibliography.

> Translated by A. P. Morton. Based on the third, revised edition. Preface by Arthur E. Waite. An often-cited book. Not an introductory treatment.

767. Gray, Eden. *The Tarot Revealed: a Modern Guide to Reading Tarot Cards.* New York: Bell, 1960. 120 pp. illus.

> Simple layouts and interpretations. Good for beginners. Does not go into the mystical aspects of the subject, however.

768. Kaplan, Stuart R. *The Classical Tarot: Its Origins, Meaning and Divinatory Use.* Wellingborough, Eng.: Aquarian Press, 1980. 240 pp. index. illus. bibliography. ISBN 0-85030-234-X.

> Earlier edition published as *The Tarot Classic* by Grosset & Dunlap (New York) in 1972. Excellent work focusing on an eighteenth-century tarot deck. A thorough introduction to the subject.

769. Kaplan, Stuart R. *The Encyclopedia of Tarot.* New York: U.S. Games Systems, 1978; Wellingborough, Eng.: Aquarian Press, 1979. 387 pp. index. illus. bibliography. ISBN 0-913866-11-3.

> The author of other tarot books, including the *James Bond 007 Tarot Book.* Kaplan also writes instructions for the tarot decks published by U.S. Games Systems (he is president of the company). Beautiful, scholarly work covering various decks throughout history, with careful descriptive notes on each card. Not a book for beginners.

770. Laurence, Theodor. *The Sexual Key to the Tarot.* New York: Citadel Press, 1971. 121 pp. illus. ISBN 0-8065-0242-8.

> "The three main reasons cards are consulted are Health, Wealth, and Sex, not necessarily in that order" (Introduction).

771. Roberts, Richard. *Tarot and You.* Hastings-on-Hudson, N.Y.: Morgan & Morgan, 1971. 296 pp. illus. ISBN 0-87100-020-2.

> Illustrated. Provides various layouts and interpretations. Accompanied by records of taped readings. A picture "index" in the margins depicts the cards under discussion. Cards from the Palladini Aquarian deck are used for the illustrations.

772. Steiger, Brad, and Warmeth, Ron. *Tarot.* New York: Award Books, 1973, 1969. 168 pp.

Includes historical background on divination and case studies of Warmeth's readings.

773. Waite, Arthur Edward. *The Pictorial Key to the Tarot: Being Fragments of a Secret Tradition under the Veil of Divination.* Blauvelt, N.Y.: Multimedia, 1971. 341 pp. illus. bibliography. ISBN 0-8334-1728-2.

Considers the historical and mystical backgrounds of tarot; also gives interpretations of meanings of the various cards.

See also item 178.

12
ASTROLOGY

Birth, n. The first and direst of all disasters. As to the nature of
it there appears to be no uniformity. Castor and Pollux
were born from the egg. Pallas came out of a skull. Gala-
tea was once a block of stone. Persilis, who wrote in the
tenth century, avers that he grew up out of the ground
where a priest had spilled holy water. It is known that
Arimaxus was derived from a hole in the earth, made by a
stroke of lightning. Leucomedon was a son of a cavern in
Mount Aetna, and I have myself seen a man come out of a
wine cellar.

Ambrose Bierce,
The Devil's Dictionary

Fascination with the heavens has existed since earliest times. The
many myths and legends based on the stars and the planets attest to
this. In addition, there has been a desire to tie fate to the heavens.
Why do some people seem to bear charmed lives, while others seem
doomed to perpetual failure? Perhaps some mystical power, based on
the position of heavenly bodies at the time of birth, determines this.
Hence, the "science" of astrology was born.

The study of heavenly bodies in relationship to man appears to
be universal. It is a practice known to have existed in the ancient
Orient—China, Japan and India—as well as the Western nations. The
ancient Egyptians saw the heavenly bodies as the key to existence. It
seems logical that when the ancient mariners learned to navigate
their boats by the stars, the power of the heavens in daily life was
confirmed.

The popularity of astrology continues to thrive today. Daily
horoscope columns are found in most newspapers and astrologers'
services are readily available through the yellow pages of most large
city telephone directories. It is possible to purchase personal home
computer software packages for astrology, and a number of long-
lived astrology magazines and annuals sell steadily and well.

A bibliographic article on astrology for supplementary reading

is by Nancy Schimmel, "Fools . . . by Heavenly Compulsion" in
American Libraries (March 1972), pp. 261-67.
Material in this chapter is arranged as follows:

- Reference Works
- Histories and Overviews
- Casual Readings
- Beginning Texts
- Advanced Texts

Reference Works

774. *Astrology Annual Reference Book.* North Hollywood, Calif.: Symbols and Signs, 1970?–

> An illustrated annual in four sections: (1) moon phases, planetary movements, etc.; (2) charts for constructing horoscopes; (3) Ephemerides; and (4) calendars.

775. Brau, Jean-Louis; Weaver, Helen; and Edwards, Allan.
Larousse Encyclopedia of Astrology. New York: New American Library,
1980. 308 pp. bibliography. ISBN 0-452-25330-6.

> A Plume Book. Translated from the French. Edited and with a preface by Helen Weaver. Consulting and contributing editors: Robert Hand, Charles Harvey, and Charles Jayne. Dictionary format in clear, simple language. An excellent attempt to update De Vore (item 778).

776. Carter, Charles Ernest Owen. *The Astrology of Accidents: Investigations and Research.* London: Theosophical Publishing House, 1970,
1977. 123 pp. illus. ISBN 0-7229-5045-4.

> An interesting exploration of some astrological events.

777. Carter, Charles Ernest Owen. *An Encyclopedia of Psychological Astrology.* Wheaton, Ill.: Quest Books, 1963, 1979. 195 pp.

> Dictionary format. Stars are linked to various human conditions, such as personality traits, behavior, and health.

778. De Vore, Nicholas. *Encyclopedia of Astrology.* Totowa, N.J.: Littlefield, Adams, 1976. 435 pp. ISBN 0-87471-858-9.

> Originally published by the Philosophical Library (New York) in 1947. Dictionary arrangement with fairly long articles. Special articles by

Charles A. Jayne and Frederic van Norstrand. Encyclopedic approach by a one-time president of the Astrologic Research Society.

779. Fleming-Mitchell, Leslie. *The Language of Astrology.* London: W. H. Allen, 1981. 102 pp. ISBN 0-352-30950-4.

Published originally by the Running Press (Philadelphia) in 1977 at *The Running Press Glossary of Astrology Terms.* Short but useful dictionary. Most entries are brief, but a few have longer definitions.

780. Gardner, Frederick Leigh. *Bibliotheca Astrologia: a Catalog of Astrological Publications of the 15th through the 19th Century.* North Hollywood, Calif.: Symbols and Signs, 1977. 2d ed. 164 pp. ISBN 0-912-50438-2.

First published in 1911 by the author as *A Catalogue Raisonné of Works on the Occult Sciences, Vol. II, Astrological Books.* Volume one covered *Rosicrucian Books.* Volume three (never published) was to cover alchemical books.

781. Hall, Manly Palmer. *Astrological Keywords.* Totowa, N.J.: Littlefield, Adams, 1975; Los Angeles: The Philosophical Research Society, 1958. 7th ed. 228 pp. index. bibliography. ISBN 0-8226-0299-7.

First published by the Philosophical Research Society. Numerous articles cover most aspects of astrology. Hall was the founder of the Philosophical Research Society and was noted for his writings on mystic societies. Very thorough.

782. Kennedy, Edward Stewart. *The Astrological History of Masha' Allah.* Cambridge, Mass.: Harvard University Press, 1971; London: Oxford University Press, 1971. 206 pp. index. illus. SBN 674-05025-8.

With David Pingree. "The study is an attempt to assemble and analyze all that is presently available of a major work by an eighth-century Jewish astrologer known in medieval Europe as Messahala and in the Near East as Masha'Allah" (Preface).

783. Old, Walter Gorn [pseud. Sepharial]. *Sepharial's New Dictionary of Astrology.* New York: Arco, 1963, 1972; Hackensack, N.J.: Wehman, n.d. 158 pp. illus. ISBN 0-668-02589-1.

Dictionary format. Contains an appendix of math. Biographies of noted astrology authors are included.

784. Sapre, R. G. *Astrology (Analytical Study of Different Eastern and Western Systems)*. Poona, India: A.V.G. Prakashan, 1968. 188 pp.

> Includes a look at the twelve houses, dashas, and the Dashavarga Horoscope. Also a long section on horoscopes cast within different systems.

785. Varahamihira. *The Brihajjatakam of Varhara Mihira*. New York: AMS Press, 1974. 400 pp. illus. ISBN 0-404-57812-8.

> Translated by Swami Vijnanananda, alias Hari Prasanna Chatterjee. Original edition issued as volume 12 of *Sacred Books of the Hindus*. First published by Panini Office (Allahabad, India) in 1912. In English and Sanskrit. Foreword and notes in English. Basic work of Hindu astrology.

786. Wedeck, Harry Ezekiel. *Dictionary of Astrology*. London: P. Owens, 1973; Secaucus, N.J.: Citadel Press, 1973. 189 pp. illus. ISBN 0-720-60173-8.

> A basic, useful dictionary of astrological terms.

Histories and Overviews

787. Bentley, John. *A Historical View of the Hindu Astronomy, from the Earliest Dawn of That Science in India, to the Present Time*. Osnabruck, Austria: Biblio Verlag, 1970. 282 pp. illus.

> A good overview. Eastern methods of astrology have had an increasing influence on Western astrology in recent years.

788. Capp, Bernard. *English Almanacs, 1500–1800: Astrology and the Popular Press*. Ithaca, N.Y.: Cornell University Press, 1979; London: Faber & Faber, 1979. 452 pp. index. illus. bibliographic references. ISBN 0-8014-1229-3.

> English edition published as *Astrology and the Popular Press*. The majority of the book covers the earlier period, with a study of predictions made at the time and of how such predictions were used politically. Describes the popularity of almanacs during various periods.

789. Darling, Harry F., and Oliver, Ruth Hale. *Astropsychology*. Lakewood, Ga.: CSA Press, 1972. 333 pp. illus. bibliographies. ISBN 0-87707-111-X.

First published in 1968 as *Organum Quaterni*. Through case studies, the authors illustrate criminal and abnormal psychological traits shown in birth charts.

790. Delsol, Paula. *Chinese Horoscopes*. London: Pan, 1973. 239 pp. illus. ISBN 0-330-23424-2.

Translated from the French *Horoscopes Chinois* by Peter and Tanya Leslie, published by Mercure de France (Paris) in 1969. Published by Hippocrene (New York) as *Chinese Astrology* in 1972. Brief introduction to the subject.

791. Dixon, Jeane. *Yesterday, Today and Forever*. New York: William Morrow, 1975. 439 pp. ISBN 0-688-02984-1.

A linkage of the twelve apostles to the twelve signs of the zodiac. Each apostle, according to the author, appears to have demonstrated certain traits which make such a comparison logical.

792. Doane, Doris Chase. *Astrology: 30 Years' Research*. Los Angeles: Church of Light, 1956; New York: Samuel Weiser, n.d. 310 pp.

An account of astrological study.

793. Gatti, Arthur. *The Kennedy Curse*. Chicago: Henry Regnery, 1976. 264 pp. index. illus. ISBN 0-8092-8213-5.

Glossary included. The author analyzes 30 charts of Kennedy family members and friends in the search for a fatal curse, as well as a curse on the presidency itself.

794. Gauquelin, Michel. *Astrology and Science*. London: Mayflower, 1972; Peter Davies, 1970. 238 pp. index. illus. bibliography.

Translation by James Hughes of *Astrologie devant la science* (Paris: Editions Planete, 1966). Published as *Scientific Basis of Astrology* by Stein & Day (New York) in 1969. A history of astrology with an overview of modern findings.

795. Gauquelin, Michel. *Cosmic Influences on Human Behavior*. New York: Stein & Day, 1973; London: Garnstone, 1974. 286 pp. illus. bibliographic references. ISBN 0-8128-1543-2.

Translated by Joyce E. Clemon. A study of statistical astrology as applied to the theory of planetary heredity.

796. Gettings, Fred. *The Book of the Zodiac: an Historical Anthology of Astrology.* London: Ward Lock, 1972. 143 pp. illus. maps. bibliography. ISBN 0-7063-1357-7.

Attractive book. Provides a good historical perspective of the zodiac.

797. Gleadow, Rupert. *The Origin of the Zodiac.* New York: Atheneum, 1968. 238 pp. index. illus. bibliographic notes.

A classical scholar describes the history and meaning of the zodiac.

798. Greene, Liz. *Saturn, a New Look at an Old Devil.* Wellingborough, Eng.: Aquarian Press, 1977; New York: Samuel Weiser, 1976. 196 pp. illus. ISBN 0-85030-148-3.

A thoughtful study of Saturn's influence in astrology, with attention to its reputation as a sinister influence.

799. Jones, Marc Edmund. *Astrology: How and Why It Works.* London: Routledge & Kegan Paul, 1977. 437 pp. index. illus. ISBN 0-7100-8828-0.

First published by McKay (Philadelphia) and Routledge & Kegan Paul (London) in 1945. A classic in the field.

800. Kenton, Warren. *Astrology: the Celestial Mirror.* London: Thames & Hudson, 1974. 128 pp. illus. maps. ISBN 0-500-81004-4.

A handsomely illustrated overview of astrology.

801. Lindsay, Jack. *Origins of Astrology.* London: Muller, 1971. 480 pp. index. illus. bibliography.

Contents include Babylonian beginnings, the Greeks, Egyptians and astrology, the Romans, pagans, and Christianity. Scholarly.

802. *Llewellyn's Moon Sign Book.* St. Paul: Llewellyn, 1906–. annual. illus.

Compact book which describes lunar influences on planting, breeding, getting rid of pests, etc.

803. *Llewellyn's Sun Sign Book.* St. Paul: Llewellyn, 1983–. annual. illus. ISSN 0-743-6408.

Originally published by Llewellyn as *Personal Guides,* then sold to Bantam, which later dropped the series when sales fell off in the early

1980s. Horoscopes and forecasts for each sun sign with hints for romance, fashion, sex, gambling, etc.

804. Lloyd-Jones, Hugh. *Myths of the Zodiac*. New York: St. Martin's, 1978; London: Duckworth, 1978. 94 pp. illus. ISBN 0-312-55870-8.

Illustrated by Marcelle Quinton. An entertaining description of the signs of the zodiac.

805. Logan, Daniel. *Your Eastern Star: Oriental Astrology, Reincarnation and the Future*. New York: William Morrow, 1972. 240 pp. illus.

Presents the twelve animal signs with traits and qualities. Based on Japanese principles, personally researched in Japan by the author.

806. Oster, Gar. *The Astrological Chart of the U.S.: 1776–2141*. New York: Stein & Day, 1976. 272 pp. index. illus. bibliography. ISBN 0-8128-1888-1.

An analysis of the country's natal chart.

807. Parker, Derek, and Parker, Julie. *The New Compleat Astrologer*. New York: Crown, 1984. rev. ed. 288 pp. index. illus. maps. ISBN 0-517-55503-4.

Harmony Books. Originally published by McGraw-Hill (New York) in 1971. Lavishly illustrated, with instructions for casting natal charts using a calculator or personal computer. Birth charts through the year 2000 are included, as well as explanations of aspects, progressions, and planetary positions.

808. Parker, Derek, and Parker, Julie. *The Astrology of America's Destiny*. New York: Random House, 1974; Vintage, 1975. 209 pp. illus. bibliographic references. ISBN 0-394-49061-4.

Contents: The Birth of the U.S., Roots of the Nation, America's Place in the Cosmic Process, the U.S. Chart, 200 Years of Growth through Crisis, and Prospects for the Last Quarter Century. (Look out for 1988–1989!)

809. Sampson, Walter Harold. *The Zodiac: a Life Epitome, Being a Comparison of the Zodiacal Elements with Life-Principles, Cosmic, Anthropological, and Psychological*. New York: ASI, 1975. 420 pp. illus. ISBN 0-88231-019-4.

Originally published by Blackfriar Press (London) in 1928. A metaphysical examination of the zodiac.

810. Wedel, Theodore Otto. *The Mediaeval Attitude toward Astrology, Particularly in England.* Folcroft, Penn.: Folcroft Library Editions, 1974. 483 pp. index. bibliography. ISBN 0-8414-9593-9.

> Originally published by Yale University Press (New Haven) in 1920 as part of the Yale Studies in English series. The study was the author's thesis at Yale in 1918.

811. West, John Anthony, and Toonder, Jan Gerhard. *The Case for Astrology.* New York: Coward McCann, 1970; London: Macdonald, 1970; Penguin, 1973. 286 pp. index. illus. bibliography. ISBN 0-356-02937-9.

> Contents: history and technique, objections, evidence, and the future of the significance of astrology. Argues for astrology as a scientific method.

812. White, Suzanne. *Suzanne White's Book of Chinese Change.* New York: M. Evans, 1976; Greenwich, Conn.: Fawcett, 1977; London: Souvenir Press, 1977; Fontana, 1978. 359 pp. ISBN 0-87131-207-7.

> "What the oriental zodiac can tell you about yourself and your future" (title page). Tells what to expect in certain years. For example, hide if you were born in a rat year and are living in a cat year.

813. Wulff, Wilhelm Theodor H. *Zodiac and Swastika: How Astrology Guided Hitler's Germany.* New York: Coward, McCann & Geoghegan, 1973; London: Arthur Baker, 1973. 192 pp. ISBN 0-698-10547-8.

> Foreword by Walter Laqueur. Translated from *Tierkreis und Hakenkreus.* Author's account of his days as Himmler's personal astrologer.

814. Zoller, Robert. *The Lost Key to Prediction: the Arabic Parts in Astrology.* New York: Inner Traditions International, 1980. 245 pp. index. illus. bibliography. ISBN 0-89291-013-0.

> Includes a translation from the Latin of *Liber Astronomiae* by Guido Bonatti. Description of how the parts were lost, and how they can be used today.

Casual Readings

815. Dahl, Arlene. *Lovescopes.* Indianapolis: Bobbs-Merrill, 1983. 246 pp. illus. ISBN 0-672-52770-7.

Glamorous movie star of the 1960s provides simple directions for using your astrological make-up to its best advantage in interpersonal relations and emotional life.

816. Dean, Malcolm. *The Astrology Game: the Inside Story: the Truth about Astrology.* New York: Beaufort Books, 1980. 360 pp. bibliography. ISBN 0-8253-0002-9.

"Eventually, the pattern became clear. One could discern the direction, if not the ultimate destination" (Preface).

817. de Jersey, Katherine. *Destiny Times Six: an Astrologer's Casebook.* New York: M. Evans, 1970, distributed by J. G. Lippincott. 188 pp.

With Isabella Tames. Six case studies from a professional astrologer's readings. "Astrology can help anyone, because it enables us to know ourselves as we really are, so that we don't waste time and energy fighting against the pattern" (p. 288).

818. Goodman, Linda. *Linda Goodman's Sun Signs.* New York: Taplinger, 1968; Bantam, 1971; London: Harrap, 1970; Pan, 1972. 484 pp.

For each sign there is a general, anecdotal description. Written for laughs, apparently, as much as for information. The author also wrote *Linda Goodman's Love Signs.*

819. King, Teri. *Business, Success and Astrology.* New York: St. Martin's, 1975; London: Allison & Busby, 1974. 377 pp.

A practical guide to developing successful work relations through astrology.

820. Leek, Sybil. *My Life in Astrology.* Englewood Cliffs, N.J.: Prentice-Hall, 1972. 205 pp. ISBN 0-13-608521-0.

Personalized account, autobiographical in nature. After her recent death, Sybil Leek supposedly was contacted in the afterlife by another medium for a tabloid article.

821. Loeper, John J. *Understanding Your Child through Astrology.* New York: David McKay, 1970. 211 pp.

Written by an educator, the book concludes with commandments of parenthood, including "cooperate with the school." Other topics covered are: astrology for the parent, short history of astrology, education and astrology, psychology and astrology, your child and astrology, sun signs, helping your child in school, planning your child's future, and your child in the Aquarian Age.

822. Lynch, John, ed. *The Coffee Table Book of Astrology.* New York: Viking Press, 1967. rev. ed. 311 pp. illus.

> A Studio Book. First published in 1962. Tables of ascendants and ephemerides of the moon are provided. Not really a text for learning how to do it.

823. MacNeice, Louis. *Astrology.* Garden City, N.J.: Doubleday, 1964; London: Aldus Books, 1964. 351 pp. index. illus.

> Appendixes provide simple tables. Basic information is given, along with nice illustrations.

824. Quigley, Joan. *Astrology for Adults.* New York: Holt, Rinehart & Winston, 1969. 245 pp. SBN 03-081860-5.

> Moon-sign ephemerides in the back. Better for casual reading than for serious study. The author also wrote *Astrology for Teens.*

825. Shulman, Sandra. *The Encyclopedia of Astrology.* London: Hamlyn, 1976. 188 pp. index. illus. ISBN 0-600-33098-2.

> Beautiful coffee-table book. International history of astrology. Not a dictionary format.

826. *Super Horoscope.* New York: Grosset & Dunlap, 1974–.

> Published irregularly, although issued recently as an annual. One volume for each zodiac sign. Includes information on moon and moon activities (such as planting, fishing, health, etc.) and the year ahead for the sun sign of each title.

See also items 39.9, 877.

Beginning Texts

827. Allan, William Frederick [pseud. Alan Leo]. *Astrologer's Library.* New York: Astrologer's Library, 1983. 8 vols.

> Edited by V. E. Robson. Written and originally published prior to World War I in Great Britain. Still considered to be a fine set of introductory texts.

827.1. *Astrology for All.*

827.2. *Casting the Horoscope.*

827.3. *How to Judge a Nativity.*

827.4. *The Art of Synthesis.*

827.5. *The Progressed Horoscope.*

827.6. *The Key to Your Own Nativity.*

827.7. *Esoteric Astrology.*

827.8. *The Complete Dictionary of Astrology.*

828. Evans, Colin. *The New Waite's Compendium of Natal Astrology: with Ephemeris for 1800–1900 and Universal House of Tables.* London: Routledge & Kegan Paul, 1981, 1971. rev. ed. 252 pp. ISBN 0-7100-0882-1.

> Originally published in 1917. Revised edition updated by Brian E. F. Gardner. Summary of how-to-do-it.

829. Freeman, Martin. *How to Interpret a Birth Chart; a Guide to the Analysis and Synthesis of Astrological Charts.* Wellingborough, Eng.: Aquarian Press, 1981. 128 pp. index. illus. ISBN 0-85030-249-8.

> Basic text without math.

830. Gallant, Roy A. *Astrology: Sense or Nonsense?* New York: Doubleday, 1974. 201 pp. illus. bibliography. ISBN 0-385-07459-X.

> Basic text and survey. Glossary included. Good overview of the subject.

831. Gaston, Wilbert. *First Principles of Astrology.* New York: George Sully, 1927. 187 pp. illus.

> "The purpose of this book is to impart a practical knowledge and understanding of the ancient science of Astrology . . ." (Preface).

832. Hone, Margaret E. *The Modern Textbook of Astrology.* London: L. N. Fowler, 1967. rev. ed. 320 pp. index. illus.

> First edition published by Samuel Weiser (New York) in 1951. The book is a result of many years of teaching astrology by the author. Includes comparison of the equal house and Placidean house systems.

833. Jones, Marc Edmund. *How to Learn Astrology.* Garden City, N.Y.: Doubleday, 1971, 1941. 190 pp. illus.

> Solid, easy-to-understand directions. Glossary included. Good instruction.

834. Kimmelman, Sydney [pseud. Sydney Omarr]. *My World of Astrology.* New York: Fleet, 1965. 378 pp. illus.

> A convincing argument for astrology. Inspirational for the beginning student.

835. Kimmelman, Sydney. *Sydney Omarr's Astrological Revelations about You.* New York: New American Library, 1973. 239 pp.

> Useful, practical introduction to the twelve sun signs.

836. Lewi, Grant. *Astrology for the Millions.* St. Paul: Llewellyn, 1969. 4th ed. 257 pp. illus.

> Classic work, first published in 1942. A quick way to learn to do a natal chart without math. "He was quiet, witty, deeply mystical and a little weird" (Llewellyn catalog).

837. Lewi, Grant. *Heaven Knows What.* St. Paul: Llewellyn, 1969, 1977; New York: Bantam, 1935. 136 pp. illus.

> Lewi's other classic work. Easy, how-to-do-it astrology for beginners. Bypasses math and other complicated methods employed for precise readings, but good for the novice.

838. March, Marion, and McEvers, Joan. *The Only Way to Learn Astrology.* New York: Samuel Weiser, 1981–82. 3 vols.

> Volume one, *Basic Principles* (ISBN 0-917086-00-7); volume two, *Math and Interpretation* (ISBN 0-917086-26-0); volume three, *Horoscope Analysis* (ISBN 0-917086-43-0).

839. Oken, Alan. *As Above, So Below: a Primary Guide to Astrological Awareness.* New York: Bantam, 1973. 344 pp. index. illus. bibliography.

> Good overview focusing on basic information for each sign of the zodiac, the sun, and the planets.

840. Raphael, Edwin. *Raphael's Astronomical Ephemeris of the Planets' Places: with Tables of Houses for London, Liverpool and New York.* Slough, Eng.: Foulsham, 1801–. annual.

> Reliable, highly regarded ephemeris. The basic positions needed to cast horoscopes are easily located.

841. Rice, Hugh S. *American Astrology Table of Houses.* Los Angeles: Church of Light, 1944. 616 pp.

> Covers latitudes from 0 to 60 degrees for the Northern and Southern Hemispheres. Includes tables which facilitate the calculation of primary and secondary directions. Prepared under the direction of the staff of *American Astrology,* a long-published magazine. A basic, useful tool which provides necessary information on longitude and latitude.

842. Sakoian, Frances, and Acker, Louis S. *The Astrologer's Handbook.* New York: Harper & Row, 1973; Harmondsworth, Eng.: Penguin, 1981. 461 pp. illus. SBN 06-013737-7.

> A good how-to-do-it book with instructions on how to interpret aspects. Well regarded in the field. Includes a cross index of aspects.

843. Sakoian, Frances, and Acker, Louis S. *The Astrology of Human Relationships.* New York: Harper & Row, 1976. 395 pp. index. illus. ISBN 0-06-013712-6.

> Glossary included. A basic text on developing the natal chart and comparing it with other charts.

844. *Simplified Scientific Ephemeris.* Oceanside, Calif.: The Rosicrucian Fellowship, 1857–. annual, with ten-year cumulations.

> Basic, necessary tables for casting horoscopes. Similar to Raphael's tables (see item 840). The early tables in this set were done by Marx Heindel.

845. *Simplified Scientific Tables of Houses.* Oceanside, Calif.: The Rosicrucian Fellowship, 1949. 312 pp.

> A basic, necessary tool, similar to the *American Astrology* volume (see item 841). Covers latitudes from 0 to 66 degrees, and longitudes and latitudes of over 4,000 cities throughout the world. Provides Placidean house divisions.

846. Valcourt-Vermont, Edgar de [pseud. Comte C. de Saint-Germain]. *Practical Astrology.* Hollywood, Calif.: Newcastle, 1973. 257 pp. ISBN 0-87877-018-6.

> Originally published in 1901. An easy-to-follow guide for using astrology to judge character and to foresee the future.

847. Vorel, Irys. *Be Your Own Astrologer.* New York: Uranian Press, 1933; Hackensack, N.J.: Wehman, 1967; New York: Samuel Weiser, n.d. 156 pp.

> Astrological Library series. Still a good, simple beginner's book.

848. Weingarten, Henry. *The Study of Astrology.* New York: ASI, 1977. 4th ed. 140 pp. bibliography. ISBN 0-88231-029-1.

> A highly regarded, standard textbook.

Advanced Texts

849. Baker, Douglas. *Esoteric Astrology.* Essendon, Eng.: D. Baker, 1982. 10 vols. illus. ISBN 0-686-45417-0.

> Treats the more complicated aspects of astrology, including theory and interpretation. The volumes are divided by houses.

850. Bills, Rex E. *The Rulership Book: a Directory of Astrological Correspondences.* Richard, Va.: Macoy Publishing & Masonic Supply Co., 1971. 428 pp. bibliography.

> "This book presents a practical list of those correspondences, conveniently arranged alphabetically as well as by sign, houses, and planets. Rulerships are included for all branches of Astrology, including natal, mundane, and horary" (Foreword).

851. Crummerce, Maria Elise. *Sun-Sign Revelations.* New York: Viking Press, 1974; London: Bodley Head, 1974. 115 pp. illus. ISBN 0-670-68329-9.

> A thoughtful, useful book which provides information on negative aspects.

852. George, Llewellyn. *The New A to Z Horoscope Maker and Delineator: an American Textbook of Genethliacal Astrology.* St. Paul: Llewellyn, 1981. 13th ed. 592 pp. index. illus. ISBN 0-87542-263-2.

First published in 1910. Revised and expanded by Marylee Bytheriver. Previously published as *A to Z Horoscope Maker and Delineator*. Although of potential value for the beginner, this book is so full of information that it can be used equally well by the advanced student.

853. James, Colin. *The Relative Strength of Signs and Planets*. Denver: Colorado Astrological Society, 1978. 273 pp. illus.

Interesting interpretations of planetary influence.

854. Jocelyn, John. *Meditations on the Signs of the Zodiac*. Blauvelt, N.Y.: Rudolf Steiner, 1970; San Francisco: Harper & Row, 1970, 1980. 277 pp. illus. ISBN 0-06-066092-9.

Thoughtful insights into some aspects of astrology.

855. Leek, Sybil. *Star Speak: Your Body Language from the Stars*. New York: Arbor House, 1975. 263 pp. bibliography. ISBN 0-87795-118-7.

Covers the effects of astral positions on the human body.

856. McWhirter, Louise. *Astrology and Stock Market Forecasting*. New York: ASI, 1977. 207 pp. ISBN 0-88231-034-8.

Originally published in 1938 as *McWhirter's Theory of Stock Market Forecasting*.

857. Mann, A. T. *The Round Art: the Astrology of Time and Space*. New York: Galley Press, 1979; Limpsfield, Eng.: Paper Tiger, 1979, distributed by Phin Ltd. 299 pp. index. illus. bibliography. ISBN 0-8317-7509-2.

Edited by Donald Lehmkuhl and Mary Flanagan. Glossary. A beautiful but complicated book on a highly mathematical system of astrology.

858. Rudhyar, Dane. *The Astrological Houses: the Spectrum of Individual Experience*. Garden City, N.Y.: Doubleday, 1972. 208 pp. bibliographic references.

Descriptions of the houses and their importance in astrology. Author (whose birth name was Daniel de Chenneviere) brings Jungian psychology and other philosophies to astrology.

859. Rudhyar, Dane. *Astrological Timing: the Transition in the New Age*. New York: Harper, 1972. 246 pp. ISBN 0-06-090260-4.

Originally published in 1969 as *Birth Patterns for a New Humanity*. A good introduction to astrological cycles and ages.

860. Tyl, Noel. *The Principles and Practice of Astrology*. St. Paul: Llewellyn, 1973–75. 12 vols. illus. bibliographies.

> Llewellyn Syllabus for Home Study and College Curriculum series. A logical progression of various considerations. A teacher's guide is also available, making this a useful set for classroom purposes. The following volumes make up the series:

860.1 *Horoscope Construction.*

860.2 *The Houses: Their Signs and Planets.*

860.3. *The Planets: Their Signs and Aspects.*

860.4. *Aspects and Houses in Analysis.*

860.5. *Astrology and Personality.*

860.6. *The Expanded Present.*

860.7. *Integrated Transits.*

860.8. *Analysis and Prediction.*

860.9. *Special Horoscope Dimensions.*

860.10. *Astrological Counsel.*

860.11. *Astrology: Astral, Mundane, Occult.*

860.12. *Times to Come.*

861. Yott, Donald. *Astrology and Reincarnation*. New York: Samuel Weiser, 1977–79. 3 vols.

> Covers retrograde planets and intercepted signs to show how they relate to reincarnation. Astrology combined with some mystic elements. Volume one, *Retrograde Planets & Reincarnation* (ISBN 0-87728-367-2); volume two, *Intercepted Signs & Reincarnation* (ISBN 0-87728-374-5); volume three, *Triangulations of Saturn & Jupiter-Mercury* (ISBN 0-87728-394-X).

13
SKEPTICS AND DEBUNKERS

Cynic, n. A blackguard whose faulty vision sees things as they
are, not as they ought to be. Hence the custom among the
Scythians of plucking out a cynic's eyes to improve his vision.

Ambrose Bierce,
The Devil's Dictionary

No sourcebook to the literature of such a controversial subject as the
occult could be complete without a few titles that disparage and scorn
the subject. A balanced view is one that scientists strive to develop
and maintain, and the more responsible investigators of the paranormal (although they may be believers) also try to be objective. Not all
are successful, of course. It is interesting to note, in the titles that
follow, that vehemence may take the place of cool logic, and bitter-
ness may accompany claimed disproof.

Since the purpose of this book is to present a variety of material
on the occult, the views of skeptics and debunkers are presented as
well as the views, for the most part those of advocates and believers,
presented in previous chapters. The number of selections is small.
But the intent of this book is not to prove or disprove the existence of
occult phenomena; rather, it is to present a sampling of the wide
range of available materials in the field.

For those who wish to delve further into the disproof of occult
subjects, an ample selection of journal articles is available through
various indexes and databases. Also, printed annotated lists are
available from Editorial Research Services (P.O. Box 1832, Kansas
City, Missouri, 64141), compiled by Laird M. Wilcox. One listing is
entitled "Bibliography on Astrology, Myticism, and the Occult." Most
of the items are anti-paranormal in nature.

The materials in this chapter are not divided into subsections.

862. Abell, George Ogden, and Singer, Barry, eds. *Science and the
Paranormal: Probing the Existence of the Supernatural.* New York: Scribner's, 1981. 414 pp. index. bibliography. ISBN 0-684-16655-0.

A compilation of essays by various debunkers on a wide range of paranormal activities.

863. Alcock, James E. *Parapsychology, Science or Magic? a Psychological Perspective.* New York: Pergamon Press, 1981. 224 pp. index. bibliography. ISBN 0-08-025773-9.

Pergamon International Library of Science, Technology, Engineering, and Social Studies series. A skeptic examines all aspects and issues of psi phenomena in detail.

864. Bok, Bart Jan, and Jerome, Lawrence E. *Objections to Astrology.* Buffalo, N.Y.: Prometheus Books, 1975. 62 p. illus.

Impact series. Reprinted from *The Humanist*, 35 (Sept./Oct. 1975). A strong argument against astrology, based on a signed condemnation by nearly 200 scientists and various critics.

865. Burnam, Tom. *Dictionary of Misinformation.* New York: Thomas Y. Crowell, 1975. 302 pp. ISBN 0-690-00147-9.

An example of a number of books dealing with fads and fallacies. Full descriptions of mysterious items and happenings often encompassed within the occult.

866. Cazeau, Charles J., and Scott, Stuart D., Jr. *Exploring the Unknown: Great Mysteries Reexamined.* New York: Plenum Press, 1979. 283 pp. illus. ISBN 0-306-40210-6.

Original title: *Great Mysteries of the Earth.* Two scientists look at the paranormal, including ancient wonders and UFOs, with ever-present skepticism.

867. Christopher, Milbourne. *Houdini: a Pictorial Life.* New York: Thomas Y. Crowell, 1976. 218 pp. illus.

Includes material on Houdini's efforts to expose phony spiritualists.

868. de Camp, Lyon Sprague. *Spirits, Stars, and Spells: the Profits and Perils of Magic.* New York: Canaveral, 1966. 348 pp. illus.

With Catherine C. de Camp. A compilation of de Camp's writings through the years on the seamier side of the occult.

869. Dunham, Barrows. *Man against Myth.* New York: Hill & Wang, 1962. 316 pp.

An argument against easy belief in the occult.

870. Eisler, Robert Isaac. *The Royal Art of Astrology*. London: Herbert Joseph, 1946. 296 pp. illus.

Very hostile to astrology.

871. *The Encyclopedia of Delusions*. New York: Simon & Schuster, 1979, 1981. 242 pp.

Examples of materials / items / occurrences once thought to be mysterious and inexplicable.

872. Frazier, Kendrick, ed. *Paranormal Borderlands of Science*. Buffalo, N.Y.: Prometheus Books, 1981. 469 pp. illus. ISBN 0-87975-148-7.

Collection of 47 articles from the *Skeptical Inquirer*, journal of the Committee for the Scientific Investigation of Claims of the Paranormal. Strongly anti-paranormal.

873. Gardner, Martin. *Science, Good, Bad and Bogus*. Buffalo, N.Y.: Prometheus Books, 1981. 408 pp. index. illus. ISBN 0-879-75144-4.

A debunking by a science writer.

874. Goldsmith, Donald, ed. *Scientists Confront Velikovsky*. New York: Norton, 1979; Ithaca, N.Y.: Cornell University Press, 1977. 183 pp. index. bibliography. ISBN 0-393-00928-9.

Papers from the American Association for the Advancement of Science Conference, 1974. Variety of scientists reject the theory that a massive planetary line-up caused certain Biblical natural disasters.

875. Hall, Trevor Henry. *Search for Harry Price*. London: Duckworth, 1979, distributed by Biblio Distribution Centre. 237 pp. index. illus. bibliographic references. ISBN 0-7156-1143-7.

A fierce exposé of Price, revealed here as a charlatan. The author has written similar books on Edmund Gurney and Ada Goodrich Freer.

876. Jackson, Herbert G. *Spirit Rappers*. Garden City, N.Y.: Doubleday, 1972. 226 pp. bibliography.

Balanced account of the Fox sisters' careers, recantations, and subsequent renunciations of their confessions. Includes material on Houdini.

877. Jerome, Lawrence E. *Astrology Disproved*. Buffalo, N.Y.: Prometheus Books, 1977. 233 pp. illus. bibliographies. ISBN 0-87975-067-7.

Contains "Objections to Astrology: a Statement by 192 Leading Scientists." Includes historical perspectives, biological versus "cosmic" clocks, and the psychology of magic and astrology. "Astrology is far from the simple predictive 'science' it appears to be on the surfaces; its inner workings are clever, complex, and subtle. Yet, for all that, it remains quite false" (chapter 1).

878. Kagan, Daniel, and Summers, Ian. *Mute Evidence*. New York: Bantam, 1984. 504 pp.

A dismissal of the rumors of cattle mutilations being caused by UFOs or as part of satanic sacrifices.

879. Keene, M. Lamar. *The Psychic Mafia*. New York: Dell, 1977; St. Martin's, 1976. 173 pp. illus. bibliography. ISBN 0-440-16849-X.

Told to Allen Spraggett. Foreword by William V. Rauscher. A confession from a fraud who spent years as a spiritualist.

880. MacKenzie, Andrew. *Apparitions and Ghosts*. New York: Popular Library, 1971; London: A. Barker, 1971. 207 pp.

Foreword by G. W. Lambert. The author compares cases of ghost sightings in the last century with present ones. He concludes that there is little or no evidence for the existence of ghosts.

881. Montagu, Ashley. *The Prevalence of Nonsense*. New York: Harper & Row, 1967. 300 pp.

An examination by a highly respected scholar on the meaning of truth.

882. Noorbergen, Rene. *The Soul Hustlers: an Exposé into the Hoax of Astrology, the UFO Mystery That Will Not Die, and What the Psychics Don't Tell You*. Grand Rapids, Mich.: Zondervan, 1976. 190 pp.

Taped interviews with psychics are analyzed in terms of voice stress and other psychological factors. Author claims that the witnesses lied when they denied any connection with the devil.

883. Randi, James. *Flim-Flam! Psychics, ESP, Unicorns and Other Delusions*. Buffalo, N.Y.: Prometheus Books, 1982. 342 pp. index. bibliography. ISBN 0-87975-198-3.

Introduction by Isaac Asimov. Bibliography divided into proparanormal and anti-paranormal sources. (More items in the second part.)

"The Great Randi," in the tradition of Houdini, is concerned with exposing frauds and frequently appears on television.

884. Sagan, Carl. *Broca's Brain: Reflections on the Romance of Science.* New York: Random House, 1979. 347 pp. index. ISBN 0-394-50169-1.

Consists of reprints of the author's works published in journals and magazines. A convincing argument for spurning the pseudosciences. Explores reasons why we still cling to occult ideas, such as their association with religious beliefs. "Practitioners of pop science were once called Paradoxers, a quaint nineteenth-century word used to describe those who invent elaborate and undemonstrated explanations for what science has understood rather well in simpler terms. We are awash today with Paradoxers" (Introduction).

885. Slater, Philip Elliot. *The Wayward Gate: Science and the Supernatural.* Boston: Beacon Press, 1977. 238 pp. bibliography. ISBN 0-8070-2956-4.

An exploration of the negative attitudes of scientists toward many occult and psychic happenings. Slater claims that science refuses to acknowledge the existence of "facts" beyond the isolation of the physical world on our planet. Easy to read, although many unusual ideas are included.

886. Taylor, John Gerald. *Science and the Supernatural: an Investigation of Paranormal Phenomena Including Psychic Healing, Clairvoyance, Telepathy and Precognition.* London: Granada, 1981; Temple Smith, 1980; New York: Dutton, 1980; Temple Smith, 1980. 192 pp. index. bibliography. ISBN 0-586-08367-7.

A British scientist investigates the paranormal, at first with an open mind, then with negativism.

887. Ward, Philip. *A Dictionary of Common Fallacies.* Cambridge, Eng.: Oleander Press, 1978. 2 vols.

Discusses the origins of various misconceptions and controversial subjects such as UFOs, tarot, alchemy, and the like.

888. White, Peter. *The Past Is Human: Ancient Mysteries Explained.* New York: Taplinger, 1976. 165 pp. index. illus. bibliography. ISBN 0-8008-6265-1.

An archaeologist presents arguments against the ancient astronaut theory.

889. Wilson, Ian. *Mind Out of Time? Reincarnation Claims Investigated.*
London: Victor Gollancz, 1981. 283 pp. index. illus.
ISBN 0-575-02968-4.

A skeptic's view of reincarnation.

890. Woodward, Ian. *The Werewolf Delusion.* London: Paddington
Press, 1979, distributed by Grosset & Dunlap. 256 pp. index. illus.
bibliography. ISBN 0-448-23170-0.

An examination of historical accounts of werewolves. Woodward dis-
counts them with more "rational" explanations.

See also item 701.

GLOSSARY

Dictionary, n. A malevolent literary device for cramping the
growth of a language and making it hard and inelastic.
This dictionary, however, is a most useful book.
Ambrose Bierce,
The Devil's Dictionary
(Ambrose Bierce disappeared mysteriously in 1913.)

Note: For more detailed definitions and additional terms, see the dictionaries listed in chapter 1.

ABOMINABLE SNOWMAN   See SASQUATCH.

ACUPUNCTURE   Chinese medical system which works on the principle of inserting needles into the skin to accomplish cures or bring about anesthesia.

AGE OF AQUARIUS   An astrological era which will begin A.D. 2740, predicted to be a new age of peace. The past 2,000 years (the Christian era) have been the Age of Pisces.

ALCHEMY   Transmitting baser metals into gold; also, the search for the ELIXIR OF LIFE. In its highest form, used as a system of purification. Its practice peaked in the late Middle Ages.

ALTERED STATE OF CONSCIOUSNESS (ASC)   A change from the normal state of mind, including dreaming, hypnosis and trance states.

AMULET   Object, charm often worn on the person, believed to bring good fortune and / or ward off evil.

ANGEL   Celestial being, emissary of God. Satan is often referred to as a "fallen angel."

ANIMISM   The belief that all natural objects have souls. Also, the belief in nonphysical, spiritual beings.

ANTHROPOMANCY   Human sacrifice and examination of the entrails for purposes of DIVINATION.

APPARITION   Spirit or phantom.

ARCANE   Secret, occult.

ARITHMANCY   The ancient form of NUMEROLOGY, primarily using the number of letters in a name. Also a method of DIVINATION.

ASTRAL PROJECTION   Being able to move about in the astral body (soul) while the physical body sleeps. See OUT-OF-THE-BODY EXPERIENCE.

ASTROLOGY   The belief that heavenly bodies affect human lives; the study and interpretation of this belief. An ancient (originating in the Fertile Crescent) and long-living "science."

AUGURY   The general art of DIVINATION.

AURA   An emanation surrounding a living body. The color and shape is thought to be reflective of personality and emotions.

AUTOMATISM   Movements of the body beyond conscious awareness, such as automatic writing and drawing.

BERMUDA TRIANGLE   Area in the Atlantic Ocean where numerous disappearances have occurred. Also called Devil's Triangle.

BIOFEEDBACK   The ability to control bodily functions by thought, or mind, control.

BLACK MAGIC   Magic and supernatural knowledge used for evil purposes; SORCERY.

BLACK MASS   A ceremony which mocks the Christian mass.

BUMPOLOGY   A modern term for PHRENOLOGY; divination and character reading by means of bumps on the head.

CABALA   (Cabbala, Kabala, Kabbalah, Quabalah) A Jewish system of esoteric mysticism. Literally means "tradition."

CARTOMANCY   Fortune-telling by cards, often through the use of a TAROT deck.

CHARM   See AMULET.

CHIROMANCY   (Chirogmanzy, Cheiroghomy) Divination by reading the lines on the hand. Similar to PALMISTRY.

CLAIRAUDIENCE   "Clear hearing." Ability to hear voices which mysteriously provide insight and information about the future.

CLAIRVOYANCE   The power to see beyond normal vision; the ability to see objects or events without using conventional sight.

COMMUNICATION (in occult) A spoken or written message divulged through a medium by or to a spirit.

CONDOMBLÉ A syncretic religion practiced in Brazil. MACUMBA. Merges the older Yoruba religion with newer gods and spirits.

COSMIC CONSCIOUSNESS A dissociated state of mind in which an individual loses a sense of self and becomes one with the universe.

COVEN A group of witches.

CROSS-CORRESPONDENCES Pieces of messages received by different mediums which must be put together in order for them to make sense.

CRYSTALLOMANCY (SCRYING) Crystal gazing to see events taking place elsewhere and / or in another time.

DEMONOLATRY Worship of demons.

DEMONOLOGY Study of demons (evil spirits).

DEVIL'S TRIANGLE See BERMUDA TRIANGLE.

DIVINATION Gaining knowledge of the future and / or unknown events by the use of omens and / or occult talents.

DOWSING The ability to locate water, minerals, and other underground materials, usually with the aid of a forked stick.

DRUIDISM Adherence to the religion of the ancient Celts. A mystical belief among priests who were magi and seers.

DRYAD Tree spirit, often depicted as a woman.

ELIXIR OF LIFE A magical substance which brings good health, lasting youth, and immortality. See ALCHEMY.

EPHEMERIS (pl. ephemerides) An astronomical table showing the positions of heavenly bodies at different times. Used in ASTROLOGY.

ESP (Extra Sensory Perception) Ability to use the senses beyond the normal range of human perception, including TELEPATHY, CLAIRVOYANCE, and PRECOGNITION.

EVIL EYE A widely held superstition that certain people are able to cast evil spells by means of a glance.

EXORCISM Ceremony to expel an evil spirit from a person, animal, or place.

FAIRY   A mythical creature with magical powers present in many folklore stories.

FAITH HEALING   Curing disease and ailments by means of prayer and religious faith.

FREEMASON   Member of a secret order promoting brotherly love.

GEMATRIA   Assigning numerical values to letters and interpreting their meaning. Often associated with the CABALA, Hebrew alphabet, and TAROT.

GEOMANCY   Divination by means of figures, or lines, drawn on the earth. Also applies to numerology based on geographic and / or astronomical configurations.

GHOST   The disembodied soul of a dead person which appears to the living.

GHOUL   An evil Asian demon, one that feeds on human flesh and robs graves.

GOAT   One who refuses to believe in PSI phenomena, as opposed to SHEEP. Also frequently a symbol for the devil.

THE GOLDEN DAWN   A secret society, dedicated to magic, which flourished in England during the late nineteenth and early twentieth centuries.

GRAPHOLOGY   The study of handwriting to learn human character.

GRIMOIRE   A witch's or magician's personal book of spells. Originally handwritten and passed down from one witch to another.

HALLUCINATION   Perception without rational basis; distorted visions.

HERMETIC ARTS   Those things relating to mystic and alchemical practices and techniques. Originally applied to the philosophy of Hermes Trismegistus.

HEX   German word for the practice of witchcraft. In current usage, generally means a spell. Hex signs used in Pennsylvania Dutch art.

HOROSCOPE   Astrological, symbolic chart of the heavens for interpretation of their effects on events, people, etc., on earth.

HOUSE   Astrological division based on time.

HYPNOTISM   Modern form of mesmerism in which artificially induced sleep creates a state in which a subject can be influenced by suggestion.

I CHING The Chinese Book of Changes. A Chinese system of mysticism based on the yin and the yang. Also used for divination.

ILLUMINATI A mystical brotherhood which flourished in Europe in the fifteenth and sixteenth centuries.

KIRLIAN PHOTOGRAPHY The process, developed in Russia by Semyou Kirlian and his wife, Valentina, of photographing auras and energies not seen by the human eye.

KNIGHTS TEMPLAR A secret order of knights which flourished in the Middle Ages. The order was disbanded on charges of satanism and heresy.

KUNDALINI A Sanskrit word referring to untapped human power sources, sometimes evident as light.

LEGEND A story handed down through history, often accepted as true.

LEGERDEMAIN Trickery and illusion as used by stage magicians; conjuring.

LEOPARD MEN Bewitched humans who become leopards.

LEVITATION Rising and/or floating in the air.

LEY LINE A relationship between significant sites which is thought to produce a form of energy or power.

LOCH NESS MONSTER (NESSIE) A water beast which supposedly lives in Loch Ness, Scotland.

LYCANTHROPY Belief in werewolves.

MACUMBA A syncretic belief practiced in Brazil, including the UMBANDA and the newer CONDOMBLÉ.

MAGIC The art of producing effects beyond the normal human range of ability by means of occult forces.

MANA Polynesian magic. "The power of the elemental forces of nature embodied in an object or person" (Webster's New Collegiate Dictionary).

MANIMALS (SHAPESHIFTERS) People who become animals.

MEDITATION Turning one's attention inward in order to achieve dissociation from the outer world and achieve intensely focused thought.

MEDIUM   A person who communicates with spirits on other planes of existence, and provides for communication between them and living persons.

METAPHYSICS   Search for the true nature. Ontology.

MYTH   Tradition and / or story, usually about superhuman beings and / or gods.

NAGUAL   Animal double (spirit) in central American Indian lore.

NECROMANCY   Magic in all its forms. Sometimes used in the narrow sense of divination by communication with the dead, and / or conjuring up ghosts.

NESSIE   See LOCH NESS MONSTER.

NUMEROLOGY   The study of numbers (such as birth date) in order to see relationships with human life and the meaning of the universe.

OBE   See OUT-OF-THE-BODY EXPERIENCE.

OBEAH   (Obiah) African sorcery (also practiced in the West Indies). In its modern form, it combines VOODOO with Christianity. Related to MACUMBA and SANTERÍA.

OCCULT   The doctrines, rites, and practice of mysterious and secret beliefs; includes magic and the unknown. Often implies supernatural powers, as well as the search for meaning outside accepted scientific methods and established religions.

OMEN   A portent of the future.

ORACLE   An interpreter of revelations from a god.

OUIJA   A board and planchette used as a means to receive messages from the spirit world.

OUT-OF-THE-BODY EXPERIENCE   The sensation of being conscious while dreaming. The impression of leaving the physical body and moving about freely. See ASTRAL PROJECTION.

PAGANISM—Non-Christian religious beliefs.

PALMISTRY   The art of telling fortunes and interpreting character from the lines and physical features of the human hand. See CHIROMANCY.

PARANORMAL   Sensory phenomena unexplainable by present concepts accepted by science.

PARAPSYCHOLOGY   The scientific study of PSI phenomena by psychologists, biologists, physicists, and other investigators.

PHILOSOPHER'S STONE   The substance believed to be capable of changing baser metals to gold. In a broader sense, the force unifying life itself and granting eternal youth.

PHRENOLOGY   The interpretation of character by studying skull shape and bumps on the head. See BUMPOLOGY.

PK   See PSYCHOKINESIS.

POLTERGEIST   Ghost, or spirit, which makes noises and / or moves things about.

POSSESSION   Control from within a person by a demon or spirit. The occupation of an individual's mind by another personality, living or dead.

POWWOW   Ceremonies with mystical aspects for celebration, expressing purpose and / or curing by North American Indian tribes. Also, the magical system of some Pennsylvania Dutch, involving the use of hexes and spells.

PRECOGNITION   An awareness or knowledge of things to come; sometimes called "Second Sight."

PREDICTION   The announcement of things which will occur in the future.

PREMONITION   A foreboding of the future. Not as detailed as PRE-COGNITION.

PROPHECY   Inspired knowledge of future events.

PSI   The abbreviation for all psychical phenomena.

PSYCHIC DEFENSES   Methods of protection on a spiritual level.

PSYCHIC POWERS   Abilities beyond the accepted, normal human range of potential based on the supermental.

PSYCHIC SURGERY   Ability to perform surgery without anesthetics, elaborate equipment, and / or medical training.

PSYCHOGRAPHY   A form of spirit writing.

PSYCHOKINESIS   The ability to move matter by PSI means.

PSYCHOMETRY   Gaining impressions and information from a physical object regarding either its former owner or the provenance of the object itself.

RADIESTHESIA   See DOWSING.

REINCARNATION   The belief that the soul, upon death, returns to earth in another body or physical form.

RETROCOGNITION   The perception of past events in the present.

ROSICRUCIAN   Member of a mystical society founded by Christian Rosenkreutz in the eighteenth century.

RUNES   Characters used by ancient Scandinavians and Germans for divination and other occult matters.

SABBAT   A sacred day of witches. Great Sabbat days are Candlemass (February 2); Roodmas, or May Eve (April 30); Lammas (August 1); and Halloween (October 31).

SANTERÍA   The African Yoruba religion mixed with Christianity practiced in the Western hemisphere. Related to OBEAH.

SASQUATCH (Big Foot, Yehti, Abominable Snowman)   A powerful, large man / beast purported to live in mountainous areas.

SATANISM   The worship of Satan, the antichrist.

SCRYING   Crystal gazing. See CRYSTALLOMANCY.

SÉANCE   A session conducted by a medium to contact spirits of the dead.

SHAMANISM   Belief in spirits who can be influenced by a shaman, or medicine man.

SHAPESHIFTERS   See MANIMALS.

SHEEP   One who believes in PSI, as opposed to GOAT.

SIBYL   Prophetess of ancient times with the power of DIVINATION.

SIGN   Astrological division, one of twelve in the zodiac (Aries, Taurus, Gemini, Cancer, Leo, Virgo, Libra, Scorpio, Sagittarius, Capricorn, Aquarius, and Pisces).

SORCERY   The art of BLACK MAGIC, often with the aid of spirits.

SPIRITUALISM   The belief in continuous life and the ability to communicate with those who have "passed over."

SUBLIMINAL   Perceptual experience at the subconscious level.

SUFI   Mystical Islamic sect.

SURVIVAL   Continuation of life after death through the personality or soul.

TABLE OF HOUSES   Astrological charts used in calculating horoscopes.

TAROT   A special deck of cards with major and minor arcanes used for fortune-telling or as paths for various esoteric insights.

TASSEOGRAPHY   Tea-leaf reading.

TELEKINESIS   The ability to move objects through thought alone.

TELEPATHY   The sharing of information between two people by means of psychic ability.

THEOSOPHY   Religious thought which claims special insights into divine revelations. The modern Theosophical Society was founded by Mme. Helena Blavatsky.

TOTEM   An object inscribed with symbols and considered to be a source of power, a focus of worship and/or personal identity.

TRANCE   A subconscious mental state.

UFO   (Unidentified Flying Object)   Flying saucer.

UMBANDA   The syncretic blend of the African Yoruba religion with Catholicism practiced in Brazil. Related to OBEAH, VOODOO, and MACUMBA.

VAMPIRE   A being, sometimes called the "undead," which sucks human blood for life support.

VOODOO   (vodoun, hoodoo, vodum)   Rites of magic practiced in the Caribbean and U.S. Related to MACUMBA and other syncretic religions.

WARLOCK   A skilled black magician. Sometimes, erroneously, considered to be simply a male witch.

WEREWOLF   A human changed into a wolf by the full moon. Variant spelling (used by the Library of Congress in its subject headings): werwolf.

WICCA   The term sometimes used to describe modern witches who follow pagan beliefs of the ancient druids. Literal meaning from old Anglo-Saxon: "wise one."

WITCH   Male or female practitioner of ancient fertility beliefs. Held in past ages to be a follower of Satan.

WIZARD   An adept, or magus figure, in folklore.

ZODIAC   An imaginary heavenly zone divided into twelve parts, or signs, usually depicted in circular chart form. Used in ASTROLOGY.

ZOMBIE   (Zombi)   A corpse brought to life to be used as a slave.

NAME INDEX

Numerical notations refer to entry numbers assigned to specific titles. Those notations prefaced by p. (page) refer to names mentioned in the text. Names indexed here include authors, editors and compilers of works, and also individuals discussed in a substantive way in the texts themselves. It does not include translators, illustrators, and authors of prefaces or forewords, all of whom are cited primarily as aids in identifying particular editions.

TITLE INDEX

Reference is to item number.

An ABC of Witchcraft Past and Present, 107

A to Z Horoscope Maker and Delineator, 852

A–Z of the Occult, 30

Abnormal Hypnotic Phenomena: a Survey of Nineteenth-Century Cases, 484

Advances in Parapsychological Research, 384

An Adventure among the Rosicrucians, 342

Adventures in Consciousness: an Introduction to Aspect Psychology, 375

The Age of Chivalry, 580

The Age of Fable, 580

The Age of Flying Saucers: Notes on a Projected History of Unidentified Flying Objects, 691

The Alchemist, 270

Alchemists and Gold, 280

The Alchemist's Handbook: Manual for Practical Laboratory Alchemy, 261

Alchemists through the Ages: Lives of the Famous Alchemistical Philosophers from the Year 850 to the Close of the 18th Century, Together with a Study of the Principles and Practice of Alchemy, Including a Bibliography of Alchemical and Hermetic Philosophy, 282

Alchemy, 269

Alchemy: a Bibliography of English-Language Writings, 276

Alchemy: Ancient and Modern, 278

Alchemy and the Occult: a Catalogue of Books and Manuscripts from the Collection of Paul and Mary Mellon Given to Yale University Library, 12

Alchemy, the Ancient Science, 39.13

Alchemy: the Secret Art, 273

Aliens from Space: the Real Story of Unidentified Flying Objects, 700

Amazing Secrets of the Mystic East, 232

America Bewitched: the Rise of Black Magic and Spiritualism, 207

American Astrology Table of Houses, 841, 845

Amityville Horror, 533

Amulets and Talismans, 239

Amulets, Talismans and Fetishes, 242

Analysis and Prediction, 860.8

The Anatomy of the Occult, 56

The Anatomy of Witchcraft, 168

Ancient and Modern Witchcraft, 176

The Ancient Art of Color Therapy, 248

Ancient Man: a Handbook of Puzzling Artifacts, 38.1

The Androgyne: Reconciliation of Male and Female, 224.6

Angels, 639

Animal Ghosts, 492

Animal Magnetism: or, Mesmerism and its Phenomena, 391.12

An Anthology of I Ching, 313

The Apparel of High Magic, 221.2

Apparitions, 457, 500

Apparitions and Ghosts, 880

The Aquarian Guide to Occult, Mystical, Religious, Magical London and Around, 47

Aradia: the Gospel of the Witches, 157

The Art of Synthesis, 827.4

Arthurian Legend and Literature: an Annotated Bibliography, 595

Arthurian Literature in the Middle Ages: a Collaborative History, 593

The Arts of the Alchemists, 263

As Above, So Below: a Primary Guide to Astrological Awareness, 839

Aspects and Houses in Analysis, 860.4

Astral Projection, Magic, and Alchemy: Being Hitherto Unpublished Golden Dawn Material by S. L. MacGregor Mathers and Others, 349